D1504086

report
2001:
a man's guide
to women

report
2001:
a man's guide
to women

hot days

hotter nights

good times

great sex

RODALE

edited by Ken Winston Caine

ISBN 1–57954–360–X hardcover

Distributed to the book trade by St. Martin's Press

2   4   6   8   10   9   7   5   3   hardcover

Visit us on the Web at www.menshealthbooks.com, or call us toll-free at (800) 848-4735.

WE **INSPIRE** AND **ENABLE** PEOPLE TO IMPROVE
THEIR LIVES AND THE WORLD AROUND THEM

Sex and Values at Rodale

We believe that an active and healthy sex life, based on mutual consent and respect between partners, is an important component of physical and mental well-being. We also respect that sex is a private matter and that each person has a different opinion of what sexual practices or levels of discourse are appropriate. Rodale is committed to offering responsible, practical advice about sexual matters, supported by accredited professionals and legitimate scientific research. Our goal—for sex and all other topics—is to publish information that empowers people's lives.

Notice

This book is intended as a reference volume only, not as a medical manual. The information given here is designed to help you make informed decisions about your health. It is not intended as a substitute for any treatment that may have been prescribed by your doctor. If you suspect that you have a medical problem, we urge you to seek competent medical help.

Report 2001: A Man's Guide to Women Staff

MANAGING EDITOR: Ken Winston Caine

EDITOR: Stan Zukowski

WRITERS: Brian Alexander, Alisa Bauman, Jeffrey Bouley, Denis Boyles, Jeff Bredenberg, Chrissy Brooks, Ken Winston Caine, Brian Chichester, Joanne Cleaver, Jack Croft, Sherise Dorf, Perry Garfinkel, Greg Gutfeld, Jennifer Haigh, Dennis Jackson, Larry Keller, Colin McEnroe, Christian Millman, Stephen Perrine, James R. Petersen, Ronnie Polaneczky, Zachary Veilleux, Tom Zoellner, Stan Zukowski

ART DIRECTOR: Charles Beasley

SERIES INTERIOR AND COVER DESIGNER: Tanja Lipinski Cole

COVER DESIGNER: Gavin R. Robinson

ILLUSTRATOR: Christian Musselman

CARTOONIST: Frank Cotham

ASSISTANT RESEARCH MANAGER: Leah Flickinger

RESEARCH EDITOR: Deborah Pedron

SENIOR COPY EDITOR: Karen Neely

EDITORIAL PRODUCTION MANAGER: Marilyn Hauptly

LAYOUT DESIGNER: Faith Hague

MANUFACTURING COORDINATORS: Brenda Miller, Jodi Schaffer, Patrick Smith

Rodale Active Living Books

VICE PRESIDENT AND PUBLISHER: Neil Wertheimer

EXECUTIVE EDITOR: Susan Clarey

EDITORIAL DIRECTOR: Michael Ward

MARKETING DIRECTOR: Janine Slaughter

PRODUCT MARKETING DIRECTOR: Kris Siessmayer

BOOK MANUFACTURING DIRECTOR: Helen Clogston

MANUFACTURING MANAGERS: Eileen Bauder, Mark Krahforst

RESEARCH MANAGER: Ann Gossy Yermish

COPY MANAGER: Lisa D. Andruscavage

PRODUCTION MANAGER: Robert V. Anderson Jr.

DIGITAL PROCESSING GROUP MANAGERS: Leslie M. Keefe, Thomas P. Aczel

OFFICE MANAGER: Jacqueline Dornblaser

OFFICE STAFF: Susan B. Dorschutz, Julie Kehs Minnix, Tara Schrantz, Catherine E. Strouse

contents

3 PROMOTE PERPETUAL PASSION

4 TUNE UP YOUR SEX MACHINE

introduction

We suggest you memorize this little-known medical fact a researcher uncovered while digging up the hottest, latest developments for *Report 2001*. It might save a life.

A study by Dutch gynecologists found that women who frequently performed oral sex on their partners had about a 50 percent lower risk of developing preeclampsia. Preeclampsia is a potentially fatal disease. Potentially *fatal*. You've gotta help your partner avoid this preeclampsia stuff.

Our scouts continue to unearth the most helpful, most entertaining, most relevant, most useful inside information for men about sex, about enjoying women, and about making life with women enjoyable. And enjoying life is what really, really matters.

We're here to help.

Here are just a few of the fascinations and cool revelations and use-it-now advice you'll discover in this power-packed *Man's Guide to Women.*

- Six ways women nag and 12 stealthy strategies to clam it

- Ways to break the ice with a pretty stranger while avoiding the risk of frostbite

- The proper way to stare at a woman's breasts and what to do when she catches you

- Mesmerizing claims from a California hypnotherapist that you can add true girth and length to your penis just by listening to hypnosis tapes

- Charisma secrets of how to enter a crowded room with style and grace so that everyone notices you and likes what they see

- What you must say *before* you open the condom if you want her to respect you as a lover

- How to satisfy that urge to, as Springsteen sang, go for a ride and never come back

- How to drive a snide mother-in-law bonkers—completely risk-free

- Why it's best not to reignite an old flame

- When and why you should (literally) hum during sex, rather than just whistle afterward

- Why you must master and employ *two* types of romance to keep a relationship purring—from Dr. Romance himself, Gregory Godek

- Remarkable ways to "Date Your Wife for Life" from the man who runs a Web site called Funinbed.com, Chris Allen, author of the *1,001 Sex Secrets* series of books

- What's it like being a daddy in your fifties? And what are the challenges of creating a second family with a second, younger wife? Twenty-six percent of Anglo, 32 percent of Hispanic, and 33 percent of Black men ages 45 to 59 are married to women ages 25 to 44. And you know what? They're making babies

- The "4 C's" secret to maintaining a happy household, from Tom Green, who lives with five wives and 25 young children. God gave him the secret one day, he says, right while he was in the middle of arguing with a wife

- Why there is hope, according to *Chicago Tribune* TV critic Steve Johnson as he surveys "train-wreck television" like *Who Wants to Marry a Multimillionaire?*, *Blind Date*, *Change of Heart*, *Loveline*, and *The Man Show* with its big-breasted women bouncing on trampolines

Hmmmm. Big-breasted women bouncing on trampolines. Wouldn't that be a great plot for a made-for-TV movie if we ever get our own *Men's* Lifetime Television network?

Enjoy,

Ken Winston Caine
Managing Editor

1
SURVIVE THE WAR OF THE SEXES

 Men and women are really the same, when you think about it. Down deep, that is. Very, very deep. Subterranean. At the chromosomal level. It can be said that men and women both have chromosomes.

Actually, when you think about it again, boys and girls are primates—and that's about the extent of our common ground. In nearly every other facet of daily life, we may as well be members of different species altogether. From our choice of friends, hobbies, snack foods, and TV programs to our opinions about sex, work, sports, sex, and, uh, sports, there seems to be precious little meeting of the minds.

Men insist, women wheedle. They have needs but won't tell us what they want. We have natural urges and daily temptations, but they dismiss them as testosterone imbalances. In this section, we offer some guidance to help you emerge unscarred (at least occasionally) in the battle of the sexes, a tumult that has been teeming since Adam caved in and ate that apple instead of the bag of Fritos that he really wanted.

TOP TEN

Conflict Soothers

Happy couples do not naturally use "active listening"—the marriage-counselor-recommended technique whereby you unemotionally or empathetically parrot what your partner has said and acknowledge that you understand it. And those couples who do use it do not have happier or longer-lasting marriages, suggests a research study that followed 130 newlyweds for 6 years of marriage. According to various interviews with the study authors, the following approaches to conflict shine through as factors in happy, successful couples' relationships.

1. **Wife gently nudges.** The wife tends to raise difficult issues in a sensitive and non-threatening and nonargumentative way.

2. **Husband appreciates.** The husband is willing to consider the wife's perspectives and is open to her influence.

3. **Male soothes.** The husband is more likely to say things and take actions to de-escalate tension, rather than become increasingly negative.

4. **Wife is playful.** The wife is likely to soothe her husband with humor.

5. **Negativity is countered positively.** The ratio of positivity to negativity in interactions is high.

6. **Partners seek positivity.** Both partners say and do things to evoke positive responses and behaviors from the other and de-escalate confrontational behaviors and tensions.

(7) Couple practices respect. Partners do not use contempt as a weapon.

(8) Neither bullies. Partners avoid being belligerent.

(9) There's no defense. The partners do not wage personal attacks and do not display defensiveness.

(10) Male is agreeable. The husband finds something in the wife's complaint that he feels is reasonable and that he can agree with.

MUST READS

Cork the Whine

From the time we were 4 years old and our mothers said in the grocery store, "Why didn't you go before we left? I told you to go, and now you're going to have to hold it until we get home," males have been pestered, harassed, harried, badgered, bullied, sniped at—in short, nagged—for doing (or not doing) something that some woman thought we should (or shouldn't) have done. Writer Jennifer Haigh turns state's evidence and throws henpecked men a real lifeline with these six sneaky tricks to end your mate's nagging.

Women nag. It is our calling and our gift, what the Lord gave us to make up for cramps, cellulite, and labor pains. Over the years, we've nagged ourselves the right to vote, hold public office, and have two cable channels devoted entirely to shopping; and we'll continue bitching until the world becomes a cleaner, fairer, better-dressed place. But why am I telling you this? If you're like my colleagues, feminine kvetching is the bane of your life and all you care about is how to stop it.

Allow me to make your day. At the risk of betraying my sex and being excluded from female restroom banter for the remainder of my life, I've agreed to reveal how any man can end the nagging in his life, without—and this is key—giving in to it. The trick? Simply understand your mate's motive for haranguing you in the first place, then employ the proper counterstrategy to clam her up.

Here you will find six ways men get nagged, six nefarious tricks for squelching those nags, and six backup strategies to use in case these tricks don't end the torture.

● The Nag: "You never tell me anything!"

She asks what happened at work today. You say, "Nothing"—a true statement in your book. Even so, she immediately gripes that you're shutting her out of your life.

What not to say: "I don't tell you anything? You never shut up long enough to give me a chance. Now where's the beer?"

Why she gets so bent: Men see communication as an exchange of useful information, so in your mind nothing you could tell your mate about your day would be of any use to her. But when she asks you what happened, she wants feelings, details, snippets of dialogue, descriptions of people's shoes. To her mind, the answer is never "nothing."

Sneaky trick to stop it: Introduce her to one of your female coworkers. Trust me, if their friendship gels, your mate will soon be telling you what's happening at your job. "My girlfriend never asks me about my day anymore. She knows she gets better stories from my assistant," says my friend Pete. One important note here: Pete's assistant, Esther, is 20 years his senior, and she's frequently mistaken for Brian Dennehy. Run this scam with plain-looking workmates only.

Backup strategy: If the office-mole strategy fails, you may not be able to squelch this nag completely. But you can make it less onerous by negotiating a moment of silence when you first come home. "Better to say that you need half an hour alone than to have the same tense conversation day after day, where you feel interrogated and she feels ignored," says Brian Kane, Ph.D., of Allentown College of St. Francis de Sales in Pennsylvania.

● The Nag: "When are you going to take out the garbage/pick up your dirty socks/churn the butter/milk the reindeer?"

There are a million variations on this one, but count on this: Whatever's not getting done in the world, there's a man somewhere who's being nagged about it.

What not to say: "If you think it's so important, why don't you do it yourself?" (These words could come back to haunt you in bed tonight. Think about it.)

Why she gets so bent: Face it, she doesn't keep you around for your looks. The trash is overflowing, the toast is dry, and Blitzen is howling in pain.

Sneaky trick to stop it: The next time you see her wash a dish, clean a window, or throw a load of a laundry into the dryer, tell her to stop. Put your arms around her. Tell her you appreciate everything she does around the house. Then take her out to dinner. See, it's not just your laziness that makes us women nuts; it's your seeming failure to notice and value all we do for you. If you shower her with enough appreciation, you might never have to do a damned thing.

Backup strategy: If appreciation fails, try sitting down and clearly dividing the household responsibilities, suggests Cynthia Lief Ruberg, a couples and sex therapist in Columbus, Ohio. Post a "to do" list on the refrigerator door.

Okay, it sounds miserable, but there are rewards, according to Sherry Lehman, a marriage and sex therapist in Cleveland. "When a woman stops resenting who does what at home, the couple's sex life often undergoes a huge improvement," she says. "It's not an exaggeration to say that picking up your socks could get you oral sex." Imagine what you'll get if you vacuum!

● The Nag: "You spend all your free time with your friends!"

She suggests dinner and a movie. You tell her you've made plans to break in your buddy's new wide-screen TV. "We never spend any time together!" she rails, even though you wake up together every morning, watch the news to-gether every night, and spit your Colgate foam into his-and-hers sinks together before bed.

What not to say: "But honey, I see you every damned day!"

Why she gets so bent: A woman needs to know that she's the most impor-tant person in your life, says Lehman. "If she feels as though she's coming in second, she'll be angry and hurt." It's even worse if you do fun stuff with your friends while your time with her is spent buying storm windows and diaper rash ointment.

Sneaky trick to stop it: Turn state's evidence. After an evening with the guys, give her a recap. You'd rather die than listen to her describe her yoga class, but she actually wants to know what you do when you're away. If she's awake (and you're sober), make your report as soon as you come home. If not, save it for breakfast. Just be sure it sounds pathetic. Once she hears that you spent 4 hours fixing the differential on his T-bird, she'll stop clamoring to be invited.

Backup strategy: If the nagging continues, you may be forced to throw her a bone. For every evening you spend with the guys, plan to do something fun with her—a dayhike or a special dinner rather than shopping for family packs of Cheerios at Sam's Club.

● The Nag: "You never listen to me!"

You're watching a particularly moving *Sanford and Son* episode when she launches into the play-by-play of an argument she had with her mother. You hit the mute button and attempt to say the right things, but she catches you trying to read Redd Foxx's lips and explodes.

What not to say: "Huh? Did you just say something?"

Why she gets so bent: You're not really wired to hear everything she says. "Men tend to communicate in a linear, logical way," says Lehman. "Women tend to tell stories, which can be frustrating for men to listen to." Then there's the matter of sheer tonnage: The average woman speaks three times as much as the average man.

"Women value communication more than anything else," says Lehman. "If she feels as if you don't listen to her, she's as upset as you'd be if she refused to have sex." And you know how that hurts.

Sneaky trick to stop it: Learn how to look as if you're paying attention. Women are masters of nonverbal listening behavior: They look at the other person, make sympathetic noises, have a million different ways of saying, "I hear you." Men don't do this as much, which can leave women feeling tuned out. The next time your eyes start to glaze over, just nod occasionally and make eye contact. When she comes up for air, give her verbal cues to let her know that you're still with her.

A simple "wow" will usually suffice.

Backup strategy: Try to outtalk her. I've found that this technique works great with chatty taxi drivers. They clam up when you start babbling.

○ The Nag: "Do you have to be such a slob in the bathroom?"
Why is it that men consider flushing optional?

What not to say: "You should have walked in here 10 minutes ago. Whew!"

Why she gets so bent: To you, pee on the toilet seat is just pee on the toilet seat; to her, it's a sign that your lives are about to lurch into a ditch. "In most cultures, women are raised to attach more importance to housekeeping than men are," says Lehman. "Trying to talk her out of feeling that way won't work."

Sneaky trick to stop it: Perform your ablutions first thing in the morning, when she's still in bed. Unless she's a true morning person, she won't be alert enough to notice how filthy the tub is.

Backup strategy: Tell her she's right about your sloppiness, then suggest that the two of you use—and be responsible for cleaning—separate bathrooms. Even money says that she'll get grossed out by your bathroom well before you do and end up cleaning it for you. She may bitch for 10 minutes afterward, but that's better than a daily tidiness lecture.

○ The Nag: "You spend too much time watching sports!"
A particularly dangerous variation of "You never listen to me!"

What not to say: "Can this wait till halftime?"

Why she gets so bent: Pro sports never go away. Season after season, year after godforsaken year. A hard-core fan can spend hundreds of hours glued to the television, wearing inane licensed apparel, getting louder and fatter with each passing week. What else do you need to know?

Sneaky trick to stop it: Some woman is going to kill me for revealing this one, but here goes: Well in advance of a big game, tell your woman how

SEX TRENDS

JUST WAIT TILL WE START DATING SOME 23-YEAR-OLD

Men who divorce in their forties become more depressed and have lower achievement goals than women of the same age, who actually become more outgoing and action-oriented. "Divorce at midlife is more empowering for women than men," says Paul Costa, behavior chief at the National Institute on Aging.

glad you are that she's not like your buddy's wife, the woman who's so needy and controlling that she can't give her man a few hours to catch a damned football game. "A relationship tends to be a large part of a woman's identity, and it's important to her that other people perceive her as having a good relationship," says Lehman.

Backup strategy: Talk her through it. Some women who don't enjoy sports simply don't understand the intricacies of the game in question. (Others do, but hate it anyway.) Invite her to watch a game with you, and mute the volume so that she can listen to your own personal commentary instead of the idiot announcer's. Throw in a back rub, and she may end up enjoying it more than you do, especially if you're an Eagles fan.

Then again, it might be easier just to let her nag.

Girls Just Want to Have . . . Something

Every man who has ever had a girlfriend or a wife or a mother knows the drill: You buy the emergency highway flares, but she wanted the pearls. You give her advice, but she just wanted a shoulder to cry on. Intuiting a woman's real desires is about as easy for a man as it is for a woman to pee standing up. Writer Denis Boyles has a better strategy. Forget about what women want—figure out what they need instead.

I don't know who said that you can't judge a book by its cover, but it was somebody with a lot more free time than I have. One glance at the cover of a book tells me all I want to know.

For example, I was down at Book Bog, a huge barn of a place, where the men and women who publish the imperishable thoughts of a great nation send giant trucks full of the stuff they can't sell at retail, even through Amazon. The Bog people use the books as table ballast and pray that people like me will pass through and find the perfect gift for someone they never liked. It was there that I saw a big stack of first-edition hardcover copies of a book called *What Women Want.*

The book, a heartfelt autobiography by the woman who speaks for all women everywhere and at all times, Patricia Ireland of the National Organization for Women, seemed to me to be an unlikely candidate for landfill status. I mean, think about it: What women want! That's a lifesaver to clueless men (and I'm sure Ireland would be happy to describe most of us that way). It's also a handy inventory for cranky women, a list of all that they don't have but wish they did. If that isn't a bestseller, what is?

Why You're Asking the Wrong Question

Nevertheless, there they were. They had all been shipped to bookstores around America, they had all been displayed by hopeful booksellers, they had all been rejected by book buyers, and now they were all stacked and marked down to less than the cost of a paperback copy of the same book. What had happened? The cover seemed to be okay—had Ireland's picture on it and everything. The leader of a women's group with 300,000 or so members? In a country with more than 130 million women? And they couldn't sell a few thousand copies of the book that claims to answer one of life's most compelling questions? Maybe once you get past the equality-respect-power trinity, all that women agree on is that they want something, and whatever it is, they want it now.

"What women want," although it's one of our species' frequently asked questions, is just the wrong question. Too bad Ireland's book wasn't called *What Women Need*. At least then we'd all have something at stake in learning what it is. What people want is frequently the opposite of what they need. Ask any teenager. So the reason we can't use "what women want" as the basis for figuring out what women really want is that the list of what women want is always on the move. (Men, by the way, don't do much better at this.) For example, here's a little history, a kind of back-ward glance at what women have wanted over the past few decades of this century.

● **What women wanted, 1965 to 1980**
Weed from Hawaii, a Germaine Greer book, a Judy Collins album, Farrah's hair, free love, a cute car, and equal access to therapy

The main thing women wanted from men: sensitivity. Until the mid-1960s, your basic guy was the prevailing model. He fought wars and invented government and worked time and a

hot **TIP!**

If you use condoms (and if you don't, give our best to the nice folks down at the clinic), be aware that mineral-oil-based feminine creams such as Replens (which treats vaginal itching and dryness) can cause condoms to tear during sex before she even has the chance to ask, "Is it in yet?" Oil-free creams, such as Gyne-Lotrimin, won't harm condoms, says Ted Rosen, M.D., of the Baylor College of Medicine in Houston. Rubbers don't mix with petroleum jelly, such as Vaseline, either; K-Y jelly is the safe choice.

half because he thought that kind of man was what women wanted and needed.

But once boomer women entered the workforce and saw that the bread-winning part was no big deal, they changed their minds about what they wanted. What they really wanted, they said, was sensitivity. By now you know the rest of this story: They wanted men to feel the things that they felt and express them the way that they did. The result was a nation of New Men—weeping as they expressed their feelings—and a career for Phil Donahue.

perfect figures

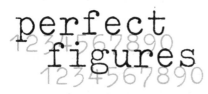

Number of single women in the United States (1998): 43.1 million

Percentage of women ages 18–44 who are single: 43

Ratio of married women to single women: 5:4

Average salary of an unmarried woman: $29,153

Average salary of a married woman: $31,148

Average salary of an unmarried man: $34,905

Average salary of a married man: $44,304

· · · · · · · · · ·

● What women wanted, 1981 to 1990
A fast-track job, a European car, South American drugs, recovery centers, Ivana's hair (and life and time), champagne, and equal access to men's military schools

The main thing women wanted from men: status. The problem with sensitive men, women discovered, was that they weren't sensitive to the right thing. Women had in mind men who were sensitive to what women wanted, especially all the spread-my-wings stuff. But what captured the attention of New Men were their feelings about themselves. What good was that?

So women decided that what they wanted was something a little more practical. By 1985, women were attending their college reunions and dragging along trophy husbands, guys more concerned with power than with protection. Women didn't just want men who could win a little bread. They wanted men who made lots of it and could serve it up on the power table at a socially barometric restaurant. Women also wanted nannies right away. For those of you who can recall it, this was a great time to be a man. All we had to do was slap mousse on our heads, drive extremely expensive cars, and be really, really irresponsible. No problemo. If women can't be specific about what they want, then we'll give them what we want.

● **What women wanted, 1991 to 1999**

Day spas, more and more Bill Clinton, crystals, Alanis Morissette CDs, Hillary's hair, a tricked-out SUV, a kid in federally funded day care, and equal opportunity to make millions as a day trader

The main thing women wanted from men: passion. What a mess. By the 1990s, half the men in America were weeping in the woods, holding on to one another for dear life, and talking about their inner children. The other half were on cell phones. Women were taking over the power positions in universities and the news media, so they were too busy to notice. But when they did, they realized that men were no longer giving them what they wanted.

So they changed their minds again. What they really wanted was passion. Not old-fashioned romance or courtship. They wanted nude megamergers. They wanted men who would be assertive about their sexuality but not about what to order in a restaurant, men who would make them feel wise all day and girlish all night. Guys who could do all this right were worshiped by women, even while they trashed the babes in the office. Men's slogan for the 1990s: "Thanks, honey. I needed that." Women's slogan: "Thanks, bud. I wanted that."

What Women Want Right Now

This brings us to Ron Geraci, one of the editors of *Men's Health* magazine. He was telling me about a guy in West Virginia who had concocted a fabulous woo plan to capture the affection of a pretty, charming, brown-haired woman in her late twenties. The centerpiece of the program: the perfect first-date, front-door gift. The guy showed up for his first date carrying not flowers and not chocolates and not a copy of *What Women Want*. He brought her venison and a bunch of fish.

"She described it as 'deer meat and trout,'" said Geraci, spellbound.

For Geraci—who has resorted to some of the most complex, elaborate, and frankly desperate dating gambits I've ever seen—it was an epiphany. "Deer meat and trout," he nearly whispered, "is a very good move."

It is a good move, and here's why: Smart women under 40 have almost no nostalgia for feminism. They realize that they can work meaningless jobs, just like men. They know that they can drive fast and smoke cigars like a big Mama Warbucks. They realize by now that it doesn't take a lot of brain muscle to slap together a career of some sort. I mean, Janet Reno has a career, for pity's sake. Meanwhile, the streets are meaner, TV is uglier, women are less safe, and kids are shooting first and asking to grow up later. "We don't need that," sensible women say to themselves. "We need a massive dose of spontaneous Eastwood. We need meat-toters."

The Swing of the Pendulum

Of course, it's not easy for some women to want something that the National Sisterhood says sucks. But just maybe Patricia Ireland's book is on the remainders table because what women want now is a man who is unapologetically masculine, a man who knows what a woman needs if only because it's a reflection of what everybody needs. Maybe it's a guy who knows that if men aren't doing what needs to be done for the wife and kids, they're likely to find themselves doing some really stupid stuff, like the stuff they'd want to do if they didn't have a wife and kids.

Maybe women want a meat man, a guy who doesn't wait for orders, doesn't wait to discuss relationships, doesn't test for hurt feelings. Maybe they want a man who knows what the right thing is and just shows up with it at the front door. And maybe if a woman can get past the pile of venison without saying, "Baloney," she's likely to find there a brave pioneer of neopatriarchy—a guy who takes his cards, walks in, puts them down on the dining-room table, piles the groceries on top, and says, "Here's the bacon. Now let's eat."

Valley of Temptation

You stop at a convenience store to buy a few items at twice what you'd pay in a grocery store. The clerk is an 18-year-old nymphet named Teena wearing a white T-shirt with, uh, no visible means of support. Unfortunately, your wife/girlfriend/mother is right behind you, so you demurely . . . what? Look away? Are you crazy? Dennis Jackson knows all about such daily man-temptations, and he helps walk us through the fire and emerge unscathed on the other side. Read on . . .

It's all Adam's fault. Adam, the proto-wuss. Any idiot knows better than to accept a helping of raw, unwashed fruit from a naked woman who talks to snakes. But Adam didn't, so now we all know about good and evil, and we feel guilty about taking extra money from a guy who charged so much to begin with. Or about looking at women and praying for nudity.

It's a battle over "impulse control"—the behavioral phenomenon that can lead men to be bad without even trying. Freudians see temptation as a dustup between unconscious impulses and conscious desires. Other psychoanalysts join your girlfriend, all her friends, and the Catholic church in thinking that man is simply compelled to fall.

Whatever the reason, says Steve Yarris, Psy.D., a New York City psychologist, a temptation is a temptation because you know it's bad but you want to do it anyway, even when succumbing could net you a smack in the face, a ruined relationship, a presidential impeachment, or a jail sentence.

So what can you do? At least venture into moral battle knowing the biggest temptations that you're likely to face and when to resist them—or, better, the least dangerous way to give in to the temptations.

To look down her blouse

She bends over and (cue choir of angels singing on high) there they are! Get this straight: Peeking is not your fault. "It's in a man's wiring," says William Winkler, Ph.D., a psychologist and sex therapist in Portland, Oregon. "Men unconsciously assess women as partners and potential childbearers." Exactly. We look at women's breasts because we don't want to see children starve, not because a perfectly formed orb of flesh with an erotic device attached to the front of it means anything to us. We're just, you know, assessing.

The best way to give in: Either go to the factory showroom—a topless bar, where potential childbearing equipment is on full display—or perform your evaluation with finesse. Women may not mind an occasional peek, but they're not crazy about all-out drooling. If you're caught in mid-slobber, you have three options.

If she sees you, flatter her. "Hey, that's a cool-looking necklace with the Sign of the Beast on it! I bet my girlfriend would love something like that. Where'd you get it?" It's lame, but it could save you a slap.

If she accuses you, revert to the Biological Imperative. "Looking at your hooters? Hardly! It was merely an expression of a biological response developed over a long evolutionary process."

If she sees you and smiles, don't look away. Averting your glance is like impersonating Jerry Lewis saying, "Oh, jeez, lady, I'm so sorry."

To go out for a bagel and wind up in Tahiti

Step out for a newspaper and never come back. Tempting, no? Men with responsibilities at home are often tempted to leave it all behind, even if only temporarily, says Edward Dreyfus, Ph.D., a California psychologist. Some aging men feel that an adventure in Rio or along the Appalachian Trail will make them feel young again. "For many men, the dream is to feel independent, to leave

Survival tips for married guys: 1) Stop watching the game. 2) Listen to what she's saying. 3) Repeat what she's just said. 4) Tell her that what she's just said makes sense to you. 5) Wait at least 20 seconds before you resume watching the game.

mortgage payments and stressful jobs and family responsibilities," he says. "The desire to flee could be a sign of fear of intimacy." Especially intimacy with a mortgage banker.

The best way to give in: Satisfy your horizon fever by taking a daylong truck ride across the state with a couple of friends, Dr. Dreyfus says. If that's too short, Ice Haven Expeditions in Alberta will take you on a rambunctious, 10-day dogsled tour through the Canadian Rockies. For around $2,000, you'll be the musher of your own eight-husky team; call (403) 845-5206. If sleeping in snow with mutts doesn't satisfy your wanderlust, there's always the Peace Corps.

● To tell your mother-in-law to take her broom and shove it
She already thinks that her daughter married way beneath her station. She rips away chunks of your flesh while advising you on how to raise your kids and commenting on your inability to fix toilets. You brood and boil, but you hold back, raising your stress level, ruining your day, your week, your life.

The best way to give in: Screaming at the old hag will just force your wife to defend the indefensible. Instead, simply treat your wife better, Dr. Yarris says, especially in front of your mother-in-law. When the biddy attacks you, turn to your wife and ask her how big her new diamond should be. "That will dump burning coals on your mother-in-law's head, because it'll be one less thing that she can say about you," he says. "If you remain placid and nonengaging, it'll drive her nuts." Then exploit the buzzard's babysitting skills and take your wife to a squalid sex motel for a few days. Or make Mom ride in the backseat with an unwashed dog. But keep smiling.

● To have a millennial kind of affair
Millions of guys have been tempted to take the virtue out of virtual by dancing modem-to-modem with a female friend. If your cyberflirting heats up, though, you could be—in the eyes of your mate—engaging in an affair.

"E-mail can lead to a very real emotional connection, and it can be filled with preoccupation, obsession, and sexual energy," says Gerald Mayer, Ph.D., a psychologist in Phoenix. "In some cases, it's a matter of true infidelity."

The best way to give in: No safe ones. Are you spending more time thinking about a nameless, faceless cyberpartner than you spend thinking about your real-life partner in the next room? If so, Dr. Mayer says, start deleting and stop replying.

● To reignite your old flame
Remember the mirrors on her ceiling? That's why you're tempted to rendezvous with your ex—euphoric recall, psychologists call it. "After we've left a

relationship, we usually don't think of all the horrible things," Dr. Mayer says. "We tend to think about how great it was that time on the beach." The reunion may start fiery, but it'll end when she nags you for snoring.

The best way to give in: There is none. This kind of recycling is a bad idea. Re-create the romance, and you'll probably end up re-creating the breakup, too.

◉ To bench-press 300 pounds just to impress the stairclimber chicks

She checked you out. Wait till she checks *this* out! So what if it's only your third session back at the gym since your holiday hiatus? All around you, rippled lads are parading their pecs, and a sudden testosterone surge tempts you to lift weights well above your personal best.

The best way to give in: Stick with lighter weights and avoid doing the one-rep max. You could permanently damage your tendons and ligaments, says John Boos, a New York City strength coach and former Olympic trainer. If you want to brag, Boos suggests, do some math. Add 33 percent to the weight that you can do for 10 repetitions. For example, if you consistently bench 150 pounds, your max should be about 200.

SEX WARS

"Honey, am I home?"

HELP ONLINE

CARTOON COUNSELING

Breakup Girl, a cartoon character with "supernatural" powers, mends
broken hearts and dispenses wise advice for the heartbroken and lovelorn.
It seems a little more geared to women than men, but it's corny
and camp and cool and kind of fun and even confidence-inspiring.
If Breakup Girl can't fix it, it's beyond repair.
www.breakupgirl.com

LIPP SERVICE

Lucy Lipps describes herself as "a radio-cable Goddess/spokeswoman/
Cyberbabe/analyst/businesswoman. Through my multiple lives so far, I
have had the opportunity to be Queen of the international party tornado of
fun and spend time with some of the world's most amazing men and women;
with years of good tips to my credit (just ask my friends), it has made me
a leading authority on romance and the art of being a contemporary
Sex Goddess." For what it's worth, she offers free advice about relationships.
www.lucylipps.com

EXTRAMARITAL EXPERTS

This site contains resources for men and women recovering from
extramarital affairs. It's hosted by a husband-and-wife team who have
been married for 44 years, having survived the 7 years of the husband's
infidelity. Married 44 years . . . guess that gives them 88 years
of experience cumulatively. And that's a lot.
www.dearpeggy.com

FIGHTING FOR LOVE

The Coalition for Marriage, Family, and Couples Education contends
that "the difference between successful and unsuccessful couples is how
they handle their differences. Successful couples disagree in a way that makes
their marriages stronger. They also have a bunch of other skills that help
them build long-term happiness and satisfaction." See the site's directory
of programs to discover a useful listing of organizations, courses,
and resources available for making marriages work, for saving marriages
on the brink, and for making good marriages better.

www.smartmarriages.com

MAN'S GUIDE INTERVIEW

Enough Already with the Blame Game

An Interview with Susan Faludi

Susan Faludi may be a feminist, but that doesn't mean she's a man-hater. She followed up her first book, Backlash: The Undeclared War against American Women, *with the more male-friendly* Stiffed: The Betrayal of the American Man. *Clearly, she knows that there are two sides to male-female dynamics, and she believes that whatever nasty stuff is simmering between men and women, we guys aren't solely responsible for it. Nor are women, for that matter. A lot of it, she believes, is simply the process of coping with profound cultural change. Not everyone agrees with her, of course. But Faludi's words carry some weight.*

She's a writer for such publications as Newsweek, The Wall Street Journal, The New York Times, The Miami Herald, *and the* San Jose Mercury News. *And Faludi has spent more than a bit of time studying and writing about the male-female thing. So just how does she view the current status of men?*

MAN'S GUIDE: In the title of your latest book, the first word is *stiffed.* That's pretty direct and to the point. How badly have we been stiffed, and what's the source of that?

FALUDI: Women often talk about what men have *done.* We talk about what men *made* happen. We talk about men dominating the scene. But we almost never talk about the social forces that act upon men.

So what I did was attempt to figure out what those forces are. I wanted to find men's hidden social history and excavate it. I wanted to understand how men got to the point they are today, where so many of them are in a lot of pain. Men are confused, they're frustrated, and a lot of them don't know what it means to be a man anymore.

And one of the big things I did in the book was to try to make sense of what's happened to men in the several decades since World War II.

MAN'S GUIDE: Okay. Why is that period of time so important to men's behavior and male-female relationships today?

FALUDI: When you look back over men's recent history—the postwar generation and the baby boom—what you find is a story of betrayal on many levels. After World War II, for example, there was a very clear promise made to men by their former G.I. fathers about what it meant to be a man.

MAN'S GUIDE: And what was that promise?

FALUDI: The fathers held up this model of manhood in which men officially became men by going out to tame a frontier, fight an identifiable enemy, and then return home to provide for their families and their communities. But that model was already outmoded.

For one thing, by the time of John F. Kennedy's presidency, the only frontier that fathers had to offer their sons was the void of outer space, a place that no one could effectively colonize or conquer.

And instead of having a clear enemy as we did in World War II when we stormed the beaches of Normandy, we had Vietnam. That was a conflict in which the enemy was decidedly unclear, and the whole mission turned into a tragic mystery.

As if that wasn't bad enough, the men returned from war expecting a culture of brotherhood like the one their fathers had enjoyed after World War II. Instead, it turned out to be a corporate brotherhood in which men's loyalty was repaid by being laid off by the millions.

And then, finally, so many men of the baby boom generation wound up married to women who were in need of support primarily because they had been forced out of jobs themselves after the soldiers came home. These were women who were

perfect figures

"I have never had a woman to give me a headache. I have never wanted a partner, and I honored my mother and father so God could spare my life."

—South African Nicklaas Amsterdam, 112, on how he managed to live so long

made artificially dependent, and they ultimately rebelled against that situation.

MAN'S GUIDE: So men returned to this whole new set of societal rules, and they returned to women who had enjoyed a taste of autonomy that was yanked away. That's where the blame began?

FALUDI: If men had been brutally honest with themselves about the source of their confusion and upset, then women—particularly those women who had found their autonomy—wouldn't have been the targets for blame.

Because if men had really looked at how they got into this fix, they would have seen that it wasn't the convenient scapegoat of feminism or affirmative action or political correctness or Hillary Clinton. Instead, they were caught up in the gears of a profound cultural change.

Men were raised with this image of their fathers being productive and hardworking, yet still engaged in the activities of their communities and their society. And then, over the course of their lives, these sons of World War II fathers watched this model of manhood, community, and family become severely devalued.

The former model of manhood was cast aside in favor of an ornamental kind of masculinity where you proved your manhood not so much by being a producer but by being a consumer. To be a man today, you need to have the most of everything. You must have the most electronics, the biggest killing in the stock market, the largest SUV, the biggest biceps.

The reality of manhood was replaced by an image of manhood. That was a major cultural shift. But it's hard to attack that because a cultural change has no real face. It's easier to go after a specific group. So some men end up saying, you know, "I don't feel powerful because women took my power away."

But the truth is that the same culture that makes so many men feel powerless makes women feel demeaned. In fact, that same consumer culture that has betrayed men first operated on women. That consumerism was part of why women revolted to begin with, because they didn't want to be treated like doormats and objects. So men and women are really being attacked by the same forces.

MAN'S GUIDE: It seems like both sides are pointing their fingers at each other, even though they aren't entirely at fault. Is one side more justified than the other? Or are men and women both equally responsible for the pickle we're in?

> **FALUDI:** Well, I don't know about equal damage. I mean, women were coming up from a lot of layers of subjugation. But the other problem with assigning relative blame is that it depends on what men you're talking about.
>
> I mean, you could be talking about men who are disenfranchised in this society, you could be talking about working-class men, you could be talking about Black men. These and other groups of men are a very different story from the very privileged upper-class men who really do have it over women.

MAN'S GUIDE: Those kinds of men have it over all of us, not just women.

> **FALUDI:** Exactly. We're being kicked in the head by the same forces. I mean, did some feminists engage in some unfair name-calling and improper generalizations about men? Sure. They were equating men in general with the men in power.
>
> In advancing a movement, people feel they need to have a clear enemy. The enemy seemed clear to feminists in the late 1960s and 1970s because everywhere they looked, there were men in power. Men were at the top of the corporate ladder, at the head of the movie studios, and at the head of Madison Avenue advertising agencies. Men were in charge of the network news. The degrading images of women were created by men. Of course, that's not all men. The truth is that maybe 1 in 10 million men owns a huge media company.

MAN'S GUIDE: So the feminists who did overreact and blame every man were confusing the men with "The Man."

> **FALUDI:** Exactly.

MAN'S GUIDE: So where are we at right now in our relationships with women and our ability to relate to women?

FALUDI: Well, there are bright spots in this otherwise gloomy story for men. The younger generation of men, for example, are much more inclined to be emotionally involved and engaged in their family lives. They are much more open and vulnerable with their children, their wives, and other loved ones.

MAN'S GUIDE: Have they become this way with the help of their fathers or in spite of their fathers?

FALUDI: I think it is in spite of their fathers. Actually, if anybody was of any help in clearing the way for men to open up emotionally, it was feminists. Feminists really championed caring roles for men. They were the ones who said there's nothing wimpy about being an involved, caring father.

The problem now is that while there has been a real positive change in how much sustenance and pleasure men can get out of their family lives, men are finding that the world outside their homes is not very welcoming to them.

The surrounding culture says to men that you have to be a winner. If you're a man, you have to be on top at all times. The message men get over and over again from the popular culture is that you're either number one or you're a loser. There is no middle ground. There is no room for the guy who is simply committed to his craft or a man who is a caring citizen in his community. Those kinds of men get no recognition.

We live in a culture where everything is about recognition. It's about how you rank and how many eyeballs are turned your way. There are only a few people who can cash in on that kind of exposure and who can rise to the top. And much of that is determined by luck.

So the rest of the men who work hard, who care about their families, and who care about their communities cannot find a place for themselves in the world. They don't feel acknowledged or valued.

MAN'S GUIDE: I know there are social and psychological differences between men and women, but are the lines starting to blur more? As you noted, we have a culture now where it only matters what your image is and how financially successful you are. As women continue to rise in the ranks of the business world and political world, are they getting the same kind of pres-

sure as the men? Is this new model of "manhood" that you mention some-thing that women have to deal with, too?

> **FALUDI:** Yeah. I mean, if there's a take-away lesson here, it's this: It really is a tragedy that men and women see each other as the enemy at a time when both are struggling with the same cultural forces. The fact is, men increasingly are being as objectified by this entertainment- and consumer-oriented culture as the women are.

MAN'S GUIDE: So genders of the world unite, then?

> **FALUDI:** Pretty much. If men and women could get beyond seeing each other as their great antagonists, great things could happen. If they looked honestly at the real source of their crises, these men who are in turmoil and the feminists who have their own struggles might recognize that they are actually each other's allies.
>
> I mean, if you look at what feminism was about, particularly in the second wave of feminism in the 1970s, a lot of it was about confronting consumerism. The movement was about confronting this whole capitalist idea that you must define yourself by your purchases. For women, that meant fighting against the expectation that they would all buy Playtex bras and lemon-scented Pledge.
>
> And with that kind of consumer culture, you have to live up to these insane images that are created by the business world—by companies that just want to sell you things. Now men are really up against that same kind of pressure. So there really is so much that men could actually learn from the feminists, who have had to deal with this issue before.

perfect figures

"She is a woman, after all. Rattling rockets and bombs— it is simply against nature."

—Russian Communist Party leader Gennady Zyuganov, claiming that Secretary of State Madeleine Albright is bringing shame to dames the world over by frequently advocating use of military force

MAN'S GUIDE: We still use terms like *war of the sexes.* Despite the growing openness of men emotionally, are we still hopelessly tied up in viewing the opposite gender as the enemy?

FALUDI: Both sexes are encouraged to view each other as the enemy. It's interesting how persistent it is. After *Stiffed* came out—a book that I sort of saw as friendly, as a kind of holding out of the olive branch—the response from women was more negative than I expected. It wasn't like all the women or even all the feminists had a bad reaction. But a pretty large number of women I heard from said, "We don't want to hear about men's pain. To hell with them. We hope they're suffering. They're the enemy. They did all of this bad stuff to us."

And a lot of men, too, reacted negatively. They said, "We don't want any empathy from women. We don't trust them. They're the reason we're miserable."

So there's still an enormous investment in blaming each other. It's easier to blame somebody else. And let's face it: It's much easier to blame a specific gender or race or person than to blame larger power structures.

It's hard to work up much fervor in blaming corporate and economic forces that we only half understand and that seem very murky and mysterious to us. It's easier to personalize everything. And for many people, of course, they've had bad experiences with the opposite sex, so they blame a gender. It's easier to say, "Well, I'm unhappy because my last two girlfriends didn't respect me."

But that's too simplistic. For most people, unhappiness springs from a much more complicated tangle of sources, not just a particular person or a particular subgroup of people.

Across America, people are less and less a part of their communities. We are becoming less knitted together in society. As that happens, we become more and more subject to the power of the marketplace.

Both men and women have this sense that they've lost their grasp on things. They feel that they are not really needed anywhere. This gener-

(**SEX** ⚥ **TRENDS**)

WE PREFER ZANE GREY

One-third of all Americans read romance novels—45 percent of all women and 16 percent of all men. Fans of the genre are most likely to be high school graduates and to live in the West.

ates an enormous sense of powerlessness. Then people become fearful about that powerlessness. And then they take out their fears and frustrations on other people, and they seek out convenient targets.

MAN'S GUIDE: Like blaming men or blaming women. Well, apart from ripping society down to its foundations and starting from scratch, what can we do to improve the situation?

FALUDI: I think the place to start is to be honest about searching out the real sources of our problems, instead of just grasping at some easy sound-bite explanation of "He did this to me" or "She did this to me."

But beyond that—and this is the hard part—we have to search for new ways of pursuing social change. We need to start rebuilding and revitalizing our public lives so that we're working toward something positive instead of basing our behaviors on finding enemies and then shooting them down.

There are indications that we're getting there. The protests against the World Trade Organization are a good example. Those protests were not about going after certain people but about confronting the global economic system and asking questions about what our collective vision is for society. You know, asking whether we want to build a world in which we're ruled by faceless transnational corporations that exploit workers halfway across the world just so that we can have our air conditioners and SUVs.

These protests brought together a diverse group of people—men and women ranging from steelworkers and service professionals to butterfly defenders and tree huggers. Also, it wasn't about "getting somebody" or winning. It was about figuring out what's wrong and what kind of world we want to make.

Part of the problem in our society is that people are subjected to worrying about short-term financial questions. They get concerned about how much more money they can make on the stock market, or whether somebody else is making more money than they are. Really, it's such a wealth-driven culture now. People aren't thinking about "Well, am I happy doing any of this?" or "What does it really mean to be a good man?"

When we start asking those questions, we can begin to build a caring, vibrant society rather than point fingers at each other.

QUICKIES

JUSTICE OF THE PEACE

Many married couples, whether newlyweds or oldlyweds, struggle with the question, "Just whose money is it, anyway?" It's jointly owned when the mortgage payment comes due, but it shifts to being a little bit more yours than hers when that spare cordless drill or graphite-beryllium putter catches your eye. To help keep the peace, consider establishing a hybrid system of bank accounts, says Ken Kurson in *Esquire* magazine. This arrangement is known in the money biz as his-hers-ours banking. Partners enjoy separate accounts to stash their own mad money but share a joint account for household expenses.

This setup offers the independence and protection of separate accounts and the ease and solidarity of a joint one (particularly useful for couples who live together without the bonds of matrimony). Drawback: Banks often require minimum balances before they'll pony up free checking, which ties up a certain amount of cash every month. So try a little smooth talking first. Your bank may lower or waive minimum balances when you keep several accounts there—or even tally up the total held in all accounts in satisfying their minimums.

HAUS-HUSBANDS DO HARD TIME

Always get stuck with dish duty? You may want to move to Europe. Last year, Germany's Green Party proposed legislation that would have forced lazy husbands to do half of the cooking and cleaning. "It was front-page news and sparked a huge debate," says Leonie Gebers, a spokesperson for the German Ministry of Women and Family Affairs. "Women here have to do all the work at home."

The German measure went down the drain (how do you enforce a scrub-the-tub decree?), but frazzled fraus in Austria have had more success. Recently, the Austrian Parliament struck down a law allowing a husband to divorce his wife for neglecting the housework, then added a new clause with a strong message: If both partners bring home the bacon, they are both responsible for cooking it . . . and for degreasing the pan.

Recalcitrant husbands won't be prosecuted, but maybe they should be. Researchers at Brown University in Providence, Rhode Island, recently concluded that in order to maintain psychological well-being, neither partner should do more than 46 percent of the housework. Of course, those numbers don't add up. Perhaps a government-funded cleaning service could vacuum away the last 8 percent. Then again, that's what teenagers are for.

BIG BENEFITS FROM SMALL TALK

Yapping with your wife or girlfriend may have its perils, but it could be less taxing to your brain than trying to ignore her. At Case Western Reserve University in Cleveland, 37 students were paired one-on-one with researchers in a room for 4 minutes. About half of the students were told to ignore the researcher; the rest could make small talk.

Afterward, all the students were given 20 difficult word puzzles.

The silent subjects quit trying to solve them much sooner than the gabby ones did. "This suggests that consciously ignoring people requires a lot of mental energy," says Kristin Sommer, Ph.D., of Baruch College in New York City, who led the study.

perfect figures

Average income per sex scene
for top female porn stars:
$5,000

Average income per scene
for male porn stars: $500

(They *pay* these guys?)

DEAR DR. MANLY

Q: _My wife accidentally (that's her story) kneed me in the crotch while we were wrestling around. Of course, it hurt . . . so bad that I almost threw up. She was mildly sympathetic, but I suspect she thought that I was digging for sympathy._ Why does getting racked hurt so bad—and why do I feel it in my gut when it's my jewels that took the knock?
—P. S., ALBUQUERQUE, NEW MEXICO

A: The family jewels are more sensitive than a roomful of Volvo owners because they're oh-so-rich in nerve endings. The singular pain that results from a tap in testicles is nature's way of ensuring your ability to procreate. Get racked once, and you'll do anything to avoid the damage to your old boys' fate in the future. Don't think of it as pain, think of it as a certain protective instinct. In fact, be grateful for it. Show it some appreciation. Just say, "Thank you, excruciating, agonizing pain that no woman could ever understand and that obviously hurts more than having a baby." No, don't say that last bit if there is a woman within 2 to 3 miles. Not if you're interested in having sex with a partner again in this lifetime. That's my best professional advice.

Regarding the tendency of this singular pain to travel north: When boys are still womb-bound fetuses, the testes begin to take shape up in the abdomen, near the stomach and kidneys. The nerves and blood vessels remain attached there even after the gonads hit dangle mode. That's why you feel pain in the very pit of your stomach after a poke in the privates. That pain is so acute, incidentally, that men can actually reexperience it simply by watching someone else receive the blow. That's empathy, man, if ever I saw it. And, jeez, women say guys don't have feelings.

Q: I'm 35, and even though I'm not the stag-in-rut that I was at 17, I still feel pretty frisky. _Why do they say that a woman's sexual peak is later than ours?_
—M. B., RENO

A: Maybe women spend their formative sexual years doing more important things. (That's why we here at _Man's Guide_ have started a campaign to ban "more important things.") The idea that a man's sexuality peaks at 18 and that a woman's peaks around 30 has no physiological basis, says Eileen Palace, Ph.D., director of the Center for Sexual Health at Tulane University in New Orleans. According to Dr. Palace, women tend to have fewer sexual experiences early on (either solo or with a partner), so they need more time to figure out what brings them to orgasm.

Men, it would seem, are driving an automatic; women, a manual transmission. Once they hit their thirties, they've had more practice and are ready to experiment more. Of course, by then we're dating their younger sisters.

perfect figures

"Women might be able to fake orgasms, but men can fake whole relationships."

—Comedian Jimmy Shubert
at the Montreal Comedy Festival

Q: *My wife recently caught my 10-year-old son masturbating. She actually burst into tears, if you can believe it. The poor kid was mortified. What should I do? Is he going to be scarred for life?*
—Z. S., INDIANAPOLIS

A: Aside from shouting out an ex-girlfriend's name in the throes of an orgasm, there's nothing worse than getting caught in the solo act by your own mother. When I was 11, my mom opened my bedroom door without knocking as I was waxing the dolphin. She was (and I'm not making this up) carrying a bowl of warm tapioca pudding for me, which ended up all over the floor. Her reaction? "We're going to take you to the doctor!" Yes, it scarred me—but after puberty, I got over it. Today it makes for a great story. Even my mom laughs now every time she retells it at family reunions and block parties and awards luncheons. I learned my lesson that day. So, of course, I've never masturbated again. Never. Not without securing the door first.

This is one arena where women just don't get it, so you're going to have to step in. Tell him, "Congratulations! You're in the club!" Since it's obviously long overdue, sit him down and explain the delightful little discovery he's made in his boxers. No need for drama. As Keanu Reeves said in *Parenthood,* playing with themselves is just what little dudes do. And big dudes, for that matter.

Explain to him that men have a primal need to let their hands explore the southern hemisphere occasionally and—until he's old enough to drive the SUV and find a helper—it's perfectly acceptable recreation for him to enjoy, in his own room, with the door firmly closed. Then assure him that you and Mom will institute a new knock-and-wait-for-an-answer policy, effective immediately. And whatever you do, don't say "masturbation" more than once. That word was invented by medieval monks to scare all hell out of kids.

Dr. Manly is a fictional character.
The actual advice was provided by a variety of
medical doctors and other qualified experts.

SUPERCHARGE YOUR INNER HUNK

The art of attracting a woman (and maintaining sway over the woman you have) relies heavily on your sense of style and grace. Simply put, it's about attitude. If you look good and you feel good about yourself and the world, you get the girl. You keep the girl. Women can smell confidence the way timber wolves smell fear. It's something they want in a man.

Fortunately for your wallet, style is more than which label should be sewn in your suit. It's a formula for living your life. Clothes + grooming + presence + bearing = how the world sees you (and how you see yourself). Frank Sinatra had the math down: He could snag a broad while wearing a welder's mask and a burlap sack. We'd put money on it. The odds are suresville, baby.

From clothes (look good without a tie, solve the most common fashion dilemmas, maximize your current wardrobe) to presentation (carry yourself with elegance and grace, radiate sex appeal), here's what we taught Frankie way back when . . .

TOP TEN

Must-Have Clothes

When you're poised on the brink of a purchase, one question consistently arises: Can I wear this with anything I already own? We can't be certain about your last purchase, but we can make some recommendations for your next one. By adding the core items shown here to your basic wardrobe, you'll make everything else in it look better.

❶ **The dress shirt.** The classic dress shirt performs double duty better than any other item in your wardrobe. Wear with a sport jacket and jeans or a patterned tie and dark suit. Ditch the French blue and comatose white for pinstripes or another subtle pattern.

❷ **The blue blazer.** No private-school crest here. The three-button styling and the classic color mean that you'll look like a guy with something to do, not like an unemployed consultant. And lose the gold buttons, please. The war's over.

❸ **Loafers.** Just call them loafers and save your pennies for a pair that'll work hard for years. Squared-off toes and suede uppers give your hooves more attitude than basic Weejuns. A thick sole is hip and comfortable.

❹ **Cargo shorts.** Trendy, but we're giving these one more year before we empty the pockets for good. Buy a pair that's long enough to reach almost to your knees. When cargoes are too short, you look like a guy shoplifting gym equipment.

5 **The polo shirt.** A fine knit says that it's more than just a T-shirt with a collar. One-button polos are dressier than the traditional three-button variety. Pair it with khakis or dark jeans if you're off duty, or toss a blue blazer over the top for a more polished look. And yes, you can button the top button as long as the neck fit is just right.

6 **The suede jacket.** More than a sport coat but less than a parka, this fall classic (in three-button style with open pockets) looks bohemian with a turtleneck and jauntily business-like with a dress shirt and patterned tie. Length? No lower than the crotch of your pants.

7 **The sweater-vest.** A dark, single-color sweater-vest can update the look of a sport coat or a two-piece suit. Think complementary colors, not contrasting.

8 **Corduroys.** In case you spent the last two decades stuck in a cubicle writing computer code for a living, we'll break it to you gently: Corduroys are back. Rule of thumb: The wider the wale (the "stripes"), the more casual the style. Go ahead and pair them with a dress shirt and tie; we'll back you up on it.

9 **The monk-strap shoe.** Not just for Pilgrims anymore. Like the classic dress shirt, the single-buckle monk-strap (in brown or black, oiled leather or suede) cozies up nicely to a suit, jeans, or business-casual attire.

10 **The black leather belt.** Yes, people do notice belts, so toss that hand-tooled Native American number with the turquoise buckle that you bought at the Grand Canyon and trade it for a medium-width belt of polished obsidian leather with a simple silver buckle.

Fashion and Style Problem-Solver

Women are carefully schooled in the fine art of clothes-as-sex-appeal from the time their first Barbie moves into that Deluxe Dream House. But nothing (not swing dancing, feminine napkins, or the political philosophy of the National Organization for Women) baffles a man as much as the nuances of current fashion. Jennifer Haigh selected some of the most common style pleas, then solicited answers from fashion experts who stake their reputations on making men look downright irresistible.

● What's the perfect year-round suit?

Almost any light- to medium-weight suit made of Super 100s wool (check the tag) can be worn year-round, according to Sal Cesarani, a men's fashion designer. "The one exception is a suit with a brushed effect—it feels almost velvety to the touch. Those should be worn only in the fall and winter," he says. If you buy only one suit, make it charcoal or light gray.

● My dad always told me to wear black shoes with black or gray suits, and brown shoes with blue or beige suits. What are the modern rules for shoe- and suit-color combinations?

Your father's conservative approach will certainly prevent you from making any huge style gaffes, but you'll find plenty of company if you sport black loafers with your khakis or even brown cap toes with a gray suit. "The modern rule is that there are no rules," says Dennis Sak, vice president at Salvatore Ferragamo. "The trendier the suit, the more freedom you have to play around with the shoes. It mostly depends on your personal style."

● I've seen photos of Frank Sinatra wearing a tie clip, and he looks kind of cool. I have a bunch of tie clips my dad left me. Can I pull off the Rat Pack look?

First off, Frank didn't *look* cool—he *defined* cool. There's a difference. And just for the record, there are three types of tie holders: bars, clips, and tacks. A tie bar extends across three-quarters of the tie's width at midchest. A tie clip is about half the size of a tie bar, and it clips to your shirt. A tie tack has a sharp pin that sticks through your tie and shirt.

All were designed to keep your tie out of the marinara sauce—or, in Sinatra's case, out of Ava Gardner's cleavage. Should you wear one? "They're unnecessary and pretentious," says Warren Christopher, *Men's Health* magazine style editor. "My advice: Don't eat spaghetti while wearing a tie; avoid fist-fights; and avoid tie paraphernalia at all costs."

● **Can I wear athletic shoes with anything other than workout clothes?**
The name of the shoes should answer your question. They're athletic shoes. Unless you're running, dribbling, throwing, sliding, or stealing CDs from the drugstore, don't wear them. When you want to go casual, there are plenty of comfortable alternatives. Almost any plain slip-on that's rounded or squared at the toe is fine to wear with jeans or khakis. If the toe is at all pointed, however, or if the slip-on has tassels, it's not going to fly as a casual shoe.

> **"** He's handsome. He's charismatic. But we really can't find out why he's so popular. **"**
>
> —Tokyo Broadcasting System's Eiichiro Inai, on George W. Bush's run for the presidency

Christopher recommends contemporary slip-ons from Bally, Bass, Dexter, Kenneth Cole, and Cole Haan. Lace-up ankle boots are also comfortable and casual, and you can wear them with just about anything except shorts.

● **I see a lot of shoes that have thick soles. How thick is too thick to wear with a suit?**
A sole about $\frac{1}{2}$ inch thick will go with just about any suit, says Robert Mingione, vice president of product development for Kenneth Cole. If your suit has a trendy cut, you can wear a sole up to $\frac{3}{4}$ inch thick. The best way to combine a traditional suit with trendy footwear is to choose a shoe with a thinner sole and a squared toe.

● **How wide should a dress belt be? And what's the style?**
For dress or dress casual (anything but jeans), you should pick up a belt that's $1\frac{1}{4}$ inches wide, according to Andy Stinson of Torino Belts. You can wear a wider one with jeans if you like. As for style, Stinson suggests narrower belts with unstitched edges and no braiding. Buckles should be rounded and on the small side. Nowadays, they lean toward silver rather than gold or brass. Belts with metal tips or metal keepers (a keeper is the little thing you slide the end of the belt under after you buckle it) are not as popular as they were a few years ago, but they're still fine for golf and other casual looks.

● **What is the proper width for pant cuffs? Does it have anything to do with how tall I am?**
Anything between $1\frac{1}{2}$ and 2 inches is acceptable, says Tom Mastronardi of Beauchamp, Mastronardi and Associates, a fashion-industry consulting firm.

(continued on page 38)

Look Smart without a Tie

For as long as almost any man alive can remember, if you wanted to be taken seriously, you had to wear a tie. Then the rules changed, and a tie was no longer required for respect. Why they changed is irrelevant. You need to know what to do about it.

◉ Know before you go.
Some occasions still demand a tie: funerals, weddings, appointments in traffic court. Elsewhere, common sense will usually provide an answer. For examples of lapses in common sense, check out the actors who show up at the Academy Awards in "alternative" tuxedos and neckwear. If you're uncertain, wear a tie. You can always remove it.

◉ Wear the right T.
Some T-shirts are dressy enough to wear solo with a suit. White ones that come in three-packs are not. "If you want to wear a stand-alone T-shirt under a jacket, buy one with a ribbed knit," says Richard Bowes, fashion director of Bergdorf Goodman in New York City.

Wear a sport coat and slacks, or a dark suit—no double-breasted jackets. Neutral or dark colors work best. Avoid pastels and bright colors.

◉ No "replacement" ties.
Ascots, bolo ties, and the like will make people think you're a character, as in, "Oh, he's a character." The world has never known a more backhanded compliment.

◉ Buy strategically.
"When you buy a suit or sport coat, purchase a few things that work with it," says Leon Hall of the E! Channel's *Fashion Emergency*. "First on the list are a white shirt and a perfect tie. Pick another shirt that has a bold color or an interesting stripe or a tattersall check." A solid shirt that's darker than your suit can also work. "A dark blue, dark brown, or black shirt looks great under a suit," says Bowes. "In the summer, a linen shirt under a suit also works well." Consider buying a black sport coat made of tropical-weight wool—it's comfortable in warm temperatures, and you can wear it with everything. Another option: a sport coat in a subtle plaid or neutral pattern, such as houndstooth.

◉ Don't button up.
If you like to button polo shirts up to the top, go for it. But never button the top button on a dress shirt that buttons all the way down the front. The nerd look is way over. Stop when you've undone two buttons—that's the maximum.

◉ Be a polo player.
In the spring and summer, try a polo shirt made of silk, linen, cotton, rayon, or

some blend thereof. A classic cotton pique polo shirt is fine with a sport coat and khakis or linen pants after a round of golf. (Pique has a raised, wafflelike appearance.) But at the office, pique will look too casual, so wear a finer-grade cotton polo, such as one made from pima or Sea Island cotton; check the label. Richly colored polos in shades such as burgundy and deep purple complement navy, gray, and black suits. "Choose one with a collar that lies nicely, and never pull the collar of your polo shirt over your jacket lapels," says Hall.

● Avoid mixing fabrics from different seasons.

Summer polos aren't meant to be worn with winter-weight tweed blazers and heavy woolen trousers. But it's fine to pair them with linen or silk.

● Add distractions.

"A solid-color crew- or V-neck sweater over a white or black T-shirt looks great under a patterned sport coat," says Ron Chereskin, a New York sportswear designer. If you wear the crew, a little bit of the T-shirt will probably peek out, which is fine. Wear a silk or cotton sweater under a lightweight jacket in warmer months and switch to a lightweight wool or cashmere sweater in the fall.

● Make a change in September.

Come fall, wear lightweight wool or silk knit turtlenecks, or mock turtles in neutral shades, such as tan, gray, and black. Avoid a super-bulky turtleneck under a jacket, however. And don't wear the cotton turtles you picked up at the end-of-winter sales. They're best worn under sweaters.

● Keep trousers simple.

For an uncomplicated look, pair a sport coat with pants in neutral colors, such as khaki and black. Never try to pass off your navy suit pants with a different jacket—nobody will be fooled.

● Before you step out, do a shoe review.

The black lace-ups you'd wear with a conservative suit and tie may be too dressy. So try a monk-strap (a shoe with a crossover strap, not laces) or a more casual lace-up with a slightly square toe. When wearing khakis, a polo shirt, and a sport coat, you can go with lug-soled oxfords or boots.

In general, a wider leg needs a wider cuff, and so does a lighter fabric. A wide cuff helps lightweight pants hang better. If you're not sure, ask a good tailor or a knowledgeable salesperson. As far as your height is concerned, if you're over 6 feet tall, wider cuffs will help balance the lower and upper halves of your body. If you're 5 feet 10 inches or shorter, consider a narrower cuff.

◉ Is it still cool to wear monogrammed shirts?

A monogrammed shirt isn't really current for business, but it can still work for casual occasions, says Leon Hall, cohost of the E! Network's *Fashion Emergency*. "The key is not to take it too seriously. Treat it like a jacket. It looks good over a T-shirt, with jeans." Another option: Encourage your girlfriend to wear it. "She can wear it over a tank top and baggy shorts and look really hot," he says.

◉ I need a new raincoat. Have any suggestions for a fresh look?

The cotton or cotton-blend double-breasted trench coat is a classic. But if you're tired of that look, there are plenty of other options that work with a suit. "Single-breasted, knee-length coats, either belted or unbelted, are very fashionable right now," says J. Stanley Tucker, senior vice president at Burberry Menswear Worldwide. "This style looks great on everyone but really tall men. If you're 6 feet 4 inches or over, you'll look as if you've outgrown your coat."

Ask a salesperson to show you coats made with microfiber fabrics. (That's a fancy euphemism for the dreaded "polyester.") Microfiber coats are lighter in weight and are easier to pack.

perfect figures

Number of times the average man shaves each week: 5.33

Number of hours spent shaving during his lifetime: 3,360

Whichever style you choose, make sure that the coat is labeled "waterproof" or "water-resistant." "Many coats sold as raincoats are not," says Tucker. If you plan to wear your new coat as a top layer in cold weather, make sure that it has an easily removable lining. And if you're the semi-sloppy type, keep in mind that navy, black, and olive green hide dirt better than tan.

◉ I often see well-dressed men wearing pocket squares. I like the look but wouldn't know how to wear one. A little help?

Three rules: 1) The square should be made of silk; 2) it should have the same general color scheme as your tie; and 3) it should never exactly match the pattern of your tie. Also, if you're wearing a white shirt, a white square will look fine no matter what color your suit is.

Here's the proper way to fold and tuck a square: Lay it on a flat surface and pick it up at the center point, so that all four corners fall downward. Grab it with your left hand, smooth the fabric, and fold it over your thumb. Now tuck it into your pocket with the points up. It should look soft, not perfectly folded, says Hall. "You can expose as many of the points as you like, but it shouldn't look like a corsage at a homecoming game."

Ooze Sex Appeal

You know a guy like this, who's possessed of rather average looks, as far as you're concerned. Certainly no freakin' Fabio. But for some reason (and this is the part that really honks you off), he's a no-fail hit with the femmes. They smile big when he talks to them, play with their hair, giggle. What's he got that you ain't got? Authors Perry Garfinkel and Brian Chichester know, and they give it to you straight in these two excerpts from the book Maximum Style.

It's nice to have style. Children adore you, men respect you, domestic animals rub against your shins. There's another side of style, however, that may matter more. It's a side that we're loath to acknowledge, mostly because we're not scoring particularly well in it. It's sex appeal.

"I think when we're young and are becoming sexual beings, we want to be seen as attractive, for our own personal satisfaction and to attract others," says Marvin Pieland of Saks Fifth Avenue Club for Men in New York City.

"Once you reach a certain age, especially if you're married, physical attractiveness doesn't seem as important," Pieland adds. "Unless you become divorced. I see that all the time. Then you realize how important looks are once you're back in circulation."

Want a second opinion? Ask the doctor.

To avoid lifeless hair, don't overuse your conditioner—once or twice a week max. Full head of dry hair? Use a product reinforced with oils. Oily or fine hair? Choose a conditioner with protein. Thinning hair? Apply only to the ends.

"There's no question. Outward appearances are our calling cards to the world. They're the first and most accessible part of your image that people see, and people will make judgments about it," says Ross E. Goldstein, Ph.D., a psychologist and president of Generation Insights, a consulting company in San Francisco.

Beauty . . . Beast?

Remember going out as a teen? You spent a huge amount of time preening before you left home. Why so much emphasis on looking good? Because it mattered. You knew that girls were judging you by your appearance.

> " It won't be so terrible to have Tarzan in pants. "
>
> —Avi Lant, a promoter in Israel for Disney's animated film *Tarzan,* on clothing the cartoon character in more than a loincloth in deference to ultra-orthodox Jewish moviegoers

Placing such emphasis on looking good was normal. And natural. And it still is, despite how superficial it may sound. As men, we keep unnaturally quiet about the importance of looking good, because outside of adolescence, it's usually viewed as vanity, a character flaw. But that denies the basic nature of life as an animal. "There's no question that attractive behavior is how a successful species adapts. It's evolution, and it's important on a deep biological level," says Hendrie Weisinger, Ph.D., a psychologist, business consultant, and author of *Nobody's Perfect* and *Dr. Weisinger's Anger Work-Out Book.*

The Science of Sex Appeal

Beauty may be in the eye of the beholder, but according to science, that's more idealism than realism. Science suggests that beauty is really hardwired in our genes and ingrained in our psyches.

"When I started my dissertation work in psychology, people believed that men were above physical beauty," Dr. Goldstein says. "The fact is that attractiveness is one of the most powerful factors in your image."

Reams of studies back this up. One well-known study of college students at the University of New Mexico in Albuquerque found that students with the most symmetrical bodies were perceived to be the most attractive. Students whose left and right sides differed by just 1 to 2 percent were found to be more attractive than those who differed between 5 and 7 percent. The prevailing theory is that symmetry implies healthier genes, and our internal mating machine, knowing this, subconsciously drives us in that direction.

In her book *The Complete Idiot's Guide to Dating,* Judy Kuriansky, Ph.D., a sex therapist and radio personality from New York City, neatly breaks down the chemical side of attraction. Among the most common chemicals, or hormones, involved in sex appeal, she says, are adrenaline (the rush), oxytocin (the cuddle chemical), phenylethylamine (natural-high chemicals), and the endorphins (the pleasure chemicals).

Our concept of beauty also is influenced by society. How else can you account for the fact that 42 percent of all *Playboy* Playmates between 1953 and 1996 had blonde hair, and almost half had hair that cascaded past their shoulders? Sociological influence works on men, too. Men of power, that is, men who are rich and famous, are generally viewed by society as the most sexy. That's a basic research premise of David M. Buss, Ph.D., psychology professor at the University of Texas at Austin and author of *The Evolution of Desire,* who surveyed more than 10,000 men and women from 37 cultures on six continents and five islands.

There are psychological factors in sex appeal as well. What rings the "attract-o-meter" for one woman might have everything to do with what's rolling around in her head. She may, for example, feel that a model man is loud, aggressive, and abrasive, because her father was like that. She may be predisposed to the scholarly, sensitive type if her first love was like that and she's subconsciously seeking to find him.

Tools of the Trade

Maybe you don't have much control over whether your eyes are more or less symmetrical, whether you're bringing in six figures a year, or whether the woman that you'd love to love has somebody else in mind. You do, however, have direct control over how appealing others find you. Realize that sex appeal involves connecting with others on an instinctual level. Sexy people are magnets, for men and women. "In a sense, you're presenting yourself in a way that pulls me toward you," Dr. Weisinger says. "You're sending out cues, almost like flirting. It's called charisma.

"Sex appeal is bonding. Does the person have a good sense of humor? Is he able to make you laugh? Is he sincere? It's emotional," Dr. Weisinger says. By realizing its importance, you'll be more likely to make the most of your sex appeal.

While physical attraction plays a healthy role in sex appeal, you're not condemned to solitude if no one's ever mistaken you for Mel Gibson.

"All is not lost if you're not attractive," Dr.

hot **TIP!**

Your belt should be 2 inches larger than your waist and should always be buckled on the third hole. And choose a color within a few shades of your shoes.

Goldstein says. "While looks might be important at first, what's behind your looks makes the most enduring and flattering impression." Here are some pointers on how you can be sexier and more desirable.

A Pickup Line by Any Other Name

Forget her astrological sign. Asking *that* is a sign in and of itself—a sign for her to steer clear of you. And forget about the time. If you can't afford a watch, or have nothing important enough going on to necessitate owning one, she won't give you the time of day anyway.

Herein lies the dilemma. You want to break the ice but don't want to get frosted.

The problem, says Dr. Ross E. Goldstein of Generation Insights in San Francisco, is that in delivering an opening line, you must appear natural in the most artificial setting. You're trying to get someone's attention without drawing too much attention to yourself.

What do you do?

"This isn't going to sound terribly profound, but the truth is that men need to understand the importance of self-disclosure when meeting a woman," says Dr. Goldstein. That doesn't mean telling her about your vasectomy. It means sharing something innocuous about yourself so that you don't appear overly interested in her.

"When you see a woman you want to meet, asking for her name is intrusive. Just giving her your name is not—it's self-disclosing," Dr. Goldstein says. "Most times, that's enough to get her to say her name in return."

○ Humor her.
Women find a man with a good sense of humor sexy. And it's not just because he can make her laugh. "Beyond displaying a playful, easygoing attitude, a sense of humor conveys a social presence, which translates into high status," says Dr. Buss. Being funny in front of others shows confidence and an ability to be on top of things without being uptight. But don't run out and buy a joke book. The sexiest way to convey a sense of humor is to learn to laugh at yourself and to find humor in everyday life.

○ Don't brag.
True self-confidence is a turn-on. But there's no surer turnoff than exaggerating your power, sexual adeptness, or athletic prowess. "Women are quite good at distinguishing false bravado from real self-confidence," Dr. Buss says.

○ Be sensitive, not simpering.
It has become a cliché: Women go for the sensitive guy. And there's a certain amount of truth behind the hype. In one study, women looked at a set

of responses to questions answered either from a masculine point of view or an "androgynous" viewpoint—meaning, a mix of both feminine and masculine traits. The women rated the androgynous male as more favorable in terms of intelligence, morality, dating, and mating potential. But don't don that Ziggy Stardust outfit or try to get in touch with your feminine side just yet. A little bit of vulnerability goes a long way.

"As the feminine side grew, sexual attractiveness declined," says study author Robert Cramer, Ph.D., professor of psychology at California State University in San Bernardino. That's because, for all the talk of making men more sensitive, the truth is that "women admire men who have firm beliefs, take control in financial or career decisions, and protect them when they feel threatened," Dr. Cramer says. The key is to exhibit emotional sensitivity without exhibiting helplessness.

So how do you walk that line?

Do's: Admit when you're wrong or ask for directions when you're lost. Feel free to tear up a little during a Meg Ryan film. Express it when you're feeling hurt or sad. Show some emotional fortitude when bad times hit.

Don'ts: Don't act helpless to get out of doing something that you don't want to do. Don't get defensive when you're in the wrong. Don't chicken out after you've made a commitment. Don't brood, sulk, or play hurt to get what you want.

● **Be nice to children.**

This is a surefire way to increase your sex appeal. Displaying affection toward children signals to women that you'll be a great dad. In one study, women were shown slides of one man in three different situations: standing alone, being nice to a baby, and ignoring a distressed infant. Women reported being most attracted to the fatherly type.

"Even a woman uninterested in having kids will notice whether a man is caring toward children, because it suggests whether he is a caring person in general," says Helen Fisher, Ph.D., a

SEX TRENDS

CAN'T MAKE FUN OF PHYLLIS DILLER ANYMORE

Will the 1990s be remembered as the decade when men became vain—or the age when they finally realized that women were on to something? The number of men in 1992 who underwent cosmetic surgery (nose job, hair transplant, liposuction, eye job, and so forth) was a paltry 55,000, compared to 1998 when 268,290 guys went under the knife.

member of the Center for Human Evolutionary Studies at Rutgers University in New Brunswick, New Jersey, and author of *Anatomy of Love*. "And that signifies whether he is willing enough to provide resources for her in the future."

◉ Watch the mirror.
A sure sign that your sex appeal is working is if you find yourself and the other person "mirroring" body language. For example, you're speaking with an attractive woman at a bar. Naturally, you lean forward as you speak. If she is

You Could Have Danced All Night

What dances should a man of style know? We asked swing dance teacher Jim Zaccaria, who volunteers with the Philadelphia Swing Dance Society; Dean Constantine, owner of Constantine Dance Studio in Minneapolis; and Gretchen Ward Warren, dance professor at the University of South Florida in Tampa and author of *The Art of Teaching Ballet* and *Classical Ballet Technique*. Here are the top seven picks.

❶ Country line dancing. "You don't need a partner, you learn the basics of every type of dancing, and it doesn't have any feminine stereotypes to scare you," Warren says.

❷ Ballroom dancing. The box step, one-two-three waltz, and fox-trot are dances that you'll do at every formal affair you attend.

❸ Jazz dancing. À la jazz musicals. Contemporary, athletic, fast-paced, hip.

❹ The hokey-pokey and the chicken dance. Yes, they're cheesy, but you'll see them at every wedding that you'll attend for the rest of your natural-born life.

❺ Ethnic dancing. "Folk dancing, like the polka, is really fun," Warren says. "You'd be surprised how big polka is. There's a vast underground subculture." If that's too scary, learn ethnic and religious dances that are important to you, such as the dance to the Jewish standard *Hava Nagila*.

❻ Modern fast dancing. Just because the polka's hard to do to something by Snoop Doggy Dogg.

❼ The tango. If one dance alone can stand you out from a crowd, it's this. But it's not for everyone. Very complex. Very difficult. Very sexy.

doing likewise, you're probably on the right track. (If she is leaning away, you are not making progress. Brush your teeth and try someone new.)

● Be an equal-opportunity flirt.

Few things perk you up like flirting. As adults, especially married adults, we forget how delicious the fruits of flirtation are. We forget how to verbally fence. To dodge, parry, and be foiled.

"How you flirt is particularly important. Some people, like salesmen, for example, may be natural flirts because of their jobs. They like people, regardless of whether they are attracted to them," explains Princess Jenkins of Majestic Images International in New York City.

The secret, she adds, is realizing that "part of flirting is acting." In other words, it's supposed to be embellished and ornamental. Just practice on everyone.

● Act your age.

"People yearn for youth," says Brad J. Jacobs, M.D., a plastic and reconstructive surgeon in New York City.

What this boils down to in sex appeal is this: The better you take care of yourself, the younger you'll look, and the more desirable you'll appear. Exercise, eat right, and diligently reduce stress. Pay apt attention to your wardrobe to keep it from dating you. But don't try hard to act younger than you are. Be natural. Wearing a toupee, showing the world your underwear waistband, and saying "dude" won't work for most of us.

Carry Yourself with Elegance and Grace

This second excerpt from Maximum Style *offers tips on how to exude charm and project a winning personality.*

Life on the arid plains of central Niger is harsh, but the nomadic Wodaabe people find time to host tribal beauty contests. Contestants preen for hours in preparation. They dress in tightly wrapped skirts, adorning themselves with elaborate jewelry, headbands, and turbans. They line their eyes with kohl, shave their hairlines, polish their teeth, and color their faces in yellow makeup to accent their noses and eyes. They dance all night to prove their grace and are poked, prodded, eyed, and ogled by friends, family, and judges until a winner is chosen.

Wodaabe beauty contests sound a lot like our own Miss America pageants. Except for one thing. All the contestants are men.

Polish and Poise

While we don't hold male beauty pageants, those same attributes—elegance, grace, beauty—cherished by the Wodaabe are coveted in our society, too.

But when we talk about elegance and grace, we're talking about something much deeper than looks or image, says G. Bruce Boyer, a private and corporate image consultant in Bethlehem, Pennsylvania, and author of *Elegance* and *Eminently Suitable*.

"Style is an outward assemblage; it reflects lifestyle. Elegance is internal; it's your confidence and comfort in yourself, your look, your smile, your demeanor," says Boyer.

Here are some hints to help you convey the essence of elegance and grace, whether you're in box seats at the ballpark or in the box at the opera.

◉ Make an entrance.

Whether it's at a cocktail party, a bustling convention center, or a crowded restaurant, the way you move through a room can convey a sense of elegance and grace, even to those who merely see you from afar. "Some people walk into a room. Other people enter it," says Jenkins. "Most of us have walked into a room and walked past three people we knew without saying hello because we didn't notice them. That's because we walked into the room—we didn't enter it."

To make a grand entrance, Jenkins suggests the following:

❶ Pause after you walk through the door.

❷ Survey the room quickly with your eyes, acknowledging whom you know at the far end first.

❸ As you walk toward them, scan nearby, nodding and acknowledging people close to you, offering warm greetings and engaging in chitchat.

❹ Continue working the room until you catch up with the people you know at the far end. By then, you will have made a favorable impression on those you chatted with—as well as on those who just observed you.

hot TIP!

A man in his socks and underpants is a man at his worst. If there's someone else in the room, always take your socks off before you lose the trousers.

● Warm up.

Appearing socially warm and approachable instantly boosts your gracefulness quotient. It starts with the basics: smiling, maintaining eye contact, listening attentively, and being sincere.

"It's what your mother taught you. If you're a good conversationalist, have good etiquette, and mind your manners, you're more likable," Jenkins says. One tactic to convey sincerity is to ask people about themselves and ask their opinions. Most people love to talk about themselves and will adore you for showing an interest in them.

● Call on your expertise.

Men who are considered elegant or graceful usually are well-versed on just about any subject. Since you can't be an expert all the time, fit in tidbits of your expertise when they're appropriate. If you know a thing or two about fine wines, share some trivia during cocktail hour. If you're not an expert, become one on a topic that's likely to come up.

perfect figures

Percentage of men who say that wearing a fragrance is part of their daily wardrobe: 40

Percentage of men who choose and buy their own fragrance: 79

"If you go to formal cocktail hours a lot, for example, learn all you can about escargot. Just don't fake anything or seem pretentious—people appreciate knowledgeable people, not phonies or know-it-alls," says Hall.

● Excel at introductions.

You'd be surprised how many people bungle an otherwise easy opportunity to look genteel. Here's a formula to follow for flawless intros.

❶ Graciously interrupt your current conversation, using the name of the person you're talking to.

❷ Introduce the newcomer by first and last name. Add some personal details.

❸ As the newcomer and the person you were talking with shake hands, introduce the latter using the same approach.

For example, "Excuse me, Tom, I'd like you to meet Bill Smith. Bill's a trademark attorney at Dewey, Cheatham, and Howe." Shake hands. "Bill, Tom Jones. He's a physics professor at Whassamatta U."

◉ Be good at chitchat.

Small talk is the mainstay of many formal and business-social get-togethers. If you're not good at making small talk, scan the newspaper before you leave home. It'll give you something to lead with. And again, ask questions—people love to talk, and they might feel just as awkward about chitchat as you do.

"Don't try too hard, though, or you could come off as patronizing or insincere. People want sincerity, not schmooze," cautions Jeff Livingston, Ph.D., an information analyst for Cisco Systems in Research Triangle Park, North Carolina.

SEX WARS

"Tell me, Jeffrey, do you still find yourself attractive?"

TURN UP THE HEAT

This is a hot site about sex appeal for guys. It even has advice for the "Weird/Fat/Ugly Guy." Among the many useful regular features is the "Latest Stratagem," which provides "proven real-world advice from plain folks and the world's leading experts that shows you exactly how to enhance your sex appeal with women." And try "The Female Translator." What's that? Here's the description: "Ever wish you could have someone translate what women say into what they really mean? Wish granted!"

www.maxxappeal.com

OUR MAIN MAN

"Clean up your act. Lose your troubles. Get in shape. Buy cool stuff. Find your style. Understand women (sort of). Close the deal. Plan your busy life." It's all here. "Make it easy on yourself and put The Man to work for you." Includes a free reminder service for birthdays, anniversaries, and so forth.

www.theman.com

COOL CLIP JOINT

E-barbershop is a super-site for men's personal care and grooming products. It has tons of national-brand products, as well as private-label and hard-to-find items and free advice from the e-barbers about personal care, grooming, sports, and romance. And you don't have to tip.

www.e-barbershop.com

MAN'S GUIDE INTERVIEW

Go from Toad to Prince to More Princely

An Interview with Stylemeister Wilkes Bashford

Cut a dashing figure and have no substance, and you might as well be mounted in a sculpture garden, because no one is going to want to be seen anywhere with you for too long. And be a bright, charming hunk wearing ghastly mismatched clothes, an extremely pungent cheap cologne, and a really bad haircut, and women will see you less as a hunk and more as a mistake. Unless you're very, very rich. And generous.

Just how much style do you need to know?

Our go-to guy for the answers is Wilkes Bashford, president of the San Francisco–based Wilkes Bashford Company, which operates an upscale seven-story apparel store and three more casual kin that sell sportswear.

Bashford also markets a line of self-named men's fragrances, shower gels, shaving cream, and the like that can be found at Saks Fifth Avenue and other upper-crust spots.

But don't assume that this man knows nothing except how to dress a guy up. When you help over a couple decades to outfit thousands of men who range from the dumpy to the princely, you learn a thing or two about how men should carry themselves in the world. And you figure out fast what the guy has to do to get the girl.

MAN'S GUIDE: Your entire business revolves around making men look good, smell good, be good. What are the critical areas of sex appeal that most men need to concentrate on but often neglect to take seriously enough?

BASHFORD: Right. Well, the first thing to know is that women are very attracted to men who are well-groomed. And by "well-groomed," I mean more than just how good your haircut is or what fragrance you're wearing. It's your general presence, the way you present yourself.

Physical details are a big part of that overall presence. That's particularly true when you're dealing with relations between middle-aged men and women, or when you're dealing with relations between men and women who are more sophisticated. In those cases, women are very, very conscious of how a man is dressed. In fact, they are highly aware of all the elements of his grooming, right down to whether he has a good manicure or not.

You're not talking about kids—really young men, are you?

MAN'S GUIDE: We're covering a pretty wide age range, but a lot of the guys who will be reading this are in their thirties and forties.

BASHFORD: Okay, great. Because I also want to mention another thing that's very important today: Men are much more health-conscious overall than they used to be. Your competition is stiffer than it used to be. Many men are really paying attention to what physical condition they're in. A lot of them are going to gyms and running and such.

The generation of people who are aging today is in so much better physical condition than people were 15 to 20 years ago. And that's because men are not afraid now to express an interest in how they look. Women, of course, have always paid attention to their looks. But it's only been within the last 10 to 15 years that men are up-front about the fact that they want to look sexy and that they want to maintain a young, vital presence.

Men are finally willing to admit that. And if you look at the average guy that's 45 to 50 now compared to what men of that age looked like 20 years ago, it's a vast difference.

> ❝ You can be seriously disfigured or whatever, and women will still be attracted to you. ❞
>
> —Actor Ben Affleck, describing the perks of being a movie star, in *Playboy* magazine

MAN'S GUIDE: But isn't it still difficult in many circles to come across as manly yet also admit that you pay attention to all the finer details of how you look?

BASHFORD: I think that it depends on where you're located. It's not a problem in San Francisco. But it might be in some other areas. On the West Coast in general, men are pretty free to pay attention to their looks, get custom haircuts, look at themselves in the mirror when other people are around, and stuff like that.

The young men of 30 to 40 years ago, especially the flower-child types, did a lot to start breaking down the barriers that made men so timid about admitting any interest in their appearance. But I've traveled around the country, and I know that paying attention to your appearance without jeopardizing your "manhood" is more difficult in some areas than in others. But things have been changing all over the country for the past several decades. It's just slower in some places compared to others.

MAN'S GUIDE: Is it possible to be really well-groomed, really well-dressed, really just have a great package, but still come across as though you didn't do much to yourself? In other words, is there a way to be really together with your appearance but not *look* as though you spent a bunch of time primping?

BASHFORD: I think that depends on the physical attributes of the particular man. Some men are fortunate enough that when they're young, they just look great, and when they age, they age really well. They have a presence that they carry with them.

But a big part of being perceived as attractive does depend on not appearing like you're trying. I think a lot of people who really care about their appearance and are attractive to others will present a nonchalant attitude. But if they do really care about their appearance, they have put some time and energy into it.

So when you see the guy who really looks fantastic but gives the appearance that he just jumped out of bed and ran a comb through his hair, chances are that he has put much more care into his appearance than is evident.

MAN'S GUIDE: For the benefit of the guys who up until now haven't spent much time on their appearance, how much time does it take? I know there are no hard-and-fast rules for anything, but what's the ballpark figure if you want to look good enough to be in the dating game?

BASHFORD: I've talked to plenty of macho guys who are my customers, so I've heard plenty of talk about their dating habits. I know that a lot of them, when they're going out on a date, change clothes three times before they feel they've gotten it right. They would probably never admit that to somebody who wasn't selling them clothes. But my feeling is that men, particularly in the younger generation, are just as conscious of their appearance and just as vain as any woman. They spend a lot of time at the process of looking good.

Having said that, I also have to point out that it's not required that you spend a lot of time primping and preening. I guess a man could get ready to go out on a date and only take half an hour to get ready.

Now, I can't see it being done right in much less time than that. But I know men who take an hour, an hour-and-a-half, or even longer to get ready for a date. With that kind of time commitment, you're talking more about the guys who really, really care how they look. You may not need to care quite that much, but you do need to care. Because, you know, the competition is a lot rougher today than it used to be.

MAN'S GUIDE: Is that because of the increased fitness of men in general, or because . . .

BASHFORD: Yeah. I mean, if you look back 20 to 30 years, guys had a paunch by the time they were 40 or 45. They didn't really pay that much attention to how they dressed. And they considered themselves middle-aged.

Well, a 45-year-old man today is often in great shape, and he is living a very active life. And he considers himself young.

MAN'S GUIDE: I remember a comedian once who joked that when you're dating, it's like a sporting event: You have to wear your uniform and run hard to get the girl. But once you have her, the game is over and the race is done. You can quit worrying about what you look like.

BASHFORD: No. Keep thinking competitively. Whether it's in business or it's in personal relationships, you damned well better stay in shape in today's world if you want to stay ahead of the pack. You need to stay in the best shape that you're able to be.

When you go out and you see guys your own age, and they're in great shape, you don't want to look like a *shlump* in comparison. There's a whole different attitude toward presentation today. And a lot of it comes from the tremendous emphasis that's been put on being fit. Every hotel you visit has a gym, and it has a spa, and people are using them.

If you don't keep up with the times, I think you're really going to suffer in the relationship game.

MAN'S GUIDE: So this is a situation where you really do have to keep up with the Joneses.

What do you think are the hardest shortcomings to overcome, things that can't be readily eliminated cosmetically? Aside from the really obvious, like being covered in weeping sores.

BASHFORD: I would say that losing your hair is pretty hard to overcome. There's not much that you can—or even should—do about that. You know, you just have to learn to create a look that works with the fact that you are either losing your hair or have lost it entirely.

> **"** He'll wear them whenever he deems fit. **"**
>
> —White House spokesman Jake Siewert, on President Clinton's choice of cowboy boots while attending a conference on teen violence

Weight is absolutely essential. It can be hard to lose weight, but you have to keep your weight in line, regardless of your age. I daresay that probably the biggest offender in killing your sex appeal is to become overweight. It really does you in.

But the most important thing you can do overall, regardless of your looks, is to project an energy. Project an interest. Project a vitality. Sometimes people become mentally lazy, and they fail to project anything worthwhile to whomever they're with. But without that vitality and without that energy, you lose a lot of appeal to other people.

MAN'S GUIDE: So it's about charisma.

BASHFORD: Sure. I mean, it goes beyond your physical characteristics. It about the aura that you create. If you project energy, people look at you in a different way.

If you're just kind of a lump, at a certain point it doesn't matter how physically attractive you are. You just won't look that appealing to people. You'll just be taking up space.

MAN'S GUIDE: Let's take an extreme example. Let's say you're really, *really* sex-appeal deficient. Your name isn't something impressive like Wilkes Bashford. Instead it's something like Herman Tinkle. Instead of being 6 feet tall, you're 5-foot-6. Instead of looking like Mel Gibson, you look like Mel Brooks.

Now that I've described myself, what can I do about it? Is it all mental at that stage in the game? Do you have to cultivate a supremely fantastic personality, or is there a combination of physical and mental things you can do?

BASHFORD: There's a lot you can do. A person in that position should focus on creating an identity. That identity should be something the guy projects over and above his basic winning personality.

A person like the one you describe should adopt a way of dressing that is interesting. Something that's a bit unique. If the guy cannot compete on a level playing field in terms of physical appearance, he has to weigh things in his favor by creating a personality that's a little larger than he is.

Part of that is in the combination of clothes he puts together. A man like this has to be aware of proportion. He has to know what works and what doesn't on his body. But more than anything, I think there should be a little bit of an off-center approach to the way he dresses and the way he presents himself.

MAN'S GUIDE: So a little quirky in some respects.

BASHFORD: A little quirky but in an appealing way. Do something that makes you interesting. You want to do something that makes people want to spend time with you. You want to stand out from the crowd in a good way.

MAN'S GUIDE: You kind of touched on this already, but how much does it hurt a guy if he looks good but can't carry himself well, or vice versa? Is that the kiss of death?

BASHFORD: It certainly is if he's planning on cultivating a long-term relationship. If the man is attractive enough, he'll probably get to first base, but he might not get to third. The thing is, people will lose interest if he doesn't pay attention to both his appearance and the way he carries himself.

If a person is really good-looking, but you talk to this person for a while and find out that he or she is really a dud, then all of a sudden that person is not so physically good-looking anymore.

The reverse is true as well. Someone might not be a dazzler when you first meet him. But once you spend time with him, and all this energy and this personality projects itself, then suddenly, for one reason or another, he looks just great. There's a beauty there that you just didn't see in the beginning.

MAN'S GUIDE: Anything else to add?

BASHFORD: I just want to stress the fact that men have been liberated. That's really important. Men today can really express who they are, or who they envision themselves to be, and not feel that somebody's going to intimidate them.

It goes back to my point that things have changed immensely over the last 20 or 30 or 40 years. As we have progressed over that time, it has become okay for men to express an interest in things that once were not considered manly. And that liberation gives them all kinds of opportunities to experiment.

I think one of the best examples of that liberation is seen in the very masculine, virile young men who are running around with their hair bleached blond. That never would have happened 20 years ago. The guy would have been in real trouble for bleaching his hair.

And I think that when you see some guy, for example, bleaching his hair blond at 16, 17, or 18 years old, he's probably going to mature into being a very interesting dresser and having an interesting presence. He's already shown a willingness to experiment, and he will likely take advantage of many of the things available on the market to enhance his appearance.

To find out more about the Wilkes Bashford Company stores and products, visit www.wilkesbashford.com on the Internet.

QUICKIES

HOW PEACOCKS MANAGE TO LOOK SO GOOD

If the guy next to you is wearing a purple tattersall shirt (a pattern of dark lines forming squares on a light background) and he doesn't look like an idiot, there's an excellent chance that the shirt was made by Thomas Pink (which is a company, not a guy). Founded in 1984, Pink quickly became known for exceptionally colorful, boldly patterned shirts that are hip but still classic. Pink's merchandising director, Tim Taylor, told *Man's Guide* how to wear the brights.

- If you're used to wearing white or blue shirts, try a soft color, such as lemon or pink. Pick up that color in your tie. If you've chosen a fairly plain shirt, you can be more adventurous with neckwear. Once you're comfortable and confident with this look, you can wear almost any color.

- Try a shirt with a small simple design, such as a check, herringbone, or tattersall. Most ties work well with them.

- If you work in a very traditional office, choose a shirt with a blue background. Blue keeps even boldly patterned shirts conservative.

- The stronger the pattern on the shirt, the plainer your tie should be. Either your shirt or your tie should speak, but two bold things together generally look awful. Remember *Cagney and Lacey*?

GET THE PERFECT FIT

Usually, we get very afraid when someone approaches our crotch with a tape measure—unless it's a tailor. A tailor is the one who can help you fool the world into thinking you're taller, smarter, and better-looking than you actually are. Chris Pamboukas, manager of Nordstrom's tailor shops, told us how to get the best from the guy poking around your inseam.

- "When you have a suit tailored, wear a dress shirt and tie, a belt or suspenders, and dress shoes with the correct height heel. You'd be surprised how many men show up for fittings in cowboy boots or running shoes," says Pamboukas.

- When buying a suit, make sure that the collar hugs your neck, the lapels lie flat on your chest, and the armholes allow enough room for movement. A jacket can be tailored to a perfect fit if these three areas fit properly from the beginning.

- Never buy pants several inches too large in the waist, no matter how much of a steal they are. Pants more than 6 inches too large involve a recut, which means removing the waistband and zipper and recutting the fabric. Doable, but that's detailed work that can get expensive and requires a highly skilled tailor.

- Don't donate that quality suit just because the current style has changed. A good tailor can give it a makeover, closing a jacket vent or tapering the legs.

- If you've gained weight, you can let out pants up to 2 inches in the waist. A jacket can be restructured to give you another $1\frac{1}{4}$ inches around the middle. You can let the pants back in again once you lose weight.

WORK ON YOUR STRONG SUIT

The only time we guys think about swim trunks is when we're escorted off the beach for not wearing them. But to accentuate your body type (or de-accentuate, as the case may be), you really need to find the right pair. Here's how to pick the suit that best fits your stature.

- Tall and thin: Look for board shorts and long bathing suits that reach almost to your knees (about 23 inches along the *outer* seam), says Nat Norfleet of Ocean Pacific clothing. The trunks should tie or snap in front. Wild patterns and loud colors look fine on lean guys.

- Big in the belly: Skip board shorts. they tend to ride low under the gut. Your best bet is a pair of volley shorts—they're similar in style to boxer shorts (about 16 inches along the outer seam) and have a drawstring waist. The shorter length draws attention away from your midsection; a dark color also helps. The shorts can be all cotton or a blend. Don't buy oversize trunks—they'll just make you look fatter.

- Short: Go with modified board shorts about 20 inches in length. Anything longer will make your legs look too short. And choose a solid color, or solid with vertical stripes down the sides, which can add the illusion of height. Skip loud patterns—they make you look even smaller.

DEAR DR. MANLY

Q: *I'm a wardrobe pack rat. I have so many shirts, shoes, and pants in my closet that I can't fit in any of the new fashions I'm buying. What's worse, I don't even wear half this stuff when I bring it home; I keep going back to my old favorites. How can I get out from under all these clothes?*
—G. T., Orlando

A: You may be a pack rat, but take heart—you're no Imelda Marcos. A recent article in the *Today* newspaper of Manila, Philippines, reported that her shoe collection alone is now at 5,000 pairs, and that's not including the 3,000 pairs seized when rebels escorted her and Ferdinand to the door back in 1986.

What you're experiencing is known as closet glut, when you keep buying more and more of what you don't need, mostly because it's the easiest thing to buy. You need a new way to harvest the clothes in your closet and save only the best of the crop.

Start by gutting the thing. Pull everything out and put it on display. Decorate your room as if it were Brooks Brothers on Madison Avenue. Then go "shopping." Don't just grab stuff and put it back in the closet, try it on. Look critically at yourself in the mirror. If it looks good, hang it back up. If there's the slightest doubt, even a tiny hesitation, trash-bag it. By the time you're done, your closet will contain only the stuff you actually look good in.

Next, take the trash bag full of clothes to a secondhand shop and trade the whole kit and kaboodle for one single thing that catches your fancy. Maybe a trench coat or a fondue set. Repeat every 3 years. If you learn nothing else from this exercise, take this to heart: What you like to wear best isn't necessarily the best stuff for you to wear.

Q: *I just moved to New York City, and I'm constantly bombarded on my walk to work with people selling brand-name merchandise. Some of it is obviously colossal crap, but how can I tell what's real and what's fake before I buy?*
—A. G., New York City

A: It's no wonder you're getting the hard sell. "Counterfeit designer merchandise generates as much money as drugs," according to Detective Robert Matthews of the Philadelphia Police Department. Before you plunk down money for faux Fendi or counterfeit Calvin Klein, look for the five dead giveaways of a street knockoff.

❶ No warranty
If the card's missing, it's probably a fake.

❷ Altered tags
Employees can steal real tags and sell them to counterfeiters, who sew them into cheap clothing, says our man Matthews. Look closely, and you may see where the old tag was removed or that the new tag is sewn in crooked. Also, if the original tag is cut in half, the garment is a manufacturer's second (defective).

❸ Low-end logos
Check logos for poor-quality stitching, colors that bleed, and other inconsistencies.

❹ Canary-colored gold
Genuine 14- or 18-karat gold has a wheat color, like your wedding ring or a Notre Dame football helmet. Bright yellow means it's gold-plated.

❺ A "ticking" second hand
One way to tell a $1,500 Rolex from a $10 fake: The second hand sweeps smoothly on most real McCoys. On quartz imposters, it moves incrementally.

Q: *Can you clean dry-clean-only clothes at home?*
—C. B., LAKEWOOD, CALIFORNIA

A: Usually, when we spill something on our clothes, we either ignore it or try washing it out with hand soap, water, and a paper towel. My brother does this because he's too lazy to go to the dry cleaner. (Plus, he owes the store money for three tuxes and a dozen silk shirts that have been in "storage" for 6 months.) So the other night, the two of us experimented on one of his rayon dress shirts using a home fabric-care kit for dry-clean-only clothes that's sold in drugstores and supermarkets. In addition to the preexisting mystery stain, I gleefully added a couple of ink and red wine blotches, all in the name of scientific progress.

The instructions are simple. First we applied the kit's stain-removal fluid to the ink and wine, which eventually disappeared just fine. The mystery stain (which may or may not be related to a wayward chunk of Big Mac) remained firmly ensconced. So we took the next step and placed the shirt and an "odor-lifting" cloth into one of the kit's bags and tossed the bag into the dryer for 30 minutes. The outcome: Stain begone! Hallelujah. Unfortunately, the shirt retained a strong scent reminiscent of carpet cleaner. Verdict? Go make nice with the dry cleaner.

Dr. Manly is a fictional character.
The actual advice was provided by a variety of
medical doctors and other qualified experts.

PROMOTE PERPETUAL PASSION

Sooner or later, the inferno abates. The fire subsides. The flames dwindle. (You get the idea. We're talking doused.) Once upon a time, the least touch would send you pawing at each others' buttons. But more and more it requires the actual expenditure of effort to ignite those passions. Especially when you factor in the effects of every other relationship you have in your life—kids, relatives, bosses, in-laws. And that same damn sandalwood smell day after day after day, no matter how much Chanel No. 5 you buy her every Christmas and birthday. Or maybe she just doesn't seem interested anymore— and especially not when you are.

You ain't watching this movie alone, Bud. We've been there, we've figured it out, and we have a few things to tell you . . .

Like what to do when you're hot, but she's not . . . the key differences between a wife and a girlfriend . . . how to master sex moves so she shakes when you shimmy. . . . These are the secrets of how to ignite and fan an eternal flame.

Sex Tricks

As a service to us guy-types, New Woman *magazine polled its readers to find out what sneaky tricks of sexual seduction turned them on most. Consider this your "to do" list.*

1 Kissing/biting her neck during foreplay ("Especially the spot between my neck and ear")

2 Having fingers like Liberace ("Right before intercourse, he presses a finger against my G-spot while he strokes my clitoris with his thumb")

3 Just being you ("I like the way he makes me laugh")

4 Massaging her feet ("He slowly undresses my feet and kisses my little toes")

5 Fondling her breasts and pinching her nipples ("The harder he does it, the better")

6 Performing oral sex ("He uses his nose in incredible ways")

7 Making eye contact ("He looks me in the eye and says 'I love you' as he enters me")

8 Pretending to be the plumber ("He acts like a repairman who comes in and discovers me 'sleeping' in bed")

9 Talking dirty ("Not disgusting, but very racy")

10 Wearing an apron ("He cooks an amazing spaghetti sauce—the smell really turns me on")

MUST READS

You're Hot, She's Not

Old joke: How do you get a woman to stop having sex with you? Marry her. For many guys, unfortunately, this is no wisecrack; it's real life. Night after night, they approach their partners for sex; night after night, their partners have headaches—or else they're taking the concept of "must-see TV" way too seriously. But a libido doesn't lag without cause. If your mate isn't as stoked for sex as you are, there's a reason. Writer Ronnie Polaneczky reveals the seven most common causes of a flagging sex life and seven ways to raise the spirit so it flies again.

● **Reason #1: You don't discuss sex, ever.**

"For all I know, my wife wants more sex, too," says Dave (not his real name), a 32-year-old computer programmer who has been married for 14 years to his high school sweetheart whom he still loves very much. "But sex isn't something we talk about. I'm afraid I'd hurt her feelings if I told her there was something wrong with our sex life. Besides, I don't think we should have to talk about sex. It ought to be one of those things that just happens, the way it used to."

Ah, the way it used to. Once that initial, steamy attraction settles into something calmer, the don't-ask-don't-tell policy doesn't cut it any longer.

What to do: If you and your wife already talk easily about other aspects of your relationship and feel happy with your marriage except in this one area, broach the subject of sex without blame or defensiveness, says Clifford Sager, M.D., a New York psychiatrist who treats couples with sexual problems.

Tell your wife something like, "I'm feeling really sexy tonight. I'd like to make love to you," or "I would really love it if we had sex tonight. I'm really turned on by you." Then give your wife a fair chance to react, suggests Patricia Love, Ed.D., a couples therapist and coauthor of *Hot Monogamy*. If neither of you has mentioned the *S*-word before, she may be stunned by its sudden appearance. But she may also be relieved that the topic is finally up for discussion.

● **Reason #2: It's the chicken-and-egg problem.**

Another reason couples stop having sex is that, well, they've stopped having sex. "When some couples get stuck on sex frequency, they polarize around it," says Helen Crohn, a New York clinical social worker and sex therapist. "He's feeling so hurt and rejected that he's become insulting, angry, and resentful. She's so defensive and upset with how he's treating her that whatever little sex they used to have has just about stopped." And things only grow worse when they look for a solution: He says that if they'd just start having sex again, every-thing would be okay. She says that everything has to be okay before she'll feel like having sex with him again.

What to do: If you and your mate are truly at a standoff and every attempt to discuss your sex life turns into an argument, make an appointment to see a marriage counselor who's certified in sex therapy. "Very often the sex problem is really a secondary problem, and there's another issue that has not been ad-dressed," says Crohn. "The point is to get the problems sorted out."

◉ Reason #3: You've stopped chasing her.

At the beginning of a relationship, a man's testosterone is usually driving him to fulfill his sexual desires. So he'll find all sorts of ways—gifts, compliments, extra attention—to make a woman feel special enough to open herself up to him sexually. In turn, she feels desired, loved, and trusting—all of which makes her especially amenable to lovemaking.

As the relationship ages, though, a man's work, family, and hobbies often take up more and more of the time he used to devote to treating his mate like a queen. This doesn't mean that he's no longer interested, but to his wife it may seem that he no longer desires her in that special way. So she becomes less interested in sex, which makes him even less inter-ested in doing the things that made her want him in the first place.

perfect figures

Of men who lived with their future wives before marriage, percentage who eventually separated or got divorced: 34.1

Percentage of divorcés among those who didn't cohabit before marriage: 20.4

What to do: Do something, man! Come home early from work and surprise her by fixing dinner; hold her hand in front of your buddies; let her know that even after all this time together, you still think she's the coolest thing going and that you're the luckiest guy in the world for being able to spin in her orbit. Then do both of you a favor: Don't slack off by being romantic only when you want sex; she'll see through that in a heartbeat. If this woman is the love of your life, treat her that way even when you're not in the mood.

◉ Reason #4: She's a new mom.

There's nothing like a baby to derail your sex life. The first months of mother-hood are a roller coaster of emotional highs, exhausted lows, and powerful epiphanies about what it is to be a woman, a wife, and a mother. An increase in prolactin, the hormone that stimulates milk production, is one reason for a drop in sexual interest, but there are other causes. "A woman may have confusing new feelings about different parts of her body, which until now she may have thought of only in a sexual way," says Karen Kleiman, director of the Postpartum Stress Center in Rosemont, Pennsylvania. Fatigue and stress, her changing body and self-image, vaginal dryness due to hormone changes, and worries about becoming pregnant again can also significantly affect libido.

What to do: Take it slowly. Even though most women can have sex 4 to 6 weeks after delivery, it often takes longer for them to feel physically and emotionally ready to rock your cradle. Give your wife space, but keep talking, too, says Kleiman. "Discuss alternatives to intercourse—holding, cuddling, and other consistent forms of affection. Or maybe you'll decide that you don't mind putting sex on hold for a while. The key is for the man not to feel rejected and for the woman not to feel as though there's something wrong with her."

● Reason #5: She's depressed.

A decline in sexual interest is one of the markers clinicians use to diagnose depression. Your girl can have what seems to be the greatest life in the world and still be felled by a sense of bleakness and despair.

What to do: If you suspect that your partner has more than a passing state of the blues, the worst thing you can do is harangue her about her lack of sex drive. Instead, tell her how much you love her, and acknowledge her depression in a sympathetic manner. "The next step is a psychiatric or psychological evaluation, including a complete physical examination," says Dr. Sager.

● Reason #6: She's concerned about body stuff.

Even if you find your partner as beautiful as the day you met her, she may be feeling self-conscious about how childbearing, gravity, and age have changed her shape. "My wife says she feels foolish having sex because everything jiggles," says Bill, a 42-year-old engineer whose partner has gained 20 pounds since their wedding day 20 years ago. "My feeling is, who cares? But she doesn't believe me."

What to do: Ask yourself whether you've been adding to her self-consciousness by nagging or teasing her about her weight or lack of firmness. If you have, you're reaping what you've sown:

Women rate agreeable men as more attractive than stubborn ones, but only if the nicer guys also have a dominant streak. If strength and decisiveness are missing, nice guys come off as meek. So put your foot down next time both of you are making plans for dinner—or, heck, deciding where to live and when to have children.

Who wants to have sex with someone who has made it clear that he doesn't like the body he's holding? Instead, keep reassuring your partner that she's immensely desirable and that your lovemaking is about more than what your bodies look like.

❍ Reason #7: She's not turned on by what turns you on.
Satisfying sex means different things to different people, and it's self-centered to suppose that other people's sexuality mirrors our own. This assumption, says Dr. Love, is the number one problem in relationships.

This was the case with Charlie, a 39-year-old architect, and Cathy, his wife of 12 years. Two years ago, Charlie looked at his sex life and didn't like what he saw: a well-meaning husband who wanted quickie sex five times a week and a loving wife who'd accommodate him, oh, every 10 days to 2 weeks. When Charlie would approach Cathy for sex, she'd complain that he was distant, that quickie sex made her feel as if she was being used.

What to do: If you want more sex with the woman you love, start creating the emotional conditions that she requires to feel like having more sex.

"I started calling during the day just to say hello," Charlie says. "I paid her compliments, asked about her day, and started talking about how I was feeling, which I hate to do. But it made her feel closer to me, and that made her want to have sex with me more. It got us unstuck."

perfect figures

In a café, French couples casually touch each other an average of 110 times an hour. American couples touch each other only twice an hour.

* * * * * * * * * *

Charlie is a numbers guy, so he's been logging his progress on a calendar (a fact he hasn't shared with Cathy, since she'd probably brain him). A year ago, he and Cathy made love 7 times in one "quarter." This fiscal, they're up to 34 times and counting. Charlie's discomfort with becoming more of a SNAG (sensitive New Age guy) is outweighed, he says, by his wife's happiness, which registers frequently in the bedroom, on top of the washing machine, under the dinner table—wherever the feeling strikes.

The Difference
between Wives and Girlfriends

The sudden and catastrophic disappearance of oral sex from the roster of received pleasures is just one of the postmarriage adjustments that a man has to face. Indeed, once dating becomes marriage, men say, a major mate-makeover takes place. But these "before" and "after" snapshots of the women we love show that the situation for married guys is far more promising than we fear. In fact, the single guys among us may be playing second fiddle, as Brian Alexander reveals in this article from New Woman *magazine.*

She sat across the table from me looking gorgeous as she lifted a forkful of crab salad to her mouth. We had just seen a movie, and now we were having dinner in a little Provençal bistro—high romance quotient—when I suddenly realized that I had not said much to her in the past few minutes besides "How's the salad?" and "Pierce Brosnan's no Connery, I'll tell ya." The conversation was lagging.

What had started as a good date suddenly seemed to teeter on the edge of becoming a bad one. I rifled through my mental card catalog of amusing-yet-gentlemanly-yet-seductive dinner conversation and drew an utter blank. The prospect of rumpled sheets, or even another date, was receding by the moment. This woman was hot, and here I was staring into my beef stew (Beef stew? On a date? What the hell was I thinking?) like a bump on a Provençal log.

Then it hit me: This woman isn't my girlfriend—she's my wife!

Coming out of my daze, I smiled at Shelley, my bride of 2 years.

"What?" she asked, puzzled.

"Nothing," I said. And then, "Do you think I'd be a good date?"

"You are a good date." (Always reassuring—one reason I love my wife.)

"No, I mean, if we were going out."

"We are out." (Always literal—a reason my wife aggravates me.)

"No, if we weren't married, and you were just my girlfriend."

She put down her fork and explained with exaggerated patience that "we would not be married now if you weren't a good date," softening the jab with an indulgent smile.

There! A girlfriend would not smile indulgently. She would summon the nearest taxi. Shelley was most definitely my wife, I concluded, winding up the internal debate. I smiled back, confident now that my "date" would sleep with me. She had to. We have only one bed.

But later I began thinking about how one really distinguishes between a wife and a girlfriend, and over the next few weeks I raised the issue with dozens of men I know. Aside from the rings on their fingers and their names on the mortgage applications, how had the women they loved changed between dating and marriage?

Somewhere along the line, men said, a woman leaves her girlfriend self behind and takes on a new set of wifely characteristics, so her partner can clearly point out differences between her "before" and "after" personas. With the exception of my brief walkabout at dinner, I can do this with Shelley, too.

So what are these differences? You may be anticipating a lot of vivacious-vixen-versus-minivan-mom comparisons, but the results of my survey were far more surprising than that. Here's what really tells a man, "This woman is no girlfriend—she's a wife!"

● Wives take more risks with their looks.

"Thong bikini," John responds simply to my wife-versus-girlfriend question. "She introduced it on our honeymoon in Jamaica. I know for a fact that she'd never worn one before then, because I asked her. But on our first day at the beach, she revealed her butt in all its glory."

John's wife wears thong bikinis even now, 5 years and one child later. "I think it's an in-your-face thing," he suggests. "The thong says, 'Yeah, I have a nice butt, and I'm married and a mom, and what do you think of that?' I think she feels like she's allowed to wear any damn thing she wants now."

Michael lets me in on a similar secret about his wife, Joanne. "She has taken to greeting me at the airport in all sorts of outrageously sexy things. Other people on the plane must think I've hired a hooker,"

perfect figures

In a survey of 3,876 newlyweds, 26 percent of men claimed to have had sexual intercourse (not oral sex) while driving.

he says, smiling. "But she couldn't care less. I think she regards marriage as a shield. If she were single, she might feel slutty. Behind the shield, she's just creatively naughty."

A wedding ring seems to confer a kind of license to experiment, and not just in clothing. My wife had very long hair throughout our courtship. It was glorious and had long been part of her identity. Soon after we got married, she came home with chin-length layers. "I just thought I'd see how it looked," she explained as I hoisted my jaw off the floor. With me in the marital bag, I think she no longer felt that she had to play it safe with a please-all style she knew looked good. She could take a chance with a cut that would actually look better.

"A year after we got hitched, my wife had a nose job," says Greg. "She said she'd always wanted to do it but waited until after she was married because she wanted a guy to love her the way she originally looked. Marriage has liberated her—though I wish she'd find a less expensive way of expressing it!"

◉ Wives are tougher.

"Why were some things about me okay before, but they need to be fixed now?" ponders Douglas. "Take my cereal bowl. We dated for 2 years, lived together for 1 year, and in all that time, I just put my cereal bowl in the sink when I was through with breakfast and cleaned it up later. And honestly, I almost always got around to it. Now it's verboten to leave a dirty dish in the sink. I have to 'rinse and stack, rinse and stack.'"

Douglas thinks the change took place when his wife realized that she would be seeing renegade Froot Loops floating in the kitchen sink every morning for the next 50 years. It makes sense; what was okay for dating, with its temporary feel, can quickly become intolerable in the permanent context of marriage.

"I haven't eaten lunch at Hooters in 4 years," Carl says. "I used to eat there maybe three or four times a year, and when Liza was my girlfriend, she never said a word about it. Not long after we got married, she felt very free to say something: 'You're my husband! Why are you hanging out at Hooters?' I never hung out! I ate a hamburger. I paid the bill. I left. But that's all over now."

"It's true that girlfriends don't sweat the small stuff," agrees Justin. "I never had those 'don't do it that way' spats with anyone I dated, including my wife. But since we got married, I have learned—and this is just a random sample—that my love of Thai food and Henry Miller novels, the way I

> **hot TIP!**
>
> *For intense, well-timed orgasms, try the coital alignment technique. Instead of holding yourself up with your arms, rest your chest on hers. Now, the tricky part: Don't slide your penis in and out. Stimulate her by rubbing your pubic bone against her clitoris. You do that by moving up and down against her body, while keeping full skin contact. It's a rocking motion, much slower than the thrusting method. Expect a learning curve, but keep with it. Many couples report orgasms that are more intense and closer together.*

pinch her butt, my system for loading the dishwasher, and my tipping habits all bug the hell out of Denise. She never said a word about this stuff when she was my girlfriend. We must have eaten in restaurants—lots of them Thai—about a hundred times, and I never tipped more than 15 percent. Was she seething inside about my alleged cheapness? What were those other girlfriends not saying? It's scary, man."

● **Wives play (and play it straight) in bed.**

Yes, the old saw about wives and oral sex does come up. Sammy expresses it most concisely: "Girlfriends give oral sex. Wives don't, because they know a husband can come in ways that require absolutely no aerobic effort on their part." Apart from that, most men told me that they think sex-with-a-wife is just as exciting as girlfriend-sex, though in different ways.

"My wife has more fun during sex than she ever had as a girlfriend," Dave says. "These days, if we fumble around, get in a ridiculous position, or one of us produces a strange sound, she laughs. When she was my girlfriend, she always seemed wound up about performing. And sex was silent. Now there's a lot of chitchat."

The laughter and communication make it easier for married partners to ask for what they really want. Though none of the men I spoke to would give up specifics, it appears that many had only requested exotic playtime activities once they'd exchanged vows. "Let's just say that I got her to buy a pair of saddle shoes," says one. "She was skeptical at first, but now she thinks it's a hoot."

Wives also start displaying bedroom personalities that they never revealed as girlfriends. "There is one particular variation—illegal in some states—that she flatly refused to even try the whole time we dated," Carl says. "Soon after we got married, and after a few gin and tonics, she leaned over and made the suggestion. She knew I'd be willing, and thought, 'Hey, we're married, let's see if it works.' Now she proposes it about twice a year, or every third gallon of gin, whichever comes first."

Of course, some sexperiments fail miserably. And at those moments, men with wives feel lucky. "If I ever misfired, every girlfriend I had, including my wife, would say, 'Hey, that's okay,' but it always sounded like she was reading from a script," Phil says. "My wife still says the same words, but she actually means them. I can tell from her tone of voice, from the way she just kisses me and goes to sleep, that it really is okay."

● **Wives have no shame.**

"Wife versus girlfriend?" begins a friend. "Wanna know the difference? A week ago, I find her in the bathroom, pants around her ankles. She goes, 'Look at this! Look at this! What is it?' Turns out, there's some small bump in a remote region where brave men fear to tread. That's a wife. As a girlfriend, she would have eaten fire before displaying that particular area to me."

I tell this story to John, who laughs out loud. "Just this morning my wife comes into the kitchen, sits down, and announces, 'I have the biggest pimple just inside my nostril, and it hurts like hell.' Girlfriends do not broadcast acne, wherever it occurs."

In fact, girlfriends often go to great lengths to draw the veil of personal privacy. "I dated a woman who loved to spend long weekends in nice hotels," Derek recalls. "It was great, but every time she needed to do anything but pee, she made me leave the room. Not just stay out of the bathroom or hang in the hallway—I had to go downstairs and wait in the lobby."

● Wives strike out on their own.
At times, wives demand more intimacy than girlfriends, but they may also insist on more independence.

"I knew that Grace liked her banking job," Robbie says, "but as a girlfriend, she was more willing to change her work schedule, leave the office behind when we went out—and I always thought that she would follow me if I ever got transferred. But after we got married, it became obvious how much she loves that job. It's a part of her that's totally separate from me, and I doubt she would ever consider giving it up. I eat alone a lot of nights."

At times Robbie resents all the nights spent cozied up with the clicker, but he says that overall he supports Grace's ambition. "She always lets me know that I am the most important part of her life," he says. "And when I get intense about work, she's equally supportive of me."

John says that his wife insists on party autonomy. "When I used to bring her to work-related events or dinners, she played the typical shy girlfriend," he says. "Now she's the one grabbing everybody's hand, talking, laughing, leading the conversation. Partly it's because she knows people better, but she says it's also because she doesn't feel like a temp. She's hired on full-time.

"Same goes for parties with friends. She's way more out front than she used to be with my crowd, and when we're with her friends, I'm definitely left to fend for myself. She won't stick with me or make sure I'm having fun. I think she feels like, 'Hey, I'm not going to hold your hand forever. We're married now.'"

● Wives don't walk away.
Men take great comfort in knowing that the women they love have sworn—in front of friends and family and their fathers, who paid for the white dress and the party—to stay married. Even though men brag in front of other people that

the U.S. atomic clock could be set according to their bathroom schedule; even though they cry at any movie involving dog death; even though their need to call Mom every week is not something that is going to go away like their wives thought.

We have all had at least one girlfriend who dumped us immediately once she tripped over our foibles or crashed into our life choices. A writer—actually, several writers I know—has experienced the instant cash-shortfall brush-off. "At first a girlfriend thinks it's very cool that you're a writer," says Warren. "Then one day she looks up, and you are still a writer, still sitting in your underwear at the computer, and you still haven't sold the multimillion-dollar screenplay to Spielberg. She says, 'Forget it. There are greener pastures.' No real discussion, no talk of compromise. It has happened to me so many times."

This man is married now, still has not hit the big time, and waxes rhapsodic about his wife. Which is not to say that marriage turns women into silent martyrs—only that a wife will work with you to find a solution to her gripes, from your puny income to your poor table manners. "She would hate it if I ever said this to her, but in a sense my wife is like my mom," Nick begins. "If I misbehaved as a kid, my mom would give me these long lectures or punish me, but there was never any question that I still got to be her kid. Now if I misbehave, I get punished, I get lectured; but there's never any question—I still get to be Andrea's husband."

Nick is not referring to breaking major vows, but to losing $100 in a bar because he had three beers and imagined he was Minnesota Fats, getting caught staring at a woman 5 years younger than Andrea, or too accurately describing certain gross-out scenes from *South Park* during one of her business dinners. "Girlfriends are still auditioning you," he continues. "How's your tap dancing? Can you sing? You make a mistake, you get cut. Your wife has already cast the husband role. The worst she will do is give you direction."

Dating is a passage, a trial, a test. We can fall hard for girlfriends, and

SEX TRENDS

JUST NOT READY FOR COMMITMENT

In 1900, men married at an average age of 26; women, at 22. Two years shy of a century later, in 1998, the average age had risen just 1 year for men, to 27. Women, however, are holding off until they're 25. Not only that, 92 percent of adults today believe that it's A-OK for the wife to be older than the husband, and 89 percent think that it's peachy if a couple decides not to have children.

even enjoy the challenge of pleasing them. But eventually every man yearns for the security and ease of knowing that he has proven himself worthy of a woman's long-lasting love.

That night in the restaurant reminded me of my recurrent anxiety dream, in which I show up for a physics final exam wearing my Spiderman pajamas. Even worse, I have somehow missed every class since the midterm. Will I pass the test? Will I get to graduate? I always wake up in the middle of this nightmare, find Shelley in the dark, and feel a rush of relief. I've had some terrific girlfriends. I deeply loved one or two. So what's the real difference? None of them gave me the feeling that I had wakened from my dream to find I'd aced the test.

Orgasmic Women Discuss Technique

There are millions of sex experts out there, and not all of them have radio shows. They're called women, and they're a hell of a lot more fun to talk to than your average Ph.D. They conduct all their research on their own bodies, and they're much more likely to let you in on the experimentation. So here's what we did: We went to the women first, and asked them what works best. (We're talking rockets' red glare here, bombs bursting in there.) Then we asked author Chrissy Brooks to consult the smartest sex docs around so they could tell us why it worked. Results are below. We'll leave the fun part up to you.

"Great lovers don't memorize complicated techniques. They master the simple things that give women pleasure," says Lou Paget, a sex educator and author of *How to Give Her Absolute Pleasure.* The more you give, the more you get. Simple, right?

● **"When I'm about to climax during oral sex, my husband flicks his tongue really fast along the length of my clitoris. A few seconds of that, and walls shake."**
Why it works: Most men think of the clitoris as just that little bud under the hood, but it actually extends deep inside a woman's body, explains Paget. When you flick your tongue quickly along its shaft, you're not only covering more territory but also creating vibrations that help carry your stimulation beyond the tongue's reach.

How to do it: The key here is to make sure that the clitoral hood is out of the way. Don't be afraid to pull it back gently and then make quick, darting motions with your tongue as far down along the tiny shaft as your tongue can go.

○ **"I love it when my man makes circles around my breasts with his finger or tongue before coming in for a nipple landing."**
Why it works: Like the ripples that circle out when you throw a rock into a pond, concentric zones of sensitivity radiate outward from a woman's hot spots. "The area surrounding erogenous zones such as the nipples tends to be highly sensitive, too," says Linda De Villers, Ph.D., a California psychologist and author of *LoveSkills.*

How to do it: Begin right at the point where her breast starts to rise from her chest, and spiral slowly inward with your fingertips until you reach the nipple. Once you hit the bull's-eye, suck and gently bite. To really tease her, try circling in until you just brush her nipple, then pulling back out for another tantalizing spin.

○ **"All of a sudden, without warning, my guy stops midthrust. Then he goes super slow, entering me inch by inch for a few minutes. It sets me off like nothing else!"**
Why it works: The key to keeping her aroused is to keep her guessing. Predictability really takes away from pleasure—not to mention that in the beginning too much of the same sensation makes a woman go numb, says Paget. But don't worry, you don't have to do anything fancy to jump-start her sensation; just stop. "Stopping and restarting a touch or a thrust builds on the previous sensation, and it lets you skip up a few rungs on the pleasure ladder," says Paget.

How to do it: Pick a thrust and stop—you can be inside or halfway out or just have the head of your penis touching her vaginal lips. Catch her eye, pause for a few seconds, and start again. For maximum effect, resume thrusting in slow motion and build back up to speed gradually.

○ **"Before we make love, my husband often stands in front of me after I've undressed and holds his fingertips right above my skin. He moves his hands all the way up and down my body. The sensation is unreal."**
Why it works: Positive anticipation is a huge part of what turns women on, says Michael Seiler, Ph.D., a sex therapist and director of the Phoenix Institute in Chicago. By levitating your fingers above the skin so they brush those fine body hairs, you're creating a delightful shiver up her spine—and making her feel as though you appreciate every inch of her body.

How to do it: Help her undress (another anticipation stoker); once she's naked, take her hand and stand facing her. Brush her hair back and let your fingertips hover over the surface of her skin. You're where you should be if the fat part of your fingerpad is touching her skin ever so slightly. Now go ahead and run your pads over her arms, breasts, belly, and thighs.

● **"I love it when my boyfriend hums while giving me oral sex. And when he follows it up with very light finger taps, I detonate."**
Why it works: There's a reason vibrators are so popular: Anything that shakes, rattles, or rolls primes a passel of nerves for peak sensation. "Any time you touch the skin with something vibrating, you transmit sensation to a wider area than you would through simple stroking," says Paget. So you're activating twice the nerves with half the work. "Top it off with a direct touch at the right time and to just the right place—in this case, the clitoris—and you'll probably send her over the edge."

How to do it: Relax your lips (think Mick Jagger) and hum a tune (think "Brown Sugar"). Bring the outermost portion of your kisser in contact with the outside of her clitoris (the hood that covers the little nub) and her vaginal lips. Move your mouth around her clitoris—very slowly. When she can't take anymore, tap gently and in a circular motion with your fingertip on the swollen nub of the clitoris; or give it a few long, languid licks, staying in contact the whole time.

● **"As he's thrusting, my guy presses hard with his hand right below my belly button. I have the most incredible orgasms."**
Why it works: On the belly-side wall of her vaginal canal lurks a quarter-size zone of pleasure known as the G-spot. The reason many women don't think they have one of these secret pleasure buttons is that the G-spot responds only to firm pressure—and that may not occur during intercourse, explains John D. Perry, Ph.D., a sex therapist in California. But pressing on her G-spot from the outside while you're thrusting inside can bring her pleasure place into fuller contact with your penis and trigger mind-blowing orgasms.

How to do it: Since the exact location of the G-spot varies from woman to woman, you'll have to play it by feel. Start by gently pressing the heel of your hand into her belly button as you're thrusting. When she screams with pleasure, you'll know you've hit the target.

● **"My boyfriend has this amazing thing he does on my nipples, private parts, and neck: He licks a small area and then blows on the wet patch. It creates these sexy tingles down my spine."**

Why it works: Remember blowing on soup to cool it off? The same principle governs the evaporation of liquid on skin: Blow it and it cools. Couple the cooling trick with a warm lick, and you have a contrast that'll make her head spin. "The further apart two sensations are on a spectrum of feeling—hot/cold or hard/soft—the more intense they'll feel done in succession," says Paget.

perfect figures

Percentage of single men who say they'll never need another "night out with the guys" after they are in a steady relationship: 39

How to do it: Creating a wet spot with water is good, but wetting with alcohol is better. Since alcohol evaporates more quickly than water, it creates a cooler effect when you blow. So bring that glass of wine into the bedroom. Swish some around in your mouth and lick a choice spot. (Try her breasts first.) Then blow gently, give it a second, and take a long, slow lick. Repeat as necessary.

● **"I love it when my man lightly bites my nipples while touching me down below. There's something about the combination that drives me crazy with pleasure."**

Why it works: Although the government hasn't yet ponied up cash for a study of this phenomenon, women and the sex experts who study them know there's often a direct sensory connection between the nipple and the pleasure nub. "For many women, lightly biting or tweaking the nipples produces a tingle in their genitals, especially the clitoris," says Paget.

How to do it: The easiest approach is to lie side by side and bite her nipple while touching her down below. Don't be surprised if she drapes a leg over your side—that just means she wants you to go deeper.

● **"One night my husband and I were fooling around on the La-Z-Boy, and he pulled up a footstool and knelt as I lay on the chair. Then he used the rocking of the recliner to help him thrust. Something about the back-and-forth motion heightened every sensation."**

Why it works: Adding something unpredictable, such as a rocking motion, can be highly erotic. "Surprise is almost always sexy—it's almost as though the rocking adds a fourth dimension to the experience," says Louanne Cole Weston, Ph.D., a sex therapist in Sacramento. Also, any position in which you're lower than she is ups your chances of hitting her G-spot by helping to angle your penis toward her front (belly-side) vaginal wall.

How to do it: Choose a recliner or rocking chair that's comfortable for her and a footstool or low table that puts you at the right thrusting height.

● **"When we're in the missionary position, my husband gets up high so his hips are above mine and enters me at a downward angle very, very slowly. Often he pauses midthrust, and I have the most over-the-top orgasms."**
Why it works: During typical thrusting, a woman's clitoris generally gets neglected. But when a man positions his hips above his partner's, he can thrust in such a way that his penile shaft remains in direct contact with her clitoris.

How to do it: From the standard missionary position, just push yourself forward with the balls of your feet and your toes so that you're "riding high." (Your hipbones should be at least an inch above hers.) Then enter and start thrusting very slowly.

● **"When my husband gives me oral sex, he also enlists his finger to provide firm pressure deep inside. The combination feels unbelievably good."**
Why it works: Although it seems logical that the clitoris and the vagina would be hooked up on the same nerve network, they actually activate separate pleasure frequencies. That's why touching inside your partner's vagina with the fingers of one hand and her clitoris with the fingers of the other hand doubles the amount of pleasure she feels, says Paget. Bonus: Many women like to feel "filled up" when they reach orgasm (having something to contract the vaginal muscles around increases sensation), so two fingers inside can make all the difference when she climaxes.

How to do it: Start by touching or licking her clitoris. Once she's stimulated, put a finger in her vagina and give her a few firm strokes. When she's about to climax, add a second finger to give her more to flex against.

SEX TRENDS

GOD KNOWS WHY

Baptists have the highest divorce rate (29 percent) of any Christian denomination in the country and are more likely to get a divorce than atheists or agnostics (21 percent). Catholics and Lutherans have the lowest divorce rates (21 percent). Jews split up more often than any other group (30 percent).

● **"I was with this guy who would pucker up his lips and seal them around my nipple. Then he'd alternately inhale and create a vacuum and exhale to put pressure on my breast. It was the most amazing feeling."**
Why it works: Just as alternating between hot and cold can heighten the effect of each, so can switching be-

tween pulling and pushing. "Pushing and pulling activate separate sets of nerves, so combining the two effectively doubles the pleasure she feels," Paget says.

How to do it: The key here is to be gentle—at least at first. Once you've taken a few spins, pucker up your lips and apply them so you create a gentle seal around her nipple. Then take in air from your nose and breathe out through your mouth. Now suck in through your mouth. Repeat, and keep increasing the intensity.

○ **"My boyfriend puts me in orbit when he gives me oral sex. It's not his technique per se, or some quirky aspect of his tongue that has me mesmerized, it's the way he seems to savor every minute of it."**
Why it works: One of a woman's greatest fears is that she smells or tastes bad below the belt. Allay that fear, and everything else you do will be golden. "When we know he's totally into it, that alone takes us to another level of pleasure," says Paget.

How to do it: Catch her eye in the midst of the action, moan, or simply tell her how much you're loving what you're doing.

○ **"My boyfriend turned me crosswise on the bed the other night so that my head fell over the edge. I thought he was nuts—until I had my biggest orgasm ever."**
Why it works: Any time you turn your head upside down, you'll feel a rush as blood pours in and oxygen is depleted. "And this head rush, combined with physical pleasure, can heighten orgasm for some women," says Dr. Seiler.

How to do it: Have her lie on her back across the bed, with her head and shoulders dangling over the edge. (Make sure that she keeps as much of her lower back on the mattress as possible, and stop if she gets too light-headed.) Enter her slowly, and show some restraint when you thrust—you don't want to knock her onto the floor.

○ **"My man puts a pillow under my butt before we get going in the missionary position. It tips me in such a way that every thrust feels a million times better and I climax very quickly."**
Why it works: When it comes to thrusting, angle is everything—when your penis slides in at just the right slant, it tickles her clitoris and makes solid contact with her G-spot. Since the G-spot is on the front (belly-side) wall of her vagina, anything that tips her pelvis back makes that hot-spot contact more likely. That same pelvic tilt also raises the clitoris, putting it in a better position to come in contact with your penile shaft.

How to do it: As you're moving into the missionary position, slide one pillow (start with a fairly flat one) underneath your partner, right where her lower back meets her butt. Let her fiddle with it until she's comfortable, then thrust as usual. Don't be surprised if your efforts produce more pleasure than you bargained for.

SEX WARS

"It was very irresponsible of you to leave a loaded gun lying around where the children and I could get to it."

BEAUCOUP BOUQUETS

It's all about flowers. They're still one of the best ways to say, "I love you," "I'm sorry," or "Hey! Look! Flowers!" These are shipped direct from the grower and are guaranteed to arrive fresh and perfect on the day you specify. Have your credit card handy. Condoms, too, if you know what we mean.

www.calyxandcorolla.com

GET AWAY FROM IT ALL

Did you know it is a scientific fact that women are 14,265 percent more likely to want sex while on vacation? Of course, it is. Here's travel advice about every appealing niche and cranny on the globe, plus daily travel bargains, information on "hot" destinations, travel tips, maps, and more. Advice is free. The rest is, well, worth it.

www.concierge.com

MARRYING MAN

Contemplating the big *M*? Avoid a big mistake. Find creative ways to pop the question, discover what you need to know about diamonds, and learn how to have an awesome bachelor party, how to pick the right tux, and how to make a memorable toast. Log on for more.

www.marryingman.com

MAN'S GUIDE INTERVIEW

How Successful Couples Keep Love Alive

An Interview with "Dr. Romance" Gregory Godek

We don't mean to be this way. It's just that very few of us were taught the importance of performing the playful rites of romance long-term. We figure, "Look, we're handling adult crises and responsibilities every day to make life work for us and our partners. Why in the world should we be expected to devote time to goofy schoolboy-woos-girl types of rituals now that we've graduated from those preliminaries and are slaying dragons in the real world?" Somehow we fail to figure out—or remember once we do figure it out—that long-term romance, when practiced consistently and well, delivers something we care a lot about. Can you spell S-E-X?

Maybe we figure that because romance is so valued by women that it's something mysterious—a female thing we could never get—like the Lifetime network. But it's not mysterious or complicated, says our expert.

Gregory Godek knows something about this. He has written more than a dozen books, including 10,000 Ways to Say I Love You, The Lovers' Bedside Companion, The Portable Romantic, *and* Romantic Mischief.

His most recent book, 1,001 Ways to Be Romantic, *actually is both his 1st and his 14th book. The first version, published in 1991, sold more than 1.5 million copies. Now he says that he's brought it into the 21st century with about 70 percent new material.*

The media have called Godek America's romance authority, America's romance coach, and even at times Dr. Romance. He has appeared on Oprah *and* Donahue *and offers romance seminars and classes to audiences as diverse as the U.S. Army, women's groups, and business organizations.*

The information in his books and seminars, he says, is simply "stuff that works."

"I'm not a doctor, I'm not a psychologist, and I don't think I have all the answers," he says. "I don't try to push my cute little idea of the way relationship psychology ought to work. I provide information based on observations from real people's relationships—people who have great relationships versus people who have mediocre ones. I explain what the people with great relationships do that most other people don't do."

MAN'S GUIDE: Clearly, you think romance is important to a relationship. How does romance change as you move from early dating to serious relationship to marriage?

GODEK: It goes downhill.

MAN'S GUIDE: Yikes. Does it have to be that way, or . . .

GODEK: If you don't work at it, it does go downhill. Here's what happens:

First of all, the average person equates love and infatuation. But they are not the same thing. Infatuation is about falling in love. Love as it exists in marriage and long-term relationships is about *staying* in love. There is a very big difference here.

When you first start dating, you fall in love. I mean, there's a reason they call it falling in love. It's like tripping; it's out of control. You don't choose whom you fall in love with, okay? It just happens, or it doesn't happen. You either have good chemistry, or you don't.

Now, I'm not criticizing infatuation, mind you. I think infatuation is one of the best feelings in the whole world.

MAN'S GUIDE: Gotcha.

GODEK: If you could bottle infatuation, you'd be richer than Bill Gates. But you can't.

The thing about infatuation versus love is that when you're infatuated, romance is easy. Even the guys whom I refer to as romantically impaired can manage to be romantic. That's because guys understand wooing. We know how to woo a woman because we like the chase. We like the challenge. Okay?

MAN'S GUIDE: I'm with you so far.

GODEK: So in the early stages of a relationship, romance is, frankly, very easy. Part of the reason is that you don't need much romance in the beginning.

I mean, think about it. At first, sitting on the couch and gazing into each other's eyes is exciting. Compare this to the same couple 25

> " It must have been one long, good layover. "
>
> —Bob Kenia, vice president of the Association of Flight Attendants, on the unprecedented number of pregnant flight attendants at British Airways

years later. They do not sit on the couch and gaze into each other's eyes. Things are different. It's simply not as exciting anymore.

This doesn't mean you have fallen out of love. It doesn't mean you have a bad relationship. But you need to *know* each other to have a lasting relationship. Infatuation is about newness and discovery.

MAN'S GUIDE: And once the newness is over, you get down to the real business of getting to know each other and figuring out if you want to stay together over the long run.

GODEK: Basically. You fall in love and you become a couple. After 6 months to a year, the relationship is, by definition, no longer new. You can still be very much in love and have lots of wonderful things between you, but it's not new.

The very nature of a long-term relationship prevents you from holding on to the infatuation. But in a good relationship, you trade the newness and discovery for depth and understanding. That's what makes a great relationship.

The problem is, most people don't do the work of building depth and understanding. It requires some effort to stay in love and to stay in touch with each other. It just doesn't happen on its own. That's where romance comes in. But before I explain, let me define a couple of terms here.

MAN'S GUIDE: Fire away.

GODEK: *Love* is the emotion, *romance* is the action.

In other words, you don't *do* love. You *feel* it. It's not really an action that you get up and do. Love is a feeling. The action that you take based on the feelings of love, that's romance.

Let's say you feel "in love." What do you do? You send her a rose. You call her on the phone in the middle of the day. You buy little gifts for no reason. You fill her car with gas. Open the car door. Bring home little surprises. You don't forget her birthday. All of that is romance.

But I also divide romance into two types. There's obligatory romance, and then there's optional romance.

Obligatory romance includes Valentine's Day, birthdays, anniversaries, Christmas, and other holidays. It's virtually a federal law that you must be romantic on Valentine's Day. If you don't send roses or chocolates, don't bother showing up at home. You know, guys, you're in big trouble here if you drop the ball.

Optional romance is coming home on a Tuesday night with a bottle of champagne. It's bringing home one rose, you know, just for no reason.

You need to act on both kinds of romance to have a good relationship. But as far as I'm concerned, the optional romance is the type that is really the most meaningful.

MAN'S GUIDE: What about pouring my wife a fresh glass of water for the bedside and opening the car door for her and things like that? Is this a subset of optional romance? Maybe something that should be called maintenance romance?

GODEK: Well, there's another way to break down the types of romance, and what you're talking about is generic romance versus creative romance.

What I call generic romance could also be called classic romance. It's all the stuff that our culture tells us is romantic. Flowers, candy, dinner, jewelry, chocolate, and so on. I also call that movie romance. The sweep-her-off-her-feet kind of romance.

Now, that's the kind of romance people think of first. It's all nice, and it's classic stuff—and it works. I mean, champagne is great, and I still give roses to my wife. However, that's not really day-to-day romance, which is maybe what you mean by "maintenance." And that's where creative romance can come into play.

You do not live your life from Valentine's Day to Valentine's Day. You don't live it from vacation to vacation. Those are high points. In the movies, they focus on the high points and really grand romantic overtures. But real people live their lives day by day by day.

MAN'S GUIDE: So the holidays and other events are peaks, while most of life is in the valleys.

GODEK: That's right. Where real love resides is in the day-to-day stuff. If you're never romantic on a random Tuesday, for example, I would say that you're not really living in a loving relationship.

❝ It takes twice as good a man to have two wives as it does to have one. If you have three wives, it takes five times as good a man if you're going to have harmony in your family. **❞**

—Polygamist Owen Allred, 86, father of 23 children and husband to eight women, and a target of lawmakers trying to polish Utah's image before the 2002 Winter Olympic Games

And that's what you're doing by randomly bringing her a little gift or bringing water to her bedside. That is a loving gesture. And if you're doing it without her asking you, that's even better. Or on the more practical side, you know, you can keep her car filled with gas. That's an expression of love.

When you are dating, there is a moment at which your definitions change, and it's no longer "you" and "me." You start thinking of yourselves as a unit. You become an "us." When my wife and I were in that transitional period of dating, officially beginning to think of ourselves as a couple, I got her a membership in the American Automobile Association. Sure doesn't seem romantic, does it?

MAN'S GUIDE: Not on the surface.

GODEK: It's just that it's not classically romantic. But I'm thinking, "Look, we're now a couple, I'm committed to her, I care about her, I love her."

And part of my taking care of her, part of my expressing love for her, is keeping her safe. Getting her a membership in AAA, for example. If her car dies, I don't want her on the side of the road helpless. I want her to be able to call somebody for immediate help. That's love, and it's a form of romance.

MAN'S GUIDE: The Auto Club. That's what really gets her engine revving? C'mon.

GODEK: Here's the problem. Some guys think just about the practical side of romance. They think that because they do the day-to-day romance, they can skimp on—or skip entirely—the obligatory romance like Valentine's Day.

Oh, no. Heck, no. You'll be in serious trouble for that.

The women will tend to argue from the other side. They'll say, "I want the sweet things, I want the classically romantic things." They might overlook the day-to-day romance if you don't maintain the classic romance, too.

The classic stereotype is a woman who is married to a really logical guy like an accountant or an engineer. Nine times out of 10, this guy does not do the classic romantic things, but he consistently does the practical things. He's taking care of her, he takes care of her car, he takes care of the house, and he's very reliable. He does all those things. In his mind, he believes he is sufficiently showing his love for her by taking care of her.

In her mind, she's saying, "Oh, I just wish he'd bring me roses more often."

You cannot do an either-or situation and expect it to work. The best relationships are made up of both kinds of romance, but doing that is up to the individual. I cannot tell you what to do. I don't care what you do. I can only tell you what works based on my observations.

If you don't want to be one of those 70-year-old couples walking down the street hand in hand, still loving each other deeply and romantically, that's up to you.

MAN'S GUIDE: Okay. So that's what we're shooting for.

GODEK: So what's that 70-year-old couple's secret? They're in love. He takes care of her. She takes care of him. They also do nice little things together. Lots of little things.

Romance is really about a building up of the little things. Or better yet, it's like the thousands of little threads and fibers that go together to make a tapestry.

With romance, you're weaving together this beautiful, creative tapestry. So when every once in a while things go wrong, it's still okay. You might have a fight, you might act the fool, but that won't ruin the whole tapestry. It just unravels a few threads.

If your relationship is based on a few big things instead of a lot of little things, you're in trouble. It's like you're hanging on one rope, one cord. And when that one cord gets frayed . . .

MAN'S GUIDE: . . . you fall.

GODEK: Yeah. You're doomed. You're Wile E. Coyote, falling down that cliff and crashing onto the valley floor.

MAN'S GUIDE: Let's get down. Let's talk to *men*. How much do the things that make her warm and fuzzy contribute to her getting hot and sweaty?

GODEK: It's definitely connected. You see, romance is the bridge between love and sex. Without romance, the gap is too wide to be crossed.

Speaking in very general terms, men tend to start with sex and move toward love. Women start with love and move toward sex. It's very easy for most guys to, you know, have sex without any love being there. They just do it. It's more physical. At least, it starts physical before it moves toward psychological.

We men need the love just as much as we need the sex. It's just that we get to the sex quicker. Men and women usually start at opposite ends of the spectrum, and it is romance that connects the two of them in the middle.

One of our problems as men is that we blow romance out of proportion. We think it's a bigger deal than it really is, and we think that it's just for the woman. "She wants me to be more romantic, so I'll be romantic. It's for her, it's for her, it's for her."

Well, if that's your mindset, you're in trouble. Because if it's all for her and not for you, that means that being romantic is a sacrifice. And nobody sacrifices for very long without resenting it.

MAN'S GUIDE: Agreed. No one wants to be a martyr forever.

GODEK: Definitely not. In my seminars, I'll say, "Guys, let me tell you something. Romance is as much for you as it is for her."

Let's just be real direct here. Would you like to have more sex?

MAN'S GUIDE: Hello. Is this thing *on?*

GODEK: Well, here's what you do: Be more romantic, and you will get more sex. Okay? That's the formula. That's the secret if you want a secret. To a certain extent, I'm making light of things. But the point is that romance can be good for the guy, too.

You know, sometimes it's about the sex, and sometimes it's about the love. It's not about having either love or sex. It's about both.

If guys want have more sex, they have to be more romantic. But the equation works the other way as well. And I would say that if there are any women reading this who want more romance, you might want to think about starting that process off by giving your man more sex.

MAN'S GUIDE: Would you say that again? Really loud. So everyone can hear.

GODEK: I give that advice with the understanding that this is being done within the context of a loving relationship. Outside of a loving relationship, it can be dangerous. Then you're trading love for sex. That can really become abusive, and people can play games, and things can get really weird.

There's one more major thing I think we need to address. Earlier on, I was talking about love versus infatuation and how you cannot move to the former without giving up the latter at some point. There's another aspect to that equation where people make a big mistake. They fail to realize that while you cannot keep the infatuation, you can keep the passion. And that's really the point of why you're talking to me, right? Ultimately, you want to find out how to keep passion alive in a relationship.

People often equate passion with infatuation. And that's just as big a mistake as confusing love with infatuation.

Passion and infatuation are different. But it's easy to get them tied together and confused, because when you're infatuated, you're also very passionate.

See, you can be 70 years old and still be passionately in love with each other. First of all, physically. And second of all, emotionally. You can cultivate passion in all aspects. Do and you move on to a place where passion cannot only survive but also grow.

QUICKIES

THE HOUSE OF LOVE

Even in a vast suburban-tract mansion, replete with dining room, 3½ bath-rooms, rec room, family room, mud room, home theater room, and fallout shelter, you won't find a sex room. Oh, sure, there's the bedroom, but sex is the least of the activities you perform there. But hey, whose house is it anyway? You can turn your entire castle into a sex palace perfect for really good, innovative, wake-up-the-neighbors sex. For instance, there's . . .

❍ The study

Swivel chairs are perfect for oral sex. Sit her down and take your place on the floor in front of her. Then get to work with your tongue while you move her, chair and all, side to side. She'll feel almost as if she were floating, says Robert Birch, Ph.D., author of *Oral Caress.*

❍ The kitchen

"Use a sturdy wooden table, which is more comfortable than the floor and at a better height than the kitchen counter," says Louanne Cole Weston, Ph.D., a sex therapist in Sacramento. Have your partner lie back on the table with her pelvis near the edge. Then reach for some food—anything that can be licked off is fair game. Giving your tongue something tasty to aim for can help you dwell in one spot longer—and she'll love that.

❍ The pool

Sex here is tricky because water washes away natural lubrication, making thrusting as much fun as putting on rubber gloves lined with sandpaper. The solution: "Non-water-based lubricant," says Michael Perry, Ph.D., a sex thera-pist in California. He suggests Wet Platinum, which is silicone-based and latex-condom-compatible. Once you're slippery, move to chest-deep water and have sex standing up. "You're almost weightless in water, so it's easy to do things you wouldn't normally be able to do," he adds.

❍ The backyard

You'll need one of those armless, three-panel reclining lawn chairs. You take the bottom position, then let her straddle you and the chair. Her legs will do all the real work—you can just sit back and watch. Now that's a house party!

● The bathroom

"Standing up works better than sitting down, unless you have a really big bathtub," says Dr. Weston. Your partner should brace herself with her hands on the shower walls. You'll enter from behind. Stand out of the stream if you're wearing a condom, since water could cause it to slip off. And don't use water-based lubricants in the tub—they can turn the floor into a slip-and-slide.

● The window

It's so much more fun looking down on your neighbor's azaleas than staring at the crack in the ceiling during sex, says Dr. Perry. Have your partner lean against a window frame (make sure the window is closed if you're a particularly vigorous thruster) and enter her from behind. If she's wearing a short skirt or dress and you keep your pants most of the way on, people below won't know what you're doing, though the shouting may give you away.

● The family room

Got a beanbag chair? "You can contour it to any shape you want, and it's almost like being in water—it'll support you in ways you're not normally supported," says Dr. Perry. Doggy-style sex works great when she's on her belly, draped over the amorphous blob (the chair, not you). So does the missionary position. "Stick a couple of thick books under the bag to keep her from sinking in too far," he suggests.

● The laundry room

Your washing machine produces more vibration than any other appliance in your home. The problem is that most people don't use it right. *You* should be the one with your butt on the lid. "The motion will be transmitted through your pelvis, essentially turning your member into a life-size vibrator," says Dr. Perry. *Hint:* Run a warm-water load.

● The closet

Closet sex works best for a quickie. "It's not the kind of place you want to linger in," says Dr. Weston. (So she says.) Pick your timing: When you're both too horny even to find your way upstairs, take her in there, pull down her pants, and have standing rear-entry sex. It's the surest route to orgasm when there's not enough space to lie down.

THE MARRIAGE COUNSELOR THAT DROOLS

No wonder Siegfried and Roy look so happy. When researchers at the State University of New York in Buffalo monitored 100 married couples at home, they found that those who had pets maintained 65 percent lower blood pressures and 22 percent lower heart rates during arguments. Karen Allen, Ph.D., the study's author, speculates that pets have a calming effect on couples. Of course, it's easy to defuse an argument when you blame everything on the dog.

FORECAST: CLOUDS, RAIN, AND A WHOLE LOTTA LOVE

Maybe it's the rhythm of the fallin' rain, but we're twice as likely to tell our wives we love them when it's dumping cats and dogs outside than when it's bright and sunny. Conversely, couples are twice as likely to argue when Old Sol is smiling than when it's wet out, according to a nationwide survey by forecasting company AccuWeather.com. Most common bitch-session topic on nice days: What are we going to do today?

"Maybe we should start giving emotional tips along with our weather forecasts," quips Joel Myers, Ph.D., AccuWeather founder and president.

Here are some other weather-related findings.

- Couples are nearly three times more likely to have sex more than once a day when it's foggy out, compared to when it's sunny.

- Women are four times more likely than men to initiate sex on a rainy day.

- Both men and women are three times more likely to eat meat on rainy days, but men are four times more likely to take a nap.

DEAR DR. MANLY

Q: *Does size really matter?*
—J. K., Gatlinburg, Tennessee

A: Let me guess—you recently asked this question of your significant other, and she said, "No! I love your erector set just the way it is." Now you're wondering if that's what *all* women say, and where'd they learn about erector sets anyway?

According to research at the University of California, the average erect penis measures 5.03 inches from base to tip when measured along the top (the dorsal side, if you prefer). Here's where the "but" comes in: If yours is smaller than average, there's still plenty that you can do to be a great lover. Of the 100 women we, uh, polled on this topic, 96 said that size *alone* doesn't matter—technique counts for a lot, as does the quality of the relationship.

If you have a size-sensitive partner, try this the next time you have sex: Have her kneel on the bed and lean forward on her forearms. As you enter her vagina from behind, lean forward, placing your hands and some of your weight on her shoulders. She should wrap her lower legs around your thighs. The weight of your body on her back and the intertwining of your legs create a tighter connection than normal, which compensates for the length issue.

Don't be afraid to bring in reinforcements either. Men are genital-oriented (not that that's a bad thing), but women realize that there are many ways to be pleasured. Use your fingers, thumbs, tongue, vibrator—whatever you can think of.

But whatever you do, for crying out loud, never apologize for your God-given package. Not only is there nothing to be sorry about, an apology puts a woman on the defensive. She'll be thinking, "Oh great, am I going to have to make excuses for my saggy boobs now?" Remember: John Thomas is just one part of your sex machine—and it's the whole package that brings pleasure to a woman.

Q: *My girlfriend says that she prefers having the skin around her nipples kissed more than the nipples themselves.* **I'm happy to oblige, but I'm confused—they always stand up like brave little soldiers when I touch them. What's the deal?**
—J. M., PORTLAND, MAINE

A: Here's some new tactical information regarding her erogenous zones that I uncovered recently. Researchers at the University of Vienna (where else?) blindfolded 150 women and gently poked their breasts with pins to gauge skin sensitivity. While thus amusing themselves mightily, they discovered that the upper breast (roughly from 9 o'clock to 3 o'clock) is the most sensitive area, followed by the outer rim of the nipple. And get this: the nipple itself was the least sensitive spot on the women's breasts.

Men like to think of nipples as little penises because both tend to stiffen up when touched. But alas, sensitivity and erectility do not go hand in hand. (Well, they do in our hands, but that's the problem.) Next time, first focus on areas of her breasts besides her nipples—and soon she'll allow you plenty of hands-on time trying to get them to stand at attention.

Q: **When I give my girlfriend oral sex, she squirms and says it tickles.** *Is there anything I can do so that she'll enjoy it more?*
—D. P., DOVER, DELAWARE

A: Sounds to me as if she's more "bashful" ticklish than poke-in-the-armpit ticklish. First off, put her at ease before you begin. Reassure her that you enjoy—nay, live for—oral sex. For some women, and I won't mention my wife's name, this reassurance is actually part of the foreplay and must be diligently attended to every time.

Next, consider your touch. Think about the head of your penis: A soft touch can make you shiver, but a more substantial caress feels like heaven. Her clitoris (and I'm assuming you know where the clitoris is, though this may be part of the problem) reacts to stimulation much the same way. Consider the classic middle-school sex-education scene from Monty Python's *Meaning of Life:*

> HEADMASTER: *Name two ways of getting the vaginal juices flowing, Watson.*

STUDENT: *Rubbing the clitoris, sir.*

HEADMASTER: *What's wrong with a kiss, boy? Hm? Why not start her off with a nice kiss? You don't have to go leaping straight for the clitoris like a bull at a gate. Give her a kiss, boy!*

For starters, rub the lips of her vagina with your hand for a few minutes to build up her arousal. Then add your mouth, but keep using your hand, too; this will help her get used to the feel of your tongue. Use plenty of saliva. Hint: You don't have to physically touch the clitoris to stimulate it.

Slowly work your way toward the clitoris. Press firmly with the flat top of your tongue—don't flick at it with the tip. That only works in porno movies. In real life, it'll make her feel like a postage stamp. Finally, try inserting a finger slowly into her vagina. Many women find the sensation of inside/outside stimulation very arousing.

Dr. Manly is a fictional character.
The actual advice was provided by a variety of
medical doctors and other qualified experts.

4
TUNE UP
YOUR
SEX MACHINE

 Once upon a time, they called them dirty old men. Those men who managed to maintain a certain sexual groove, despite getting a little long in the tooth. They were oddities because, everyone thought, the older you get, the less sex you're supposed to have. Or even want. Everyone thought.

Ah, but then along came Viagra (sildenafil), and even the Granddaddy of Sex, Hugh Hefner, bless his heart, has girlfriends again. Four, in fact. And he's pushing three-quarters of a century. The words impotence *and* erectile dysfunction *have become household words, thanks to the nightly chatter of former presidential candidates and TV news anchors.*

As Martha Stewart would say, it's a good thing.

We want you to enjoy that good thing. In this section, you'll learn how to keep your love motor roaring smoothly, even if it idles roughly now.

TOP TEN

Performance Enhancers

For lifelong tip-top sex, keep your body systems purring and in tip-top shape. Here's how.

① **Schedule annual checkups.** Check your blood pressure and cholesterol levels, prostate, heart, colon, and so forth, and nip problems early, as they arise.

② **Stay physically active.** Get 40 or more minutes of vigorous activity at least 3 days each week. Sweat. Get your heart rate up a bit and keep it up. Better yet, do it with a friend. Having a partner makes it easier to stick with a program and creates what psychologists call a social network, which is good for stress reduction—and that's good for a lot of things.

③ **Lift weights.** Strength training not only makes you look and feel hotter, it builds your immune and circulatory systems, helps firm up flab, increases your flexibility, and gives you a chance to make pal talk with pretty young ladies with tight bodies if you do it in a gym.

④ **Cut your pressure.** Keep your blood pressure levels down in the healthy ranges, and if diet and exercise don't do the trick, take medication. Healthy blood pressure staves off stroke, heart disease, and memory loss, and, best of all, it makes for optimum orgasms.

5 **Live frugally.** You don't need to be a miser, but overextending your finances creates incredible stress that is hell on marriages and other cohabitation relationships and causes physical damage that impairs your immune system and your ability to get and sustain erections.

6 **Look at them tomatoes.** Eat 10 or more servings of tomato-paste-based foods each week. They have to be cooked with oil, preferably olive oil, to bring out the great prostate-protecting substance, lycopene.

7 **Have sex.** Often. Have more, it's on us. Frequent pleasurable sex (of the safe variety) reduces the mortality rate. It feels pretty good, too.

8 **Avoid smoke.** Passive smoke damages those little veins and arteries that your penis counts on so much and exposes you to nearly all the health hazards that smokers suffer.

9 **Know your genes.** Knowing what diseases and conditions you are prone to will help you develop healthy strategies for postponing, avoiding, or fighting them. It always helps to know what the enemy looks like.

10 **Brush and floss your teeth.** It makes you more attractive, and some of us can use all the help we can get. Also, medical science now is finding that the plaque-forming bacteria damage arteries, which can wreak havoc throughout your body.

MUST READS

Savor the Fruits of Passion

Good food is like good sex: Open mouth; eat something warm, juicy, and delicious; moan with pleasure; beg for seconds. A more fitting metaphor you couldn't ask for. Still, there's an art to culinary love, as writers Jeff Bredenberg and Alisa Bauman so tastily point out in this guide to lusty cuisine from the book Food Smart.

When you first met her, you got turned on by watching the way she wiped the spaghetti sauce off the corner of her lip. Just hearing her ask you to pass the peas sent chills down your spine. You were like Jack Nicholson and Jessica Lange in the steamy, kitchen love scene from *The Postman Always Rings Twice*, smashing dishes in a wild frenzy of passion. It was that great.

Now, the culinary thrill is gone. Each day you eat, not necessarily together. Then you lie on the couch and watch the evening prime-time lineup, sharing a bag of barbecue Fritos. She reads women's magazines with articles like "87 Things That Are Better Than Sex." Every once in a while, you glance at each other, and both of you silently think, "Maybe tomorrow."

It's time to bring food back into your sex life.

"If you are well-fed, you are more likely to think about sex than if you are not well-fed," says George Armelagos, Ph.D., professor of anthropology at Emory University in Atlanta and author of *Consuming Passions.*

Eating for Pleasure

When most guys think about food and sex, the first thing that probably springs to mind is whipped cream. That's not what we're talking about here.

But stay with us. We'll get to that later. We're talking about ways you can eat smarter for more sensational sex, because when you get right down to it, the food you put in your body is ultimately more important for sex than the food you smear *on* her body. Here are some helpful hints.

● Make a B-line.
The B vitamins thiamin, riboflavin, and niacin are all needed for a healthy sex drive. If you drink alcohol on a daily basis, you may want to take a daily 100-milligram thiamin supplement, because alcohol depletes that vitamin. Otherwise, you can get it by eating whole grains, asparagus, and raw nuts. Riboflavin is found in asparagus, bananas, broccoli, and lean meats.

Niacin dilates blood vessels, creating better bloodflow, and it synthesizes sex hormones. But if you take it in supplement form, it can irritate your stomach, causing ulcers. It's found in fish, lean meats, peas, and beans.

C about a supplement.

Vitamin C helps keep your various sex glands running smoothly and your skin smooth and elastic. It also keeps sperm strong by protecting them against free radicals that make them cling together in immobile clumps.

Vitamin C is found in citrus fruits, strawberries, kiwifruit, tomatoes, and green vegetables. If you're looking to be a dad, taking a 250-milligram supplement a day may improve your sperm's chances of fertilizing an egg.

Dial E for excitement.

Vitamin E aids sex hormone production and improves circulation. Be careful about taking large doses, however, because it can increase blood pressure. If you are taking supplements, start below 100 IU. It is naturally found in nuts, seeds, beans, whole grains, fruits, and vegetables.

Be Zeus with zinc.

The body needs zinc to produce testosterone, the male sex hormone. It also increases sperm production and the volume of ejaculate and may protect sperm from vaginal bacteria. Either too little or too much zinc can negatively affect your sex drive. You can easily get your Daily Value of 15 milligrams by eating steamed oysters, pumpkin seeds, sunflower seeds, garlic, and spinach.

Foods of Love

Many items considered as aphrodisiacs work for a very simple reason: because you believe they will. Your brain is your biggest sex organ. If it thinks something turns you into a love machine, it will, says Dr. Armelagos. So if you believe salted crackers will fire up your libido, chances are they will.

Some aphrodisiacs, such as oysters, work because they contain nutrients that your body needs. But they only work if your body needs

hot TIP!

Finally score a big date with Helga from the mailroom? Put down the shaving cream, Mr. Smoothy. Shaving gels and lotions lubricate your beard better than foam, helping prevent irritation and unsightly razor burns that clash with your new tie. "Keep the beard hairs moist, and it'll decrease by two-thirds the force you need to cut them," says dermatologist Neal Schultz, M.D. Our favorites are Alba Botanica Mango Vanilla Shave, One Touch Inverness Gel, and the fragrance-free Aveeno Therapeutic Shave Gel. Prefer to see your stubble as you shave? Go for gel in a tube—pressurized goop tends to lather quickly.

perfect figures

Amount of blood it takes
to make your penis erect:
3 ounces

• • • • • • • • • •

those nutrients. Oysters are packed with zinc, so if you are zinc-deficient, oysters may help you feel sexy. If you're not zinc-deficient and oysters make you feel sexy, it's probably your brain doing all the work, Dr. Armelagos says.

There is scientific evidence to back up some other aphrodisiacs. Here are a few.

● Caffeine

Daily coffee drinkers are almost twice as likely to describe themselves as sexually active. And coffee-drinking men report fewer erection problems. "Some caffeine will wake you up. If you feel sluggish and caffeine wakes you up, then you're going to say, 'Oh, I'm horny,' instead of, 'Oh, I'm going to go back to sleep,'" says Jeanne Shaw, Ph.D., a certified sex therapist and clinical psychologist in Atlanta.

Once you move beyond moderate drinking (a couple of cups a day), however, you can reverse the effect. Too much caffeine can make you so hyper that you can't focus on feeling turned on.

● Chocolate

It has a number of ingredients that make us feel good. The stimulants theobromine and caffeine get our hearts beating. And a component called phenylethylalanine is thought to produce an "in love" sensation that dulls pain.

● Celery

If you want her to crave you instead of a magazine, this is what you want to eat. Androsterone, a potent male hormone, is thought to attract females, and it can be found in celery. Researchers speculate that when you eat celery, you can release the androsterone through perspiration after digestion. The woman can't smell it consciously, but she'll want to get her nose near your skin.

● Pumpkin pie

You don't have to eat it. Just bake it. Researchers at the Smell and Taste Treatment and Research Foundation in Chicago measured bloodflow to the penises of 31 men as they smelled different scents. The combination of pumpkin pie and lavender really got the blood moving. Other penis-picker-upper scents included doughnut combined with black licorice, pumpkin pie combined with doughnut, and plain old orange.

● Serotonin

It's a chemical that your brain produces when you eat a food that contains the amino acid tryptophan along with some carbohydrates. Low levels of serotonin have been linked to low sperm count, poor ejaculation, and low virility. Stress will deplete serotonin. But when you eat the tryptophan-carbohydrate combination, it calms you down and replaces the needed serotonin to boost your sexual desire. Try combining about 3½ ounces of fish, poultry, or lean beef with bread or pasta.

A Menu for Love

There's a reason watching her wipe spaghetti sauce off her lip turned you on a year ago but now barely distracts you from thinking about what's on TV tonight. When you first met, your body produced chemicals that put you happily in love. Then it stopped. You can't turn back the clock, but you can make dinner more sensual.

● **Reserve a table for two.**
First of all, to have a sexy dinner, you need to see each other while you eat. Often couples are too busy to eat together. "Dual-career couples who don't have time for each other are stressing their own growth by not having some ritual in the day when they are together," says Dr. Shaw. "Dining together is a ritual that has more nutrition in it than just the food."

● **Have a slow hand.**
One of the worst sex sappers is stress, and if you wolf down your meal, it contributes to stress. So take it easy. Chew. Taste. Savor it.

Stump the Sexperts: The Quiz

Think you know a lot about sex? Let's see how you do on this quiz. Then turn the page for the answers.

❶ Which of the following has at some point during history been used to perk up a man's penis? (a) Beheading a male partridge and having the doctor eat the heart and the patient drink the bird's blood mixed with water; (b) smearing oil, pepper, and nettleseed on a dildo and sticking it up the anus; (c) eating hippopotamus snout; (d) eating hyena eyes; (e) all of the above.

❷ What food did the ancient Egyptians mold into the shape of a penis and why?

❸ The sea slug has been considered an aphrodisiac by the Arabs and Chinese partly because it displays a trait that is similiar to the male penis. What is it?

❹ What creature was used to make Spanish fly?

❺ Which of the following is a man more likely to do after having sex? (a) Get something to eat; (b) have a beer; (c) smoke a cigarette.

Bonus question: When the Aborigines of central Australia ask "Utna ilkukabaka?" it can mean one of two things. One is, "Have you eaten?" What's the other?

Stump the Sexperts: The Answers

If you're just browsing, turn back a page to find "Stump the Sexperts: The Quiz." No fair peeking at the answers below.

❶ The answer is (e).

❷ Bread. In his book *Consuming Passions*, Emory University's Dr. George Armelagos says that the Egyptians may have made the association between bread and the male sex organ because bread swells as it bakes.

❸ It swells and grows when touched.

❹ Also known as cantharides, Spanish fly was made from a beetle found in southern Europe. The bug was dried and pulverized. When eaten, it irritated the gastrointestinal system and dilated blood vessels, causing erections of the penis or clitoris. The bug's damage to the kidneys, though, was fatal in some cases.

❺ The answer is (a). About 6.8 percent of men usually eat after sex, compared with 5.7 percent who have a drink and 3.4 percent who smoke.

The answer to the bonus question is: "Have you had sexual intercourse?"

❍ Feed each other.
You hold the spoon for her while she eats. Need we say more?

❍ Pass the salt before she asks.
Throughout the meal, do little things that will warm her heart. "These little acts of kindness at the dinner table can really create feelings of warmth and unity and enhance feelings of sexuality later in the evening," says Doreen Virtue, Ph.D., a psychologist in southern California and author of *In the Mood*. Don't wait for your mate to ask you to pass the salt or whatever other seasoning she usually uses. Offer it to her without being asked. If you've been paying attention at all, you know what she likes. If you haven't been paying attention, start. Now.

❍ Cooperate, don't criticize.
It's good for a couple to cook together, but it's not good if their being in the kitchen together turns into a power struggle. "The man might stand there and tell the woman how to chop onions a certain way. She's going to feel offended and criticized," Dr. Virtue says. "If he's really into how onions should be chopped, he should do that."

Build a Better Bedroom Body

Forget working on that hook shot, and never mind perfecting your parallel skiing. If there's one physical activity that men want to be good at—nay, perfect at—it's that most gentlemanly of sports, love. In the book Powerfully Fit, *authors Brian Chichester and Jack Croft outline the simple workout routines (and the reasons behind them) that will transform you into a marathon man of romance.*

Like many other vigorous activities, sex requires physical grace and skill if you want to reach your objective. And yes, it does require a certain degree of fitness if you want to be really good.

"The evidence is pretty conclusive. Besides the fact that exercising increases your well-being and confidence—both of which figure into the sexual equation—a regular fitness routine also enhances your physical ability to have sex," says James White, Ph.D., professor emeritus of exercise physiology at the University of California, San Diego.

Science backs that up. In one study of sexual behavior, Dr. White found that men who regularly worked out enjoyed a 30 percent boost in their sexual appetite. But more important, the exercisers also reported a significant increase in sexual performance; specifically, they were lasting longer and having more orgasms.

And you thought exercising would only make your muscles hard.

Stretch for Sex

A scene from life: You're sitting in front of the TV, channel surfing for the game, when your remote accidentally lands you on a free preview of the sex channel. Suddenly, you've forgotten all about the game. Right now, you just want to know how those incredibly skilled actors managed to get into that position.

But you'll never know, because just then your significant other marches in, wondering what all the moaning's about. You switch channels so fast you get a cramp in your thumb. A bit sullen now, you watch the game, but you're still wondering: How'd they do that?

The answer is flexibility, chum.

"If you want to do well and keep from hurting yourself in any physical endeavor, you have to have flexible, supple muscles. It doesn't matter whether it's basketball or sex," says Jeff Friday, a strength and conditioning coach. So unless you want to end up with, say, a groin pull in the midst of an Olympic lovemaking session, take a few minutes every day to limber up those libidinous muscles.

Eric Gronbech, Ph.D., professor of physical education at Chicago State University, who researches the link between fitness and libido, recommends trying the following stretches to get you started. If you have a fairly new mattress, it's perfectly okay to do these stretches on your bed. But if your mattress has a furrow in it from years of, ahem, overuse, do these stretches on the floor. And then go out and buy a new mattress.

> " I had a lot of things I was going to do when I became the first First Man. "
>
> —Ex-politician and paid Viagra spokesman Bob Dole, lamenting his wife Elizabeth's withdrawal from the 2000 presidential race, during a lecture at Kansas State University

● Raise some calves.
Men have a tendency to overflex their calves in the heat of passion, resulting in muscle spasms a bit lower in their bodies than they might have been expecting, says Dr. Gronbech. You can corral potential calf problems by lying flat on your back on the bed, with one leg bent, foot flat against the mattress. Keeping the opposite leg straight, raise it as far as you can, until it's pointing toward the ceiling. Now flex your foot, pointing it toward your chest. Hold the stretch for a 10-count, relax, then do it two more times. Now switch legs.

● Arm yourself.
Certain positions—the missionary leaps to mind—put quite a bit of stress on your shoulders, says Dr. Gronbech. So do a shoulder flexor: Sit up, cross your wrists, then raise your arms above your head as though you were about to be tied to the headboard (hmm, *there's* an idea). Now, straighten your arms and extend them back behind your head as far as you can, while still keeping your wrists crossed. Hold the stretch for a count of 10, relax, and repeat two more times.

● Float like a butterfly.
No two ways about it, your groin muscles work overtime in the sack. The best way to keep them flexible and avoid embarrassing and untimely muscle cramps is with a butterfly stretch. Lie flat on your back in bed, knees bent, feet flat on the mattress. Pull your heels toward your buttocks; now turn your ankles so that the soles and heels of your feet are touching one another. Your knees should naturally point out to the sides. Now let gravity do its thing—let your knees slowly drop toward the bed. When they're as far apart as possible, hold for a count of 10, then bring your knees back up. Relax, repeat twice.

❷ Be hip in bed.

What do an F-14 and your sex life have in common? Neither one gets anywhere without thrust. The F-14 relies on a jet engine; your libido depends on the thrust generated by your hips. To get hip to great sex, try this: Stretch your legs out straight, spread them apart, then lean forward from the hips as far as you comfortably can. Keep your legs relaxed and your feet upright. For stability, keep your hands in front of you. Hold for a count of 10, relax, and repeat twice.

The Great Sex Workout

Having a well-muscled body can improve your sexual performance in two ways. First, being in good shape will allow you to last longer. Second, the better you look, the more likely you are to attract partners interested in lasting longer with you. Here's all you need to get rock hard, right now. And then again, later.

❷ Exercise abs for amore.

Along with your hips, your abdominals help power the thrusting motion so useful during sex. A basic crunch will serve you in good stead. Do three sets of 10 and work your way up from there.

"If you can get up to three sets of 20 repetitions, you'll have all the thrusting strength you'll need for sex," says Dr. Gronbech.

❷ Be a muscle missionary.

Just as the shoulders need to be stretched, they (along with the arms) also need to be strengthened. If you're on top, you need to hold yourself up as long as you stay up. Collapsing onto your partner because your arms gave out is hardly the kind of climax most guys imagine. Pushups are the most natural choice for sex-training. In the weight room, you can build up your shoulders with—what else?—shoulder shrugs as well as upright rows. If you don't already know how to do these exercises, check out "Your Own Personal Trainer" at www.menshealth.com or buy a weight-lifting book or ask a trainer at a gym.

SEX TRENDS

REBUILDING THE HOUSE OF LOVE

Viagra has put the sex back in the Playboy Mansion. Seventy-four-year-old Hugh Hefner credits the blue diamond with saving his life. "I've got four girlfriends now," all under 25 (including twins), he told *Newsweek*. "It's the best legal recreational drug out there."

Powerful and Plentiful Orgasms

In the arena of sex, there's one muscle group that you want to be sure to work, but you'll never find a circuit machine for it. The muscles in question are the pubococcygeus, or PC, muscles. Besides performing such handy tasks as anchoring the base of the penis to the pelvis and stopping the flow of urine on command, the PCs also contract like crazy during orgasm.

Many experts say that by exercising your PC muscles, you can unlock the door to a whole new bedroom of sexual potential, one where you can prevent premature ejaculation, control the timing and intensity of orgasm, and even develop the capacity for multiple orgasms.

But before you do any of these things, you need to strengthen those PCs with a series of exercises called Kegels, named after the doctor who first devised them. Alan P. Brauer, M.D., a psychiatrist, sex therapist, and director of the TotalCare Medical Center in Palo Alto, California, recommends that for starters, you should do 5 sets, with 10 reps per set, of each of the following Kegels. Each week, add 5 reps per set, until you're doing 30 reps per set.

● Slow clenches

Squeeze your PCs exactly as if you're trying to stop the flow of urine. Hold each clench for a slow count of three.

● Flutters

Clench and relax as fast as you can.

● Push-outs

Bear down on your PCs as though you were trying to force out those last few drops of urine. You'll know you're doing it right when you get your lower abdominals into the exercise.

Once you've reached your 30 rep-per-set goal, try these advanced exercises.

● Super Kegels

Tighten the PCs and hold that clench for a full 20 seconds. Don't give up if you start to feel the clench fading, just keep renewing the contraction. Do 10 Super Kegels spread out over the course of a whole day.

● Towel raises

This is one PC exercise that wouldn't be very P.C. to do in public, seeing as how it requires an erection. Once you have one (how you get there is up to you), gently hang a damp washcloth over the end of your penis. Now, using the PC muscles,

○ Treasure your chest.
In the film *Kiss of Death,* actor Nicolas Cage portrayed a volatile crime boss named Little Junior Brown who bench-pressed strippers to stay fit. While your partner might offer more than a little resistance to that offbeat training idea, doing bench presses the conventional way can certainly help your love life. Although your chest does minimal work under the covers, Dr. Gronbech reminds us that developing a better physical self pays major psychological dividends. "It allows you to have a more traditionally masculine appearance—you'll look better and feel better about yourself," he says. "It's very useful for attracting a sex partner, in a cosmetic sense if nothing else."

○ Remember: All muscles matter.
Finally, just as a good lover never focuses too long on any one part of his partner's anatomy, when you're working out, don't neglect the rest of the muscles in your body. "During sex, there might be a few muscles that work harder than others, but from an overall performance standpoint, be sure you're doing a full-body workout, because sex really is a full-body experience," says Dr. Gronbech. And the more you can do with your entire body under the weights, the better you'll do with that body between the sheets.

make your penis jump up and down 10 times. As your strength increases, add more weight—move up to a hand towel, then a bath towel.

After a few weeks, you should experience firmer erections and more pleasurable contractions during orgasm. But more important, Kegels give you finer control over your ejaculations. As you reach the point of no return, by clenching your newly strengthened PCs—with one long squeeze or two medium squeezes, just like tapping a brake pedal—you can bring ejaculation to a screeching halt.

Then you can take a long, deep breath and continue with the business—or pleasure—at hand.

If you've been training with Kegels and you can hold the squeeze for several seconds, you can achieve orgasm without ejaculation or losing your erection. Admittedly, this takes practice, and the first few times you try it may not yield the most satisfying results. But the more you try it, the better you'll get. More important, you'll be working toward that Holy Grail of sexual achievement, multiple orgasms.

Amorous Aerobics

They may not rank number one, but your heart and lungs are a close second on the list of organs important for great sex. "When we did our studies, we found a direct correlation between aerobic activity and sexual performance," says Dr. White. And no wonder: Aerobic activity—figure on three to four sessions a week of 30 to 45 minutes each—is the single best way to improve cardiovascular fitness and train your heart and lungs so you don't hit the wall in the final moments. Try these.

perfect figures

Average number of times per year American men have intercourse: 148

Average number of times per year French men have intercourse: 151

● **Work out with your woman.**
There are some obvious reasons to work out together. You get to spend more time together, and you're doing something that makes each of you look and feel better. But here's something you may not know: When her face is flushed at the end of the workout, it may not be entirely from exercise. In a study of women, Chicago State University researchers learned that almost one in four had experienced sexual arousal or even orgasm while exercising. Step aerobics, anyone?

● **Walk for your woman.**
There's an old adage: "It's all right to get your appetite walking around town, just as long as you eat supper at home." And like most sayings, it contains a kernel of truth.

"Walking is a good, light aerobic exercise, and certainly won't hurt as a libido lifter," says Dr. White. Just make sure that it's part of a more involved workout. In Dr. White's study, men who only walked didn't report nearly the sexual increases of men who walked *and* combined it with more vigorous exercises like running, swimming, and weight training.

● **Take the stairway to heaven.**
When exercise trainers say that stairclimbing can build explosive power, they're not exactly referring to sex. Nevertheless, a few sessions on the stairclimber at your club, or running the stairs once or twice a week at the office, will put some spring in your sexual stride. Other good aerobic jump starts include swimming and cycling.

● **Have more sex.**
It may not be as aerobically powerful as an hour on the stairclimber, but sex does qualify as an aerobic activity—and the more sex you have, the more you

can have. "It's like any activity—the more you do it, the better you get," says Dr. Gronbech. "If your sexual frequency is a few times a week, you're much better off—in a lot of ways, obviously—than the man who only has sex once a month."

He Shoots, He Scores!

With all the time, money, and effort you've put into not getting anybody pregnant all these years, it stands to reason that trying to make a baby should happen pretty easily. You just forgo the contraception ritual, and bada-bing, bada-boom, 9 months later Junior You comes to visit. The reality, however, is that 50 percent of hopeful couples, most of whom are perfectly healthy and fertile, don't get pregnant in the first 3 months of unprotected sex. Here, Zachary Veilleux lays out three key steps to better your baby-making odds.

Step 1: Protect Your Ammo

You contribute only one ingredient to the baby-making process, so your primary duty before trying to conceive is to make your sperm as plentiful, strong, and capable of sneaking into your wife's egg zone as possible. Here's how.

● **Don't fry the little guys.**
Nothing sautés sperm faster than direct heat. Sitting in a hot tub or sauna, sleeping on a heated water bed, or even running a fever can fatally damage developing sperm months before they're actually ejaculated. In fact, your scrotum hangs the way it does in order to provide your sperm with a cool environment, away from the heat of your body. Since it takes 75 to 90 days for sperm to mature and be ready for firing, give up your steamiest pleasures 3 months before trying to conceive.

One thing you probably don't have to worry about: your choice of underwear. A study from the State University of New York at Stony Brook found that neither briefs nor boxers noticeably altered scrotal temperatures.

● **Reach orgasm often.**
Here's the green light you were looking for back in high school: If you're not already firing your

The top nine cancer-fighting foods are: 1) broccoli; 2) tomatoes; 3) spinach; 4) oranges; 5) garlic; 6) apples; 7) soybeans; 8) carrots; and 9) green tea.

A Man's Greatest Fears about Fatherhood

- No matter how hard you try to protect the baby, something will go wrong.

- Leisure time as you know it will be over.

- Adventure and spontaneity as you know it will be over.

- Your youth as you know it will be over.

- You'll degenerate into a short-fused, gin-and-tonic-guzzling, work-complaining, business-page-reading, potbellied paradigm of fatherhood.

- She'll love the baby more than she loves you.

jets three times per week, try to reach that level before you start attempting to conceive. "If you don't ejaculate for a while and then suddenly start having a lot of sex, that can stress the glands that manufacture semen, causing them to become inflamed," says Larry Lipshultz, M.D., former president of the American Society for Reproductive Medicine. Also, regular ejaculation, whether through sex or masturbation, can help ensure that the old sperm are skimmed off, making room for younger, healthier swimmers.

● **Trim your beer gut.**
In large enough quantities, body fat can convert male hormones into the female hormone estrogen, slowing or halting sperm production, says Dr. Lipshultz. What's more, being overweight (having more than 30 percent body fat) can raise the temperature of your genitals, further reducing your chances of having healthy sperm.

So put yourself on an exercise program. Working out not only will trim your waistline but also will help you alleviate stress, another possible sperm damager.

● **Clean up your act.**
Recreational drugs, smoking, and excessive drinking can all be toxic to the testicles. So at least 3 months before you try to conceive, give up the first two vices and cut back to a few drinks per week. That's also a good time to start taking a multivitamin that contains vitamin C, vitamin E, and beta-carotene. These three antioxidants help counteract the chemicals that can damage sperm, Dr. Lipshultz says.

Step 2: Check Your Range

Timing isn't everything when it comes to conceiving a kid, but consulting a calendar can help. Here are some factors to think about.

The season

Researchers from the University of Rochester in New York analyzed semen samples donated to a fertility clinic over the course of a year. Their findings: The sperm counts of samples donated during the winter or spring were 16 percent higher on average than the counts of samples donated during the summer or fall. And cool-weather sperm motility was 7 percent higher. "I don't think it's a coincidence that the highest sperm counts occurred in the cooler months and the lowest occurred when it was warm," says Grace M. Centola, Ph.D., author of the study.

The week

A woman releases just one egg each month, and within a week of its release, the egg can no longer be fertilized. Consequently, there are only 4 or 5 days each month during which conception is possible.

Some women claim that they can tell when they're ovulating, but you shouldn't depend on it. "We know of no reliable physiological event in a woman that marks her fertile days," says Allen J. Wilcox, M.D., Ph.D., chief of epidemiology at the National Institute of Environmental Health Sciences. And drugstore ovulation-prediction tests are still too crude to be of much use. Your best bet? Use Dr. Wilcox's formula.

1. Ask your partner how many days are in her shortest and longest menstrual cycles. (The average is 28 days.)

2. Subtract 18 days from her shortest cycle. This tells you how many days after the beginning of her period her fertile days start. Now subtract 14 days from her longest cycle. This tells you how many days after the beginning of her period her fertile days end.

3. Count the number of days since the begin-

A Woman's Greatest Fears about Motherhood

- No matter how good a mother she is, something will happen to the baby.

- You'll leave her for a 25-year-old blonde who can eat anything and still wear spandex shorts without tying a sweatshirt around her waist.

- She'll think of sex as something she used to enjoy without having to be begged or cajoled by you.

- She'll never get rid of that "baby weight."

- She'll feel guilty every day about having a career.

- The baby will love you more because you're the fun one.

ning of your partner's most recent period. If the number falls in her fertile window, she's at her most fertile right now. Stop reading and get to work!

Researchers estimate that 85 percent of all conceptions take place during this window. If she has passed her most fertile days, you've missed your best chance for this cycle. But your next opportunity is only a few weeks away, so stay in practice.

● The hour

The afternoon is when women are most likely to receive the hormonal surge that triggers egg release. Ovulation follows 12 to 20 hours later, says Dr. Centola. Sex just before bedtime may help ensure that viable sperm are around when the egg first makes itself available.

Step 3: Pull the Trigger

We're assuming you have the "insert tab A into slot B" stuff down already. But aside from the basics, research shows that how you have sex can make a difference in conception.

hot TIP!

To avoid turning your Viagra pill into a $10 Life Saver, wait at least 90 minutes after a lavish dinner to take it. High-fat foods prevent you from fully absorbing Viagra (sildenafil). "If I hear a man say that Viagra didn't work for him, it's usually because he took it too soon after a fatty meal," says Ken Goldberg, M.D., a urologist in Dallas. You can also take Viagra 90 minutes before eating. It'll be absorbed by the time you eat, and you'll have 12 hours to enjoy the effects.

● Position

Enlist the help of gravity, advises Louanne Cole Weston, Ph.D., a sex therapist in Sacramento. She recommends a modified version of the missionary position: Your partner lies on her back, knees curled to her chest. You slide your thighs under her lower back and enter from a kneeling position. "This allows for deep penetration and leaves her vagina turned upward, which helps her retain more sperm," Dr. Weston explains. When you're finished, she should stay put for 15 minutes, so your sperm can swim the first lap downhill.

● Intensity

A study from Cardiff University in Wales found that women who reported having great sex were nearly twice as likely to retain sperm in their cervical mucus as women who thought the experience was just so-so. "More powerful muscle contractions may help create a kind of suction that draws sperm up into the reproductive tract," suggests Jacky Boivin, Ph.D., the lead researcher. Another theory is that chemicals released as she becomes aroused may help reduce levels of acidity in her vagina, making it more hospitable to sperm beginning a long swim.

◉ Repeat performance

Given the proper environment—the warm, moist climate of a vagina, for example—sperm can live as long as 4 to 5 days after they leave your body. But there's no need to wait for all your soldiers to die before you draft more. In Dr. Wilcox's study, couples who had sex daily had a 37 percent chance of conception per cycle, compared with 33 percent for those who did it every other day and just 15 percent for the weekly crowd.

SEX WARS

"You'll like it here—we're a pretty disobedient bunch."

HELP ONLINE

WHAT THE DOCTOR ORDERED

If it's about your physical self, you can find reliable answers here. You can
even fire away personal questions at real live docs in real time for free
in a medical chat room, where the docs will answer your questions but won't
diagnose or prescribe—or even keep you waiting for long. Is that amazing
or what? We know you hate to go to the doc, and that's another reason
that we especially like the idea of this site of cyberdocs.

www.americasdoctor.com

SHAPING UP

FitnessLink offers no-fluff, commonsense information about building
muscle, losing weight, taking supplements, and staying motivated.
Visit the virtual gym where "you'll be guided by former Mr. California,
Mr. America, and Mr. Universe bodybuilding champion Doug Brignole.
Doug will explain the use of dozens of machines and apparatuses commonly
found in fitness clubs, revealing how to get the most benefit—
and the least risk—from a weight room." Of course, you won't build any
muscle clicking a mouse. Still, you can shower down in the virtual
men's locker room, and you may want to after ogling an extremely muscled
femme pinup of the week, if that's your taste.

www.fitnesslink.com

MEN'S STUDIES 101

All the superstars of the men's movement can be found here. Talk up men's
issues and find information and support for all aspects of male living.
You'll find men's stories, articles, poems, and interviews, as well as book and
tape reviews dealing with contemporary men's emotional, spiritual, and
health issues. Does this help you get more sex? Hell, we don't know. But here,
at least, you can find someone who'll cry with you.

www.vix.com/menmag/

MAN'S GUIDE INTERVIEW

Going Deeper, Deeper before Getting Down

An Interview with Hypnotherapist Wendi Friesen

You're becoming very relaxed, even drowsy. Your eyelids are getting heavy. In fact, you can hardly stay awake. Sle-e-epy. Your lids are drooping now, so heavy . . . sliding shut so tight. So-o-o-o sle-e-e-epy.

If you're like most men, that's probably what your penis is whispering to your brain right after every session of hot sex. You blast off, then you drop off.

But what if an actual person were whispering relaxing, hypnotic words to you? What if the woman in your life could entrance you for her pleasure and yours? Soften up your inhibitions a little? Lead you to erotic fantasy worlds with nothing more than a few choice words? Control your ecstasy so that you last and last—and finally explode with a passionate fury you haven't known since your first time?

What if you could do the same to her?

According to certified clinical hypnotherapist Wendi Friesen, all of that is possible—and more. The author of the book and audio set Hypnotize Your Lover, *Friesen says that many forms of sexual dysfunction, like arousal problems and premature ejaculation, can be helped with hypnosis.*

It's even possible, she insists, to increase penis size and a woman's breast size. Now, isn't that every man's dream? Your penis. Her breasts. Bigger, bigger, bigger. Man's Guide *must point out that science is a bit light on this. Nonetheless, Friesen does cite some impressive-sounding studies on breast growth as well as pitches her practice, books, tapes, and other mesmerizing offerings and services at www.wendi.com. But you don't want to go there yet. Right now, you just want to focus on how it feels to read these words and, in a moment, on the count of three, imagine that we are talking with the master hypnotist herself . . . 1 . . . 2 . . . 3 . . .*

MAN'S GUIDE: **One of the more interesting selling points you've noted regarding hypnosis and sex is that you can use hypnosis to increase penis or breast size. So my first questions would have to be "How so . . . and how much? And how quickly?" Like, I have a date tonight with a woman I'd really like to impress . . .**

> **FRIESEN:** Well, as for "how so," think about how cuts heal. Your brain knows how to replace the cells that are no longer present and do all the other things necessary to put you back to normal.

And now there is research showing that using your mind to increase breast size can produce permanent results in 8 weeks or so. I had a friend who basically did that. She did not use hypnosis exactly, but she "talked" to her breasts and asked them to grow.

After a month, she grew a full cup size. A year later, they still had not shrunk.

MAN'S GUIDE: Talk about an interesting form of biofeedback.

FRIESEN: Oh, yeah. Based on this stuff about breast size, one guy asked me if I could produce a hypnotherapy tape for him to increase the size of his penis. I didn't think it would work for a penis, but I figured, "What the heck?"

So I made a tape for him to get his brain to create some kind of positive connection to that part of his body and create change. I had him imagine that he could observe the growth process in his genitals and could increase bloodflow, increase cell growth, increase the flow of hormones and all the other things necessary to increase not just his erection but also the actual size of his penis when it was not erect.

That was one side of the tape. The other side was designed to put him on a timeline, imagining a future with a bigger penis. Imagining what it's like to be bigger, more confident-feeling, more secure about his appearance.

MAN'S GUIDE: Sort of the ultimate in self-visualization. Did it work? Did it last? Did he need mental "booster shots?"

FRIESEN: Well, he listened to my tape during a monthlong period when he and his fiancée were in completely different parts of the country. When she returned, the two of them found that not only was his penis bigger, but it was large enough to cause some initial discomfort.

A year later, he e-mailed me again and said, "You know, maybe it's our imaginations, but my wife insists I'm still growing, and I haven't listened to your tape since that very first month."

MAN'S GUIDE: Why would that be?

FRIESEN: I suspect that when he was visualizing a future timeline of being bigger, more confident, larger, and all that, his subconscious never really established an ending time.

What's interesting is that he's not the only guy to experience this. I got an e-mail from a man recently who was playing one of my tapes on an endless loop while he was asleep. He told me he had grown 2½ inches in length and added a bunch of girth, and he said, "It's hard for me and my girlfriend to have sex, because it kind of hurts her, and I'm hoping that there's some way we can bring it back down a notch."

MAN'S GUIDE: So are you going to have to add a penis-size-reduction tape to your product line now?

FRIESEN: I joked with him that he should play the tape backward. But he did need help, so I arranged a telephone session with him to work on asking his subconscious to find the perfect size that will bring him and his girlfriend pleasure.

But it is interesting that when you change your body image in the subconscious, actual changes in your body can follow. There was a really interesting case of a woman who had undergone breast-reduction surgery, and she went from being a DD down to a B. Six months later, her breasts had grown back to a DD.

I told her, "Wow, that's amazing. I never heard of that." And she told me, "Well, apparently, the doctor has heard of it, because he said regrowth happens fairly often."

So they took away all that tissue, but her subconscious still had this image that she was supposed to be a DD. So her brain went to work, and it all grew back.

MAN'S GUIDE: Is this similar to "dressing for success," when you put on nice clothes, walk with good posture, and keep a smile going—and you actually begin to feel better?

FRIESEN: It really is true. Except that with hypnosis, you do the reverse. You change your mental outlook first and then something physical happens. For example, if we send hate to our bodies by saying, "Oh, God, I despise my flat chest," or "I hate my penis because it's too small," then we don't do ourselves any good. What you will get is more of the same bad stuff. The more negative images you put in your mind, the more they take hold.

But I was really surprised about the guys who ended up with the problem of becoming too big as a result of hypnotic suggestion. It's kind of funny in a way. It reminds me of the saying, "Be careful what you wish for; you might get it."

MAN'S GUIDE: Well, we've talked about increasing the size of the private parts. But size, as they say, isn't everything. What about the more important aspect of sexual activity? In what ways can hypnosis enhance your sexual relationship with a woman? In what ways can it help the experience?

FRIESEN: Our sexual desire originates in the mind. Really, the biggest sex organ you have is your brain. The mind holds the keys to experiencing wonderful, immense pleasure or, at the other end of the spectrum, terrible guilt and fears that make us unable to enjoy sex.

It's pretty common that women, for example, feel a lot of guilt over how long it takes for them to have an orgasm. And men, if they have fears about impotence, often get so frightened that they talk their brains into giving them the very erection problems that they wanted to avoid.

The mind plays a powerful role in sexual relations. I know of hypnotists who have done demonstrations in which they talked women into having orgasms without being touched. And that's not odd at all. After all, men and women alike have dreams that cause them to have orgasms.

So if you think about the potential for the brain to produce not only arousal but also orgasm without physical stimulation, you can imagine how we could amp up our sensations and pump up our sex lives by putting our minds in the right place.

MAN'S GUIDE: Sounds like a nice goal.

FRIESEN: Yes. And as a result, I made a tape called *The Ultimate Orgasm.* Essentially, it helps your brain assign five different levels to the orgasm or erection. If a man has been having problems with his erections, he would learn how to trigger his body to move him into each successive level of arousal. Same for a woman who may be having difficulty achieving or maintaining orgasm.

That's one use of hypnotism. Another use would be to make your entire body more sensual and more receptive to pleasure so that your body could feel orgasmic from head to toe, not just in your genitals.

Of course, almost all people can experience intense pleasure in parts of their bodies other than the genitals, such as the nipples or toes. But what I'm talking about is the ability to go even further so that you tell your brain that your knee, when rubbed, will become aroused.

MAN'S GUIDE: Are you always going to get such obvious sexual successes with hypnosis?

FRIESEN: No, not always. You're not always going to become bigger or multiorgasmic or more sensitive. Many people who buy my tapes, particularly in the case of sexual dysfunction, do so because they are trying to alleviate fears that they are inadequate, too small, or whatever. And they may get relief even if they do not get the precise physical results they are seeking.

Some people, for example, tell me that they didn't grow in size from listening to my tapes, but they still think the tapes were a success. They tell me things like "I'm *enjoying* sex so much more. I really do feel more confident, and I am so much more pleased just being in the moment." There really is a benefit to focusing your mind on the idea that you deserve to experience pleasure.

MAN'S GUIDE: Is there a risk that hypnotism can be misused? Could somebody covertly hypnotize his partner and start mucking around in her head a bit? Or is this a completely safe and innocuous type of thing?

FRIESEN: That's tough to answer definitively. Some professionals will tell you adamantly that people cannot be hypnotized against their will. I don't think that's 100 percent correct. But for the most part, especially as an amateur using trance states with your partner or spouse, you are not going to get someone to do something that she doesn't already want to do.

That's particularly true if you try to hypnotize someone covertly. The woman would almost certainly break out laughing at what you were trying to do—long before you'd begin to have any effect on her hypnotically.

On the other hand, a very few people really do know what they are doing when it comes to hypnotism. And there can be a strong mixture created between sex and hypnosis. If someone has a weak constitution, mentally speaking, and a person taps into his or her sexual desires in the right way with hypnosis, there could be some misuse and manipulation. But the combination of factors that would allow something like that to happen and the level of skill that would be required of the person doing the hypnotizing are exceedingly rare.

MAN'S GUIDE: So it's pretty much like any other intimate activity. If you have a weak spot or dysfunction already, a person could manipulate it anyway—with or without hypnosis.

FRIESEN: Sure. And if the other person is confident and fulfills the desires, it's like . . . well, it's like a scam artist who's going to take money from old people. He knows how to fill their needs, how to make them feel like their dreams can come true, how to tap into their deepest desires. It's a con, and it doesn't require hypnotism.

The thing with sex and hypnotism, though, it that sexual desire is something that goes deep into our core. If you can get to that place in the person's mind, you could possibly insert suggestions like, "The only way you'll feel any sexual desire is with me," or "The only voice that will make you feel aroused in any way is mine." Those kinds of things have happened. But very, very rarely, and it can be undone. The truth is that a very unique combination of things has to come together for hypnotism to be misused.

MAN'S GUIDE: So, aside from those extremely rare situations then, hypnotism is reasonably safe and healthy.

FRIESEN: Very healthy, actually. Even seeking out hypnotherapy or hypnosis tapes can be a very positive experience, because it gets couples talking about things that they might have been unable to talk about before.

A couple who had been married 10 years came to my office, even though they were having a good sex life, because they wanted something a little bit more. They wanted some adventure. Hypnotism offered that for them. They wanted to do things like plant little suggestions in each other's minds. Like if he stroked the back of her hand or said a certain word, it would produce a certain response in her.

But one of the specific things they were interested in was a subject I cover in *Hypnotize Your Lover* about how to get your partner to love giving oral sex. His wife told me, "I would like to be able to enjoy giving him oral sex, but I just don't like doing it." And of course, he told me, "Yeah, I'd like it if she enjoyed doing it, too."

So what I did in our hypnosis session was talk to her about the things that made her feel really loved and really sensual and really sexy. And I attached those feelings to the act of giving oral sex. I helped her create a mindset in which she would not simply selflessly give him pleasure but also receive pleasure for herself from performing the act.

perfect figures

Number of U.S. patents given to hair-growing drugs since 1990: 58

· · · · · · · · · ·

They were just as pleased as could be by the results. He was ecstatic, of course. She said, "You know, I didn't expect anything to happen, but I've got to tell you, it really worked. I really love oral sex now, and there's no reason to avoid it. I really, really like doing that for my husband."

Now, isn't that nice?

MAN'S GUIDE: You won't get any argument from me. I think that's quite nice.

FRIESEN: So they both got to come out ahead . . . well, maybe that's not the best choice of words. Let's say that they both really benefited. It wasn't like he was making her perform oral sex against her will. She wanted to be able to do it. But this is a good example of a couple whose sex life was healthy but they wanted some little changes, and hypnotism helped.

MAN'S GUIDE: Is there something about hypnotism—about the whole concept of mind control, however harmless—that just strikes an erotic chord in most people?

FRIESEN: Definitely. There's a lot of mystery. People think of it as something almost magical, like making a wish and having it come true. But the important thing about hypnosis and hypnotherapy is that in most cases it is needed, because people tend to focus on their fears and what they don't want. Few of us really focus on convincing our brains to give us what we want. We dwell on the negatives. If a man obsesses on the fact that he's having trouble getting erections and says, "I can't even try because it probably will fail," then he will fail.

What's so simple in theory, yet so hard to do in fact, is to tell yourself, "Okay, every time that I have sex, it's going get better, and my brain is going to know what to do. I'm going to lose myself in the moment, and my erections are going to be dependable, stronger, and harder."

People come to me and pay me a lot of money to help their subconscious minds focus on what they really do want. Hypnosis can be really fun and mysterious, and it can help you create states of mind that you have never experienced before.

QUICKIES

PAUNCH ALARM

William Shatner knows the value of sucking in his gut—for years he fended off that Homer Simpson look by holding in his stomach rather than doing situps. But if you're the absentminded type, James Stage of Aberdeen, Scotland, has a product for you. He holds a new patent on a contraption that reminds you to pull it in for a good impression. The device, which attaches to your belt and rests against your stomach, trembles like a pager set to "vibrate" when you let your beer belly sag. Stage views this gut-sucking as a workout—his patent application says, "Continual holding in of one's stomach is a form of isometric exercise." Talk about busting your gut.

AVOID A HEFTY PROBLEM

We've always thought extra-large condoms were like $100 bills: Most guys carry them only to show off. But a yearlong study at La Trobe University in Australia found that men with slightly thicker (not longer) penises may actually need larger condoms. Of the 184 men studied, those whose penises had a circumference greater than 6 inches (5.2 inches was average) were three times more likely to break regular condoms during sex than the men with thinner penises.

"One size does not fit all," says Anthony Smith, Ph.D., author of the study. "Condoms must fit snugly enough to stay on, but they shouldn't be overstretched." To find your girth, wrap a measuring tape around your erect penis 1 inch up from the base. If the measurement is more than 5¼ inches, you should try a larger condom.

SPEAKING OF EXTRA-LARGE...

Looking to spend the last of their grant money before the deadline, evolutionary biologists at the University of Manchester in England dutifully measured the testicles of 80 men and chronicled their sexual proclivities over the past decade. (What do biologists tell their mothers they do for a living?) Turns out that men with small testicles, roughly the size of white grapes, had experienced fewer sexual encounters than men with large testicles—think golf balls

> **❝ I hope the doctor will write me a prescription for a girlfriend. ❞**
>
> —Norwegian bachelor Elder Huse, responding to his government's 23-point advisory that includes the recommendation that adults should have sex at least twice a week for good health

(no pun intended). Men with average-size equipment fell right in the middle. And for reasons yet unknown, small men were more faithful to their wives than their bigger counterparts were. (Go ahead and take a feel—we know you're curious.)

A GOOD REASON TO GIVE HER A DOSE

Researchers at the University of Southern California in Los Angeles think that they've found the perfect vehicle to transport experimental vaccines for chlamydia, genital warts, and HIV into women: sperm. Within 5 years, says Virginia Scofield, Ph.D., an immunologist, women may be able to insert vaccines for sexually transmitted diseases into their vaginas via a foam, and then—as a necessary second step—have sex. "The vaccine would lock onto sperm, and the sperm could ferry the vaccine deep into the cervix to produce a potent, local immunization," she says. Several intercourse-delivered vaccines are under development. The method might also work for birth control drugs. Now's the time to start planning for that second career at the health clinic.

DEAR DR. MANLY

Q: *Recently, I climaxed while having sex, but I didn't ejaculate.* **To make matters ironic as well as disturbing, my girlfriend thought I was faking the orgasm. What happened?**
—M. R., BURLINGTON, VERMONT

A: Your little misfire was probably a "retrograde ejaculation." Normally, when you reach the point of ejaculation, it becomes the point of no return because the neck of your bladder slams shut to keep semen out and headed down the right pipe. Occasionally, it doesn't close fast enough, and your prostate propels semen into your bladder rather than out through your urethra.

Rest easy. If this happens every once in a while, it's harmless. But if it happens often, you should see a urologist. Even then, it's still probably nothing to lose sleep over, but a doctor can rule out certain causes, such as diabetes, nerve damage from an injury, or complications from prostate surgery.

Q: *During sex with a new partner, I've occasionally had an erection that lasted a couple of hours. Back when I was 17, I dreamed about this, but now I'm worried. Is a perpetual boner dangerous?*
—F. L., AUSTIN, TEXAS

A: You were too busy to notice, but your hardness fluctuated slightly during that time to let the blood circulate. That's different from priapism, an erectile disorder in which the blood vessels clamp shut and stop blood from circulating altogether. If the penile tissues don't relax within 6 to 8 hours, they can be permanently damaged. Priapism can be a side effect of antidepressant or impotence drugs. It has also been reported in young Viagra (sildenafil) users who didn't need the drug in the first place.

If you ever have a rock-hard erection that won't subside after you ejaculate, take a cold shower, try to urinate, and apply a towel-wrapped ice pack to your penis. Not all at once, necessarily. You can do these things in stages. If what's gone up has not come down after 2 hours, go to a hospital. One injection of adrenaline or ephedrine, which will con-strict the vessels and let the blood flow out, can save your sex life.

Q: *How many times should I be able to reach orgasm in one night?*
—G. B., CLEVELAND

A: I love your initiative, but it depends mostly on your age. A fit man in his twenties—on a night sure to become legendary—might muster six orgasms over the course of 5 hours. For a man in his fifties or sixties, figure one a night. Between the ages of 30 and 50, though, the average healthy dude who's not skunk-drunk or taking any medications that affect orgasm (ask your doctor) should be able to ejaculate two or three times with no problems. But remember, a real champ can deliver a knockout punch on the first round, so don't get too hung up on quantity. Quality still counts.

Dr. Manly is a fictional character.
The actual advice was provided by a variety of
medical doctors and other qualified experts.

ORCHESTRATE SIZZLING DATES

 One of the surest ways to put a twinkle in her eye, whether she's your girlfriend of 2 weeks or your wife of 20 years, is to treat her to a great night out. Or to a great day at the races, an afternoon in the park, or a week in Jamaica. Heck, even knowing which restaurant has the all-u-can-eat jazz-and-lobster buffet is a step on the road to becoming a real datemeister. But if you want to take it to the next level—we're talking Richard Gere–in–American Gigolo level—you'll need a few tricks of the trade under your belt.

And you'll find some sneaky tricks in this section: How to give her a compliment that'll bring the dew to her lilies. How to give her the perfect foot rub, the king of all sexy massages. How to turn a simple "first date" into the first of many. And, perhaps most important, how to track her hormonal cycle and factor PMS into your planning when scheduling a romantic getaway.

TOP TEN

Deal Closers

She looked in your general direction, but maybe she was scouting around for a friend or trying to find someone with a watch. Then again, maybe she's digging that dark green Regis Philbin shirt-and-tie combo you're wearing. What to do? Incorporate our top 10 steps for buying her a drink in no time.

1 **Smile when she looks over.** Catch her eyes briefly. Be patient. Your goal is to keep her intrigued but guessing.

2 **Mirror her signals.** If she turns her body toward you, turn your body toward hers. If she leans her elbow on the bar, you do the same. Don't make eye contact while you do it, though; otherwise you'll look calculating. Mirroring gives the subtle impression of having something in common.

3 **Approach her from the side.** This makes you less threatening and increases her interest. It also allows you to deflect gracefully if her boyfriend suddenly returns from the john.

4 **Wait for a break in conversation, but don't hover.** Forget clever lines. Say hi. Give her your name. Wait for her to give hers. Talk to her like a relative you actually get along with. She's reluctant? Don't give up (unless she's flipping you the bird). Both men and women are overly ready to feel rejected.

⑤ Keep your eyes above her neck. Glue them in place if you have to.

⑥ Leave soon, but briefly. Don't promise to be back, just say, "Excuse me for minute, I have to catch up with my buddy. It was great meeting you."

⑦ Return to your pals for 10 minutes. Stay out of her line of sight, but let her see you every now and then.

⑧ Approach her again. If she has picked up another suitor, act relieved instead of jealous. The more the merrier. Calmly evaluate her response to the other fellow. He probably has nothing on you.

⑨ Reel her in. Once you're in her group, motion with your head for her to lean in—there's something you don't want others to hear. Say, "You're probably just killing time until your boyfriend gets here."

⑩ Run off with her if she laughs and shakes her head no. Ask her to sit at a booth away from the crowd. Take it from there.

MUST READS

The Dating Game

You caught her eye, you bought her a drink, you made her laugh, you drove her home, and bingo! You got her phone number. The hard part's over. But how's your follow-up? Do you have what it takes to craft a first-rate first date?

Not to worry—author Sherise Dorf lays out a no-fail strategy for a romantic rendezvous that won't blow up in your face. Dorf, who recently left the dating game to marry a nice Jewish boy she met on a blind date, has written for Salon.com, P.O.V., Cosmopolitan, and others. She now seeks vicarious thrills by setting up friends and professional acquaintances on both coasts.

I have been on about, oh, 1,132 first dates in my life, give or take five. And don't think I didn't take notes. Every girl does. Besides, whatever I don't remember, my girlfriends do—and most of the time, it's the stuff I've spent years trying to forget.

On the plus side, there was Elan, who knew the art of wining and dining (8 hours' worth, at six different stops, each unique). Then there was sweetly goofy Jonathan, who arrived with daisies and a Snickers bar in hand, because he thought it was a good idea to woo me with flowers and chocolate before taking me to see Jerry Seinfeld in concert.

Good moves, these. But for every smooth first encounter, there's at least a dozen clunkers, the ones that my sisters-in-dating and I endure with the aid of a lukewarm smile and an internal clock that ticks off every single minute until we can get home. A typical story: Matt, who took me to a sports bar and proceeded to watch an entire Knicks game over my head as I contemplated putting a nick in his.

The irony is that a few basic strategies can turn your self-doubts into a self-assured second nature that's smoother than Puff Daddy's. I've spent the last 12 years of my life doing hands-on research. My female first-date panel has a few more decades under their collective belts. So it's time to listen up, Romeo—we're going to teach you something here.

The Phone Call

Being kind of a chick-about-town, I was always surprised when I met a guy who seemed sure of himself, gave him my number, and then, in return, got a message on my machine a couple of days later than contained more "uhs" than information. "Hey, uh, call me back, uh, when you, uh, get this, uh, message, so I can, uh, ask you, uh, something. My number, uh, is 5, uh I, uh, 2, uh . . ." To which I say: *Uh!*

If you ask a woman for her number and she gives it to you without hesitating, clearing her throat, or looking nervously around the room (or bar) for help from a friend, then she wants you to call her, preferably in the next couple of days. No waiting period required. Be confident, and don't be vague. "'So, you want to hang out sometime?'" laughs Leslie, 30, director of a legal aid organization in Chicago, "makes me think, 'What is this, high school?'"

"Any type of hesitancy, overt shyness, vagueness, or downright fear is a turnoff," echoes Diana, a 34-year-old writer in Atlanta. Calling with specific plans in mind, however, will generally earn rave reviews.

perfect figures

Number of 21-year-old women in 12th grade in 1998: 18,000

Number of 21-year-old men in 12th grade in 1998: 3,000

When is a specific plan not a good idea? When it gives the woman unattractive information about you and your traits. "A guy called me and asked me if I wanted to go to a restaurant with him because he had coupons that he had to use up before they expired," shudders Elaine, 28, a student in Chicago. He ended up using them—without her.

Dress for Success

Once the date is set, make a concerted effort to look good. If you're rolling your eyes right now and thinking, "I don't want to go out with anyone who doesn't accept me for who I really am," then fine. Skip this section, continue wearing ripped jeans with cross-trainers, and enjoy wondering why you can't seem to score any head-turners.

Looking good doesn't mean breaking out your fanciest duds. That, too, might be a turnoff, as it signals that you're trying too hard. "I was staying at my grandmother's house, and a guy came to pick me up for our first date wearing a suit and carrying a single red rose," says Gina, a 30-year-old professor in Waterville, Maine. "Contrary to what I thought my grandma's reaction would be, she looked at me as he was walking up and said, 'Isn't that a bit much?' I agreed with her. It wasn't sweet. Somehow it was almost creepy."

"*Appropriate* is the key word," adds Diana. "Wear a sport coat if it's a nice dinner out; nice shorts and shirt if it's a summer concert."

Take Charge

Yes, it's the dawn of a new millennium, but guess what? *You* asked *her* out. That means you plan the itinerary. Period. If you are going to dinner (or lunch or drinks), research several options, and take into account the food, the service, the lighting, and the mood when making a final selection. Make reservations so that you and your date don't have to wait 45 minutes for a table. (If you do encounter a wait, suggest a drink from the bar.) And if you don't know where the restaurant is, call ahead and get directions. On that note, if you're picking her up, get directions to her place as well—and don't lose them.

"I was so excited about this date with my friend's agent," says Lisa, a 29-year-old composer in Los Angeles, "but on the night of our date, he was 20 minutes late, and I get this call from him on his car phone asking me for directions. I'd already given them to him earlier that day, so I was kind of turned off, but whatever. I told him again. He picks me up, and then asks me how to get to the restaurant he'd chosen. At this point, I thought, 'How the hell should I know?' He ended up getting directions when he stopped for gas. I was completely disgusted now. Why didn't he run his errands before he picked me up?"

And finally, *you* pay. If she insists, tell her that you'd be happy to let her pick up the check another time. "When the check is put on the table," explains Lisa, "pick it up immediately and put your credit card or cash down. Don't make the poor woman try to guess whether you want her to offer money. Just pay the bill." Please read that last sentence again. Now inhale. Make a mental note: She always wants you to pay on the first date. Now exhale. We're moving on.

Do Your Homework

Most women say, "It doesn't matter what we do, as long as he has a plan." That's what they say. What they really want, in the words of Jillian, a 32-year-old actress in Vancouver, is a *flexible* plan so that "if I don't like his choices, we can do what I want."

While she'll likely agree to anything, you'll get much more credit if you have taken some time in advance to plan an activity that you know she'll like. "Subtly find out what kinds of things I enjoy," says Jillian. "Make sure that there are people around so I don't feel threatened." That doesn't mean you can't be cozy. Gina feels that "good food at an intimate, but not over-the-top, restaurant or cafe is a great starting point for a date, because it allows for good conversation, in which we tell each other selective accounts of our life stories."

Veronica, 30, who works for an oil company in Washington, D.C., says that if your date likes the outdoors, weekend daytime activities are great for the first get-together. "If you do something like hiking, horseback riding, or sailing, it allows for easy conversation without any awkward silences," she says. "It also gives you ideas for making small talk." Just make sure to come up with a backup plan if the weather doesn't cooperate.

Talking Points

Unless you are friends who are moving the relationship toward another level, the goal of the first date is to get to know each other; to establish whether or not you have anything in common, whether you are attracted to one another and whether you can spend 5 minutes, 5 hours, 5 years, or 5 decades together.

Thus, first-date movies are generally a bad idea. "If we go to a movie," says Amy, a 31-year-old artist in San Francisco, "I will know as much about you at the end of the date as I did at the beginning: nothing."

What you talk about is also important. The idea is to reveal information about yourself (as well as impress with how cool, funny, smart, and debonair you are) and get her to reveal the same. It's all about dialogue. "I like it when the guy asks me questions about myself," says Lisa. "And when it looks as if he's actually listening to my answers, he gets double points."

If you're worried about the initial conversation, it might be a good idea to think about some potential topics ahead of time. It's also a very good idea to encourage your date to talk about something that she's passionate about. Be sure to gauge her comfort level when you throw questions her way, however, to make sure you're not putting her on the spot for information that she's not ready to give you.

perfect figures

Percentage of men who say that it's important to look good when they're . . .

On a date with their girlfriend or wife: 95

At work: 79

Out with friends: 73

At school: 23

At home: 13

If you're having a good time at dinner, ask your date if she would like to continue the conversation with coffee, dessert, or drinks at another location. This gives her an out if she wants one—and gives you a positive sign if she chooses to stay.

Conversation Taboos

Two cardinal rules of first-date conversation: Don't get too political, and don't get too personal. No rants about abortion, or soliloquies about past loves or personal health issues. "You will discuss these things at some point," says Judy Kuriansky, Ph.D., a sex therapist from New York City, radio's "Dr. Judy," and author of *The Complete Idiot's Guide to Dating*, "but not the first time you spend time together. It causes too much conflict."

An anecdote: I had a date once with a guy named Richard. Let's call him Dick, because I wanted to at the time. Dick spoke at length throughout our too-long date about himself and, specifically, about his ex-wife. According to Dick, she was mentally ill, and when they divorced, she was placed in a mental hospital. From time to time, she successfully escaped the hospital and somehow found her way to his house, popping through the window and surprising him on more than one occasion.

Oka-a-ay.

Sending Signals

Almost every woman out there believes it's crucial for a guy to tell her that he's having a good time. This doesn't necessarily mean overtly blurting it out. "Compliment her on things that no one else would notice," advises Dr. Judy. "Point out genuine things you find appealing about her. Tell her you love the way she holds her fork, or that she looks so pretty without having to wear a lot of makeup. Everyone loves to be acknowledged."

Gina knows the date is going well if it includes some sensual gestures. "If he whispers in my ear, or touches my cheek, or strokes my hair, that's a great sign. If we're laughing a lot, that's even better."

A follow-up call is good form— 2 to 3 days is the general rule. "He should tell me he had a good time and wants to see me again only if it's true," says Veronica. "But call me a couple of days later to ask me out again—don't press the issue that night, and don't put me on the spot."

"Be honest," insists Diana, "and be polite. Say something like, 'I enjoyed spending time with you; I'd like to do it again soon.'" Avoid those three little

SEX TRENDS

NO GLOVE, NO LOVE

These days, an unwanted pregnancy is the lesser of two evils when it comes to using a condom. More than one-third of sexually active men between the ages of 25 and 49 use a prophylactic. Of those, 79 percent say that they wear one primarily for birth control; 81 percent say that they cover up mostly to protect against unwanted diseases.

words—"I'll call you"—if you don't intend to follow through. In fact, avoid them altogether, on principle.

The Moment of Truth

To kiss or not to kiss, that is the question. The answer? "Depends," says Lisa, "but a kiss on the cheek if you had a great time is usually appropriate and sweet." If things have gone well, some lip-locking is generally welcomed. "I like a kiss on the first date," says Veronica, "but the guy needs to use some good judgment. If I'm being distant and not getting near you, don't go for the kiss."

Finally, unless you've known her for a while in some other capacity, fantasies of taking your first date under the sheets are usually just that: fantasies. "He should never ask her to spend the night, no matter how hot the date has been," offers Gina.

Now, on the second date . . .

Bachelor for a Week

If you don't count eating an entire bag of Doritos for supper, watching Baywatch *with the mute on, and closing down a sports bar at 3:00 A.M. on a Sunday morning, cruising for women is perhaps the one bachelor pastime that married guys miss most. So what happens when you turn back the marital clock? We took Stephen Perrine—a very married, middle-aged father of two—and paid for him to live the glorious single life for 7 days. What was left of him filed this report.*

The blonde model with the pouty pink lips is on her knees, her high heels twisted awkwardly behind her, her blue dress riding up, her silky hair splayed across my thighs. As her eyes meet mine, I note a stunned expression that says, "I never expected anything like this." And, of course, she didn't. Her head is in my lap for one reason: I tripped her.

I apologize profusely and help her to her feet. Still unsteady from the drinks she's ingested, she staggers off to find a restroom. I watch her make her careful way through the nightclub, her teal-wrapped tush swinging like a church bell, and I think, "This is definitely not a place for a guy like me." But that's fine, because tonight—this whole week, actually—I'm not a guy like me.

This is an experiment we're conducting here. Take one standard-issue American man, early 1960s model. Two kids, one decade-plus marriage, 3 years into a 30-year mortgage. Now, by a remarkable confluence of circumstances, give him the chance to live wholly unencumbered—the bachelor lifestyle—for 7 days. No diapers. No "I'll be home soon." No reason to lower the toilet seat. No need to go to bed, or even come home, at anything approaching a decent hour.

It's actually my wife who first suggests it, when a new job in another city arises and we fumble for an alternative to changing houses, schools, and lives. "You could get an apartment," she says. "A bachelor pad." Then the editors at *Men's Health* up the ante: Live like a bachelor, really, and we'll cover your expenses for a month.

Within a week, my wife is walking around the city with real estate agents, finding the perfect spot for her ineligible bachelor. She takes special joy in picking out furniture, stocking the refrigerator, buying the bath towels. Just days later, I'm ready to settle in.

That's when my education begins.

Lesson #1:
Don't Let Your Wife Set Up Your Bachelor Pad

What I have in my swinging new apartment:

- Diet soda
- Penzi's all-natural Alfredo sauce with wild mushrooms and garlic
- Cotton balls

What I don't have in my swinging new apartment:

- A stereo
- Chips
- Beer

I have never before lived on my own: I moved right in with my future wife after finishing college. I have never gone for want of a well-made bed or a home-cooked meal. Or sex. What will happen to me when I'm left to my own devices? What happens when a tame animal is returned to the wild?

Bill Route might know. He's a wildlife biologist for the International Wolf Center, and he's seen what happens when a wolf is taken from the wilderness at a young age, then later released back into the forest. "He's likely to get torn to pieces by the pack," Route says. And if he manages to avoid the pack and tries to live as a lone wolf? "Once he's been brought into human contact, he loses the ability to hunt big game," says Route. "He could be gored by a deer, or he could simply fail to bring down a big animal."

So the socialized wolf just can't make it in the wild? I ask.

"Not if he has to hunt big game alone. But it's possible he could survive," Route says. "If, say, there were enough beaver around."

Yes. Well, then.

REMOVING MY EYES from the model I tripped, I turn back to the woman seated beside me. Her name is Stephanie, her hair is brown, and her neckline plunges like the Dow when Alan Greenspan has a head cold. We are talking closely. She occasionally places a hand on my forearm. I make a point of letting her see my left hand, devoid of the gold "reserved" symbol I've worn for 10 years. This is going very well. It feels almost natural.

The week didn't begin this way. My first night out without a wedding ring—what a strange sensation. My thumb would play unconsciously with the bare skin on my third finger. Several times on the street, my head whipped around, scanning the sidewalk, sensing I'd dropped something. Then a cool flash of relief would come as I realized what I was looking for, and that it was safe in the back of the third kitchen shelf, behind the All-Bran.

That first night, at about 9 o'clock, I went to a bar around the corner. Alone. Oh, I called my old buddy Evan, a man so renowned for his college-era antics that at a dorm Halloween party, three different people came dressed as him. I hadn't seen the guy in years. Let's get together, have some laughs. But no. He and his wife were going to the theater. Who else did I know in this city? Jesus, a bunch of old married people. So I went alone. Had a couple of beers, watched the Yankees win. At 11:00, I went home and made myself dinner.

- Number of nights out of seven I ate dinner alone on the floor in front of the TV: three.
- Percentage of those nights on which dinner consisted of frozen Pizza Pockets left behind by the bachelor who had lived in the apartment before me: 100.

Lesson #2: Singlehood Is a Permanent State of Temporariness

The walls have been repainted, and all the furniture is new. But within days, my apartment is chaos. Every bad habit I've sublimated since college (clothes hangers? why?) has reemerged. It's as if I've picked up a vibe from the guy who lived here before me, the vibe that says, "Why bother?" I know I won't be living here forever. He knew he wouldn't be living here forever. Every bachelor in every apartment in every city is a man waiting to move on. At the house I share with my family, every corner is filled with evidence of our lives: pictures, tchotchkes. At the apartment, it's as though unpacking, emotionally and physically, is too much of a hassle.

STEPHANIE EXCUSES HERSELF, stands up, brushes back her hair, and slides past me—cleavage precisely at eye level, thank you very, very much—on her way to the bathroom.

"Dude, she is digging you," my friend Dave says. "I've been watching. She's leaning into you and looking in your eyes. You're there!"

Okay, we need to call an official time-out here and consult the rule book: I can talk. I can flirt. But I can't do anything that I won't be able to tell the whole truth about at the end of 7 days. So by the rules of this particular bachelor game, what we're looking at here is catch-and-release. Just getting a woman's phone number, I decide, will count as a conquest. It's as near to the fire as I'm willing to walk.

I see Stephanie heading back to my table, and then—the way you see any tragic event, in slow motion—I see a swirl of friends intercept her and sweep her off to another part of the club. But though I don't get Stephanie's number, it has been a successful night. I flirted a little, and I came close to landing a date. I go to bed happy.

Lesson #3: When You're a Bachelor, Women Distract You from Life

"Let's say you're in a room, and there are two people you can choose to talk to," says my friend Robert. "One is the most fascinating Nobel laureate of our time. The other is a cute woman who works in a supermarket. Who are you going to talk to?" Married guys have an option. They can pursue the platonic unabashedly. Single guys, on the other hand, are like plane-crash survivors in the desert. They like stimulating conversation, but there's this little matter of food and water that needs attending to . . .

"For a single guy, there's no such thing as a quiet, relaxing night at home," says Robert, who is a bachelor. "If anything is going on, and there's even a remote possibility you might meet someone, you go. Anywhere you are, if a woman you're even somewhat attracted to walks in, everything changes. That becomes your focus."

Indeed, losing focus is a big problem. On day five, I wake up panic-stricken. I'm due at work, and I have just remembered what I blew off doing the day before: laundry. This is a problem because, having vowed not to wear the same pair of underwear I've worn the past 2 days (it has but two sides, after all), I am without a support team.

This whole self-reliance thing takes some getting used to. In my married existence, I put things into the hamper, and, a few days later, they mysteriously reappear in the top drawer. In the world of bachelordom, this ceases to happen, which is why I wind up at a discount clothing store, forking over cash for fresh briefs while under my dress pants my team of acrobats is operating without a net.

That afternoon, my new underwear and I are invited to a dinner party. After successfully flirting with Stephanie, I know just how I should conduct myself. I've not only remembered how to talk to strange women, but I've also struck a balance between fantasy bachelor and real-life married man. It will be a fine evening. There's just one problem.

"LIBA. LIKE 'LIBRA,' without the R." Oh, my.

She's sitting between me and my friend Danny. Liba's skirt is little more than an unfolded napkin across her lap, and I can feel her thigh rubbing through my khakis beneath the table. She's talking about her career as a lawyer, how she wants to do more, how she knows she could do something creative. And I'm fascinated by every word she says, for three reasons:

❶ She's very pretty.

❷ She's very flirty.

❸ She's already asked me for a ride home.

We've been laughing together for hours, and somehow, at some point, I've erased that yellow caution line I drew across my conscience at the outset. My thoughts aren't about getting her number. In fact, they're being swept up in a turn of events that I have neither the will nor the biological imperative to fight.

Liba and I finish our wine and say a quick goodbye to our hosts. She pops a mint into her mouth, offers me one. The elevator comes. Liba is leaning into me, vaporized chardonnay mixing with Certs as her face gets near mine. Then we're in the lobby, we're on the street, a cab's there immediately, she's in, I'm in. We are heading uptown.

Okay, events have gotten serious. I've been married 10 years, and though I'll admit that I haven't pitched a perfect game, at least so far it's been a shutout. And now, well, now the bases are loaded.

The cab races up the avenue, and I'm trying to remember, God, how does one do this again? "Let's stop at my place for a nightcap," I say, with what I remember as my long-dormant "let's get it on" voice.

"I don' tingk so," she says, her voice curiously muffled.

What? Oh, of course. "We should head straight up to your place . . ."

"That mint didn' go well wi' my wine," she murmurs uncomfortably.

"We could whip up a late snack. What's the address again?"

"I heat Amana throw rugs!"

She turns to me, alarmed, her eyes wide and her hand to her mouth. "Pardon?"

"I said, I think I'm gonna throw up!"

The cab pulls up in front of my building. I hand Liba a twenty for the fare, step out onto the curb, and watch the yellow cab with the pretty, flirty, nauseated girl drive toward the horizon. Sure, maybe she was really sick. Or maybe she just wanted to get rid of me. I'm good at taking hints.

I ride the elevator to my apartment, where I have an epiphany. This adventure has taught me something I would never have learned inside the constraints of marriage: I am a hideous, disgusting, unlovable man, and women are repulsed by me. I drink two beers and pass out.

Lesson #4: Bachelors Don't Have Life Preservers

Upon waking, I remember that (a) acetaminophen can cause liver damage when combined with alcohol, and (b) I am, in fact, married and hence—theoretically, at least—capable of winning a woman's love. I realize now why so many of the single guys I've talked to want to be married. A wedding ring is irrefutable evidence that yes, you are worth something to someone. Lose the ring, and you're dog-paddling through an emotional ocean without a life preserver. It's clear to me now that I'd never make it as a bachelor. My ego just can't swim that well.

On the final night of my single life, I drag myself out to a party. I'm feeling pretty defeated and ready to be married again. Suddenly, there's a tap on my shoulder. It's Stephanie. "What a coincidence," she says.

"You know, I never did get your number," I say. She hands me a card, smiles, and wanders back off into the mix. I look down at the white embossed calling card. Bingo—a success. Just in time. Because tomorrow my

SEX ✠ TRENDS

NO, I INSIST— I'LL GET THE CHECK

Men and the women they date still expect the boys to pay the freight for dates and romancing. Nearly 85 percent of adults say that men should foot the bill for flowers and dinner, and 64 percent say that they should pick up movie or concert tickets, too.

own little wolf pack is coming into town, and I'm returning to the fold. I crumple the card into my pocket, hail a cab, and go home. Fishing my ring from the kitchen cupboard, I secure it back on my hand.

All seems right again.

Lesson #5: Married Guys Are Luckier

In the end, if I learned one overriding lesson, it's this: Married men fantasize about being bachelors. Bachelors fantasize about married life. But married guys get the nod for one reason: They know that if they really wanted to, they could go back to being bachelors. A lot of us do it. A lot of us do it against our wishes, in fact. But a bachelor, especially once he reaches a certain age, well, he doesn't really know if he can do the married thing. He doesn't know if he's capable of commitment, and he doesn't know if he'll ever find one woman with whom he can settle down, raise a family, build a future.

Especially one who'll let him play bachelor for a week.

Epilogue

A few days later, I'm sitting at my desk, surrounded by pictures of my wife and of the kids wrestling with a cat. Beside me is a packed bag; I'm heading to our house in the country for the first time in more than a week. The phone rings.

"Hello?"

"Hello, Steve? It's Liba! Remember me?"

Tricks of the Trade

Vital guy-smarts include changing a flat tire without smearing grease on your shirt, popping a bottle of champagne without putting out an eye, and carving a turkey without carving your thumb. But guy-smarts won't get you far with women, as Larry Keller and Christian Millman reveal in the book Guy Knowledge. *Here are two girl-smarts you should know, too.*

How to Compliment a Woman

Perhaps you consider yourself a pretty savvy investor. You have a few bucks tucked away in your retirement account. You keep a trained eye on the market and maybe even dabble a bit overseas.

Well, lend an ear, friend, because we're about to drop the hottest investment tip of your life on you. For a couple of seconds a day, we can make you rich beyond your wildest dreams. And you can't beat the price.

"If you give a woman the gift of a compliment, you're going to get back her love, respect, admiration, and devotion," reports Ellen Kreidman, Ph.D., a relationship expert and best-selling author of *Light His Fire* and *The 10-Second Kiss*. "Your cost? Nothing. Your reward? A woman who responds to your needs in return."

Sound like a pretty good deal? It is.

Be a Golden-Tongued Romeo

You may not know it, but you're being quizzed:

HER: "Do you love me?"

YOU: "Yup."

Bzzzzzz. Unfortunately, you get zero points. Well, maybe a tiny fraction of one for at least answering in the affirmative. You see, questions like this one are your opportunity to shine, to really lay a sparkling compliment on her. It's all about being specific.

It's not enough to mutter generalities when you're complimenting the love of your life. You need to go into hard-core detail. "It takes a little practice, but it's worth the extra effort," explains relationship expert Dr. Ellen Kreidman. "Sometimes a 5-second compliment can make her feel wonderful for 4 hours." For example, instead of mumbling, "You look nice," try saying something like, "Wow, that red dress looks beautiful on you. It shows off your sexy legs," or "You're a

knockout in that outfit. Every man at the party is going to envy me."

And what do you say after your wife or girlfriend has just cooked a delicious meal? Instead of the perfunctory, "Good dinner," tell your sweetie, "This is the best fried chicken I've ever tasted," or "That was terrific. I'm the luckiest man alive to be with such a fantastic cook."

Get the drift? Yes, it seems somewhat corny. That's because it is. But it shows that she's so special to you that you're moved to hyperbole. She wants to be your apple tree blossom of a thousand perfumes.

So what's the answer when she asks if you love her? "Do I *love* you? I worship you! I love you more than life itself. I can't imagine how I ever lived without you," suggests Dr. Kreidman. Write that one down on the palm of your hand for the next time you get a pop quiz.

It's not necessarily your fault if giving compliments is a bit foreign to you. "Many men simply haven't learned what a woman wants to hear," Dr. Kreidman says. In relationships, we often unconsciously mimic what we saw in our own houses growing up. If your dad's idea of a compliment was grunting at the meat loaf your mom cooked, chances are pretty good that you didn't take away a whole lot of valuable lessons from that. All is not lost, though—an old dog can learn new tricks. Here are a few things to keep in mind.

● Say something.
Anything. "When you say nothing, people always take it as a negative," says Dr. Kreidman. She got her hair cut? Pipe up. New dress? Sing out strong. "If you're thinking that she already knows that you like the way she looks, the way she cooks, or that you're proud of her, it isn't enough. It has to be verbalized," she says.

● Look for the little opportunities.
There are countless ordinary occasions that are perfectly suited to a compliment, says Joan R. Shapiro, M.D., a Denver psychiatrist and coauthor of *Men: A Translation for Women*. "If you like the way she looks when she steps out of the car, say so," she says. Tell her what a wonderful mother she is. "That means a lot because we always doubt that."

● Show her off to others.
Complimenting her in front of other people is extremely powerful, no matter how much she shyly protests. "It's like when you got married and you said in front of everybody, 'I choose this woman,'" says Dr. Shapiro. "It's like saying it all over again."

"It always has three times the impact when you compliment her in front of other people," calculates Dr. Kreidman.

● Keep the glow going.
When she comes home from work beaming about something she has accomplished, it's because she wants to share it with you. "Express pride in her," Dr. Shapiro says. "Show her how impressed you are." Your opinion matters to her. Make sure she knows it.

● Know her buttons.
There are certain specifically female areas you need to be extra-sensitive around. One is a woman's fear of getting older and becoming less attractive to you. How many times has she asked you, "Honey, will you still love me when I'm old and wrinkled?" You probably joked around and told her, "No way,

you're out the door for a 20-year-old." Har-har. Funny to you, not to her, says Dr. Kreidman. "She wants to hear how she grows more beautiful with every year that passes," she says.

● Be her support team.
If she's trying to overcome a personal problem like smoking or overeating, she needs you in her corner. Never, ever mock her attempts to better herself. "She really needs to hear how special she is for trying to improve herself," says Dr. Kreidman.

● Make a game of it.
Did she remember to put the cap back on the toothpaste? Did she remember to slide the seat back in your car so you don't have to cripple yourself getting in? Did she remember that you like crunchy, not smooth, peanut butter? Make a game of seeing how many small things you can notice about her, and point them out with a compliment.

● Do it daily.
"Don't let a day go by without taking time out to notice that wonderful woman," says Dr. Kreidman. "Compliment her every day on something she has done, who she is, or her physical appearance."

You have only two choices here: to criticize or to compliment. Both start with the same letter but end far differently. Here's what happens when you criticize. "You'll have a woman who's unresponsive, cold, and unloving," says Dr. Kreidman. And you know what often happens then? "We fall in love because of the way we feel when we're with another person," she says. When a woman stops feeling beautiful and sexy and appreciated with a man, she's tempted to find those feelings elsewhere.

Here's what happens when you give a compliment. "A woman who feels good about herself when she's with you is automatically motivated to satisfy your needs and care about your feelings, and will try to please you," says Dr. Kreidman.

Tough choice, huh?

Give Good Foot Massage

In the movie *Pulp Fiction*, Vincent (played by babe-magnet John Travolta) says it all: "You're saying a foot massage don't mean nothing, and I'm saying it does. I've given a million ladies a million foot massages, and they all meant something. We act like they don't, but they do. That's what's so cool about them. This sensual thing's going on that nobody's talking about, but you know it and she knows it." And in a few minutes, you'll know it, too, buddy.

There are 52 bones in your feet, making up about a quarter of the number of bones in your body. Add to that 66 joints, 214 ligaments, 38 muscles, and a bunch of tendons, and you have a rough idea of how intricate your feet are. Topping that all off, women have about four times as many foot problems as men, likely a result of wearing high-heeled shoes so often.

No wonder she feels so good when you give her a foot massage.

Let's face it—nobody has the time to give a full-body massage as often as he (or she) would like. But, in a paltry couple of minutes, you can win your sweetheart's undying gratitude by massaging her aching feet. Here's how, according to certified massage therapist Elliot Greene.

● **Trim your nails.**
The bottom of your partner's feet isn't the place to buff your fingernails. It's essential to make sure that they're cut short, or else you may get a knee-jerk tickle reaction right in the kisser.

● **Assume the position.**
It's best to have unrestricted dual-hand access to the bottom of her foot, so don't sit side by side. Instead, kneel on the floor while she lies on the floor or sits on a comfy chair (a real princess-on-the-throne fantasy for her here—hint, hint).

● **Smile and make eye contact.**
Remember, Grasshopper, this isn't about rubbing her foot—it's about . . . well, you know. It may not look like sex, but it's certainly another form of it, so try not to appear as though you're digging earthworms out of a bait bucket. Sensuous massage is a dance best choreographed through improvisation. Feel free to explore, caress, touch, alter. Ask her to speak up (in moans or words) if something feels particularly good, if she wants you to concentrate more on a certain area, or if there's something she doesn't like, Greene says.

● **Speed kills.**
Bear in mind that old Pointer Sisters song, "Slow Hand." There's a reason they sang it with such fervor. Women routinely complain that men are too hurried and too rough in their touching,

hot TIP!

Condos are so-o-o 1980s—but that's only if you're stuck owning one. Renting, on the other hand, is a great way to score a hot vacation deal that's cheaper and more spacious than many hotel rooms. Condominium Travel Associates coordinates vacation rentals in the United States, Caribbean, and Mexico, starting at just $450 a week. For more information, visit the Web site www.condotravel.com.

notes Bernie Zilbergeld, Ph.D., a sex therapist in Oakland, California, in his book *The New Male Sexuality*. A gentle and slow touch is associated with thoughtfulness, intimacy, and love. Before you start your massage, gently rest your hands on her for a few minutes while you talk about nothing in particular. This acclimates her to your touch before you begin the actual work.

○ Give her some grease.
Nothing says, "Girl, you're just like a sister to me" more than some half-assed dry-rub. Plunk down a few bucks for a lightly scented massage oil. You won't need much. But whatever you do, warm the oil in your hands instead of squirting it straight and cold from the bottle. Cup your hand and fill it with a dab of oil about the size of a quarter. (You can always add more as needed.) Then rub your hands together vigorously a few times to get the oil toasty warm before you smooth it on.

○ Start big.
Put your right hand flat on the sole of her foot, with the heel of your hand snug in the arch. Use your left hand to hold her leg gently but firmly just above the ankle. Slowly push your right hand into her foot, stretching her toes forward toward her knee. Hold for about 10 seconds.

○ Go small.
Hold her heel with one hand and use the thumb of your other hand to make firm, small circles on the sole of her foot. Cover the entire sole with this motion, but pay particular attention to the arch and ball of her foot.

○ Pull the piggies.
Work up to her toes by gently squeezing the topside and bottomside of each between your thumb and forefinger. Tug softly as you slide from the base of the toe right off the end. Be warned: The skin *between* her toes is extremely sensitive, unpleasantly so for some women, so venture there at your own risk.

○ Head for the ankles.
With your thumbs braced against the heel of her foot, curl your fingers around the inside and outside edges of her foot. Using a gentle, circular motion, rub the area beneath the protruding anklebones.

○ Bring her home gently.
If there's any oil residue left, wipe it off with the towel you've stashed nearby. Finish the massage by gently holding her foot in both hands for a few moments, one hand on the bottom of her foot, the other on the top, to impart the warmth of your body.

○ Think ahead.

If you're going to play the love slave, do it right. Don't be in any rush to bring her back to the real world, says Greene. Your thanks will come soon enough. When you're finished with both feet, and she's resting there all aglow with eyes at half-mast, inquire as innocently and innocuously as possible if there's any-place else that she'd like you to massage.

SEX WARS

"We have to be missing twenty-four hours before I consider us lost."

HELP ONLINE

MR. SUAVE

Who should know more about wooing women well than Don Juan, right?
The Don Juan Center freely shares secrets of successfully attracting,
meeting, and dating desirable women. You'll find discussions, jokes, articles,
tips, and a "success coach" to answer all your personal love challenges.

http://sosuave.com

CUPID'S EROS

Step-by-step instruction for hot talk, flirting, and giving the
perfect, erotic massage—all of which certainly is our idea of a sizzling date.
And you'll find a whole lot more at this Web site of the Society
for Human Sexuality. This site is about sex and more sex.
That seems especially comforting to us.

www.sexuality.org

DO-IT-YOURSELF ROMANCE

The Romantic's Guide offers 1,000-plus creative ideas on love,
dating, and romance. That's 1,000 more than most of us
usually come up with. We'll take it.

www.theromantic.com

MAN'S GUIDE INTERVIEW

How to Date Your Wife for Life

An Interview with Author Chris Allen, of Funinbed.com

Dreading the prospect of yet another night of prime-time TV with your wife? Sick of going to the movies every Saturday with the woman with whom you cohabit? Can't stand the "same old, same old" with the lady you profess to want to spend the rest of your life with?

You don't have anyone to blame but yourself. If you're in a rut, chances are that you dug that rut yourself—with a little help from your woman. Still, we like you; we feel for you. So we found someone to help get you back on a smooth road leading toward a little fun and excitement.

Chris Allen is the man behind Funinbed.com, a Web site where, as he says, "couples can go to learn how to keep the variety and the passion alive both in the relationship and in the bedroom. Because that's really the biggest challenge that couples face today—keeping it fresh and maintaining their relationships at a point where they don't simply want to stay together but are also having a great time."

Allen is also the author of several books, including The Foreplay Gourmet, 1,001 Sex Secrets Every Man Should Know, *and* 1,001 Sex Secrets Every Woman Should Know.

Although his books and Web site are slanted heavily toward keeping things steamy in bed, we thought we'd ask him primarily about what comes before that. Namely, setting the mood, planning great dates, and keeping your relationship lively no matter how long you and she have been together.

MAN'S GUIDE: How substantially does the concept of dating change once things really get serious—once you're living in the same place or, for that matter, once you get married?

ALLEN: Mainly, the date becomes something that both of you do for the sheer fun of it rather than as a getting-to-know-you exercise. If it's done right, you can have some fun and have an adventure.

In a long-term relationship, the date doesn't have to be something where the two of you have to sit and talk and find out more about each other. You already know about the other person, and you know that she is the person that you want to be with. So you can just focus on having some fun, doing something off the beaten path.

MAN'S GUIDE: But is it sometimes more of an effort to get into "dating mode" when you're in a marriage or other live-in relationship? Is it harder to say, "Let's go on a date" as opposed to "Well, let's just go out and see another movie and grab some dinner or something?"

ALLEN: Yeah, I think that definitely can be a challenge, because you no longer have to invent an excuse to see the person. She is going to be there whether you get off the couch or not—well, up to a point, at least. If you don't get off the couch after a while, there is a good chance that she won't stick around.

But it is true that it takes more of a conscious effort to say, "Well, we haven't done anything in a while. We need to get up and go out." Still, it's something you need to do. Mind you, just sitting and watching TV together can make for some great evenings. But you can't do that consistently and expect a relationship to continue moving forward.

MAN'S GUIDE: So you would say that dating remains viable, and can flourish, no matter how long the two of you have been together.

ALLEN: Definitely. I think it's not only viable, it's *necessary.* You know, you have to keep things going. There's never really a time when you can just coast through the relationship. Dating is part of the effort that you have to put in to make sure the relationship stays fresh and stays fun.

MAN'S GUIDE: So how do you keep it fresh and fun after 5 or 10 or 20 years—or more?

ALLEN: Once you've been together a while, you have to put more emphasis on the nature of the activity. You have to have something a little bit more special planned.

When you're dating in the early stages, just the fact that you're going to be with the other person makes the evening special. But once the two of you are together long-term, you have to give serious thought as to how you are going to make this day different from just any other day.

When my wife and I were first dating, it didn't matter really what we did, as long as we were together. That was the main thing. But now, I have to scan the paper to see if there's a concert coming to town or some kind of art exhibit coming up that I know she'd want to see.

MAN'S GUIDE: Do you also need to do something special in terms of how you ask her out? It's not like when you were first dating, when there was still a strong chance that she might have other plans . . . or a better prospect for dating. Some of that spark and spontaneity is missing.

ALLEN: If you can put some special spin on the way you ask, that always helps in terms of making the date more romantic. But basically, there are two ways you can ask, and I think you need to alternate between the two pretty frequently.

First, you can have the surprise. You have something planned that you know she will want to do, but you don't spring it on her until right at the last minute. You might even want to get her in the car and not even tell her where you're taking her. That's the ultimate surprise.

But on the other hand, especially if the date you're planning is a ways off yet, it can be really nice to tell her early and give her something to look forward to.

MAN'S GUIDE: Like you said earlier, when you are in a newly minted relationship, you're just thrilled to be with the person. The romance and the passion are all tied up into each other. Do the distinctions become a little bit more polarized when you're in a long-term relationship? Does it become an either-or thing, where dates are either romantic or passionate? Or do the romance and passion still stay pretty well mixed together?

ALLEN: I think that if you consistently work on the romance, then the passion will take care of itself. Passion is one of those things that is hard to predict or control. But with the romance, you can exert a lot more control over that. And when you work on the romance, everything else will fall into place.

But you are right, romance does tend to take the place of passion a little bit. When you become more familiar with that person, your heart isn't always going to be pounding. When my wife and I were first dating, just reaching over and holding her hand could make me feel as if I had to breathe into a paper bag to keep from hyperventilating.

But you're not going to sustain that level of intensity. You can't. That doesn't mean you love the person less. But that's also why I think that romance really is the key. If you work on the romance, then the passion will take care of itself.

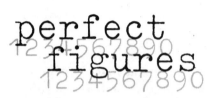

perfect figures

McDonald's food costs about one-third less in Memphis than it does in New York City.

MAN'S GUIDE: So instead of constant intensity, you save it up for the big game.

ALLEN: Yeah, exactly. Yeah.

MAN'S GUIDE: Even with feminism and women's liberation and all that, the responsibility for asking someone out and planning a date generally falls to the man. When you're married or cohabiting, does it become a bit more egalitarian?

ALLEN: No, I don't think that it ever changes. It can be really confusing to guys, because you don't always know. With some women, you open a door for them, and they're insulted. But if you don't open the door, that's the time a woman is going to be insulted because you aren't a gentleman.

But some things are eternal, and asking the woman out is one of them. Even when you are together long-term, I think the roles are still pretty clearly defined. It's almost always up to the man to ask the woman out, no matter how long you've been together.

MAN'S GUIDE: So what are some good plans that a guy can make if he really wants that date with his wife or live-in girlfriend to be movie-quality romantic?

ALLEN: When I hear from women, the top activity they always mention is dancing. Women really respect a guy who can at least hold his own on the dance floor. That really makes for a lot of romantic evenings.

So women are very impressed with a night out dancing. But guys don't give dancing enough credit or attention. And the thing is, you don't have to be Fred Astaire or anything. Just make sure that you know a few steps. Just a few basic steps so that you won't trip and embarrass yourself on the dance floor.

MAN'S GUIDE: Anything else along those romantic lines, especially for those of us with two left feet or an unshakable fear of dance floors?

ALLEN: Well, I'll go right back to my comments about surprises. Surprise your woman with something: a gift or a special evening or anything like that.

Any time it's clear that you've put some thought into the evening, you're more than halfway there. That is a really great way to a woman's heart. Underplanning is the greatest pitfall for any kind of date.

Women love it when it's obvious that you've put immense thought into the evening. And the more preparations you've made, the more romantic it is to her. Take care of arranging for a babysitter. Make the reservations. If you're going to go out to a hotel or something afterward, have some champagne already chilling in the room. The more premeditation you put into the date, the better.

MAN'S GUIDE: Basically, let her know that she's in your hands and that she's taken care of.

ALLEN: Oh, yeah. I've gotten so many letters from women that basically describe variations on that theme. And when they describe their most romantic night or the sexiest night of their lives, it always starts off with the guy being in charge of the situation. Women will write to me and rave about how "I came home from work, and there was already a dress laid out for me" and things like that. Women just love that stuff.

MAN'S GUIDE: Well, you've already said that romance will often lead to passion. But do you have any other, more specific tips for guys who want to guide the evening more firmly into the erogenous zone? I mean, we're guys. We ideally want the evening to end in raucous sex.

ALLEN: Well, there are some specific physical things that many women say really relax them and open them up for a more passionate evening. And there are three things I almost constantly hear from women in that regard.

Number one: giving her a back rub. Number two: massaging her feet. And number three: brushing her hair—women really melt for this one.

MAN'S GUIDE: If we just had enough hands, we could do all three at once. Would that get things going or what?

Seriously, though, hair brushing?

ALLEN: Women really, really love it when you brush their hair, and it's something you don't even have to be on a date to do. You can just be sitting and watching television, and then you go get her hairbrush. You have her sit down in front of you, and while the two of you are watching TV, you just brush her hair. Women just turn to putty when you do that. They really go crazy for it.

But, yeah, those are three things that women really, really respond to.

MAN'S GUIDE: You're telling me that the best sex toy a guy can have is his woman's hairbrush?

ALLEN: Exactly. Yeah.

MAN'S GUIDE: So you said that underplanning a date is a surefire mood killer. Let's expand on that.

What other things do guys do that make her say to herself, "Why the hell did I even marry you? Why did I ever date you to begin with? What was I thinking?"

ALLEN: I think any kind of situation where you make it painfully obvious that you're just going through the motions. When you make it clear that you are just going along for the ride. If you are not enthusiastic about the date, and you make sure that she knows you're just doing it for her sake, that's just about the biggest turnoff there is.

I'm talking about the eye-rolling, looking-at-your-watch kind of date. I'm talking about those times when a guy takes his girl to see a "chick flick," and he's sitting there going, "Yeah, yeah, yeah. When's this going to be over so we can get something to eat?"

She can't really enjoy herself knowing that you're just sitting there waiting for it to be over. And if you do that to her, she'll probably reciprocate the next time you guys make love by giving you the same lackluster response.

MAN'S GUIDE: So the gates to paradise will be closing, then.

ALLEN: Oh, yeah. Yep.

MAN'S GUIDE: Okay, for the extremely romance-challenged guys out there, what are some places where you just don't want to take your wife in 99 percent of all cases?

ALLEN: I think monster truck rallies would be a bad start.

MAN'S GUIDE: Not the right mood, huh?

ALLEN: Nope. And I think I'd probably stay away from sporting events, too, and stuff like that unless she is specifically interested in it. Those kinds of events are more for the guy than for her.

It's not likely to go over well if you say, "Hey, honey, I got Bulls tickets for tonight. Let's go on a date." If she loves the Bulls, obviously that's cool. But most of the time, that kind of date is not going to work out well for you in the end.

MAN'S GUIDE: You know, it occurs to me that something I used to see in my single days was guys taking their girls to strip clubs. How good an idea is something like that?

ALLEN: Definitely a bad idea in most cases. If you go to a topless joint, you are putting your partner in a position where she's almost going to have to compete for your attention. That's bad news. It's funny you brought that situation up, though, because I've seen it before, and I don't understand what those guys are thinking.

MAN'S GUIDE: So let's assume the guy keeps his wits and doesn't make an ass of himself. Everything's going nice, and you head home, or you head to the hotel room. You rub her back, you brush her hair, you massage her feet . . . What are some other things that you can do to take that slow burn you have going and turn it into a nice, big fire?

ALLEN: Well, another thing I often get from women is this: It seems like one of the most romantic things that a guy can do is put rose petals on the bed. I did a survey once on the Web site and asked, "What's the sexiest thing a guy can do for you?"

And I seem to recall that something like three-quarters of them said, "Rose petals on the bed." Women just really, really love that.

Another big one was drawing a bath for her. And I don't mean a sensual thing where you guys are going to bathe together. I mean the guy just draws a bath, maybe has some candles going in the bathroom, maybe gets her a glass of wine or something, and just puts her in there and leaves her alone. Just lets her sit there and soak so that the stress of the day or the week can melt away. And guys, give her plenty of time.

Especially nowadays, with so many men and women both having jobs, a lot of women have told me that it's just the ultimate when they come home from work and their guys have drawn baths for them.

If you do special things like that, it pays off so much. Later on, she will really let you know how much she appreciates your effort.

Another thing that women really love is when a guy buys a particular piece of lingerie. Sexy lingerie or something like that. Because a lot of women don't enjoy picking that stuff out for themselves. The problem is that if they buy it themselves, they may like the lingerie, but they're not sure if the guy will like it.

But when the guy buys her something, then she can be absolutely sure that that's one of his favorite pieces. Again, that kind of thing shows that he put some thought and some effort into his actions, and that means a lot to the woman.

QUICKIES

CONDOM COURTESY

If you're in bed with a woman whom you've recently met, chances are you've made a decent first impression. (Please, tell us she's not passed out.) But according to an experiment done at Arizona State University, you can improve your already high standing by doing some condom play-by-play. Women watched videotaped scenarios of a man and woman starting to have sex, then they rated the man's maturity in each one. They considered the man to be more mature when he told his partner he was going to put on a condom, rather than letting the ripping foil do the talking. Announcing deployment wins you points for poise and reassures her that you're confident enough to be cool about contraception—and that the tearing noise wasn't just you breaking wind.

DO THE "FUNKY FREUD"

Here, if you need it, is another reason to resist getting dragged onto the dance floor whenever the DJ plays "What I Like about You." Your command of the Funky Squirrel could give away hidden aspects of your personality, says Leesa Dillman, Ph.D., a communication professor at the University of Nevada in Las Vegas. Here are her observations.

● **Waving your hands in the air**
This shows that you're a happy, jolly sort who rarely feels stressed-out. Or your hair is on fire.

● **Wiggling your butt**
You're uninhibited and passionate, and you enjoy wild relationships. You're trying to draw attention to yourself, maybe because no one's dancing with you.

● **Staring at the floor while dancing**
You're shy, anxious, and obviously overly concerned about staying in rhythm. Or you're dancing to Alanis Morissette.

● **Repeating the same steps**
This suggests single-mindedness, no imagination, and too much self-consciousness. Or you're trying not to spill your beer.

● **Clicking your fingers or clapping your hands**

You're sociable and you crave interaction with others, so you're trying yet another way to draw attention to yourself. And you're probably the drunkest man on the floor.

● **Dancing with fists clenched**

You find it hard to relax. You're defensive, tense, or easily stressed. You should not be allowed to join the hokey-pokey line.

DECODE HER EMOTIONAL DAY-TIMER

A woman's monthly cycle strongly influences her sex drive and her moods—but hey, if you've ever had a wife or girlfriend (or mother or sister or aunt . . .), you've already learned that the hard way. But most guys blunder from month to month, surprised by the swing of the pendulum. Having a working knowledge of her biological highs and lows can spell the difference between having a relaxed, carefree vacation or hot night out and enduring one spent walking on eggshells, playing duck-and-cover. Here's how to read her ebb and flow.

" These guys dance like a 12-year-old kicking around a dead squirrel. "

—John Dvorak, computer columnist and TV host of *Silicon Spin,* describing how a crowd of computer-industry moguls, including Bill Gates, looked while dancing with their dates at a Las Vegas club

● **Follicular phase**

When it occurs: Days 1 to 12

What's happening: She sheds the lining in her uterus. Bleeding usually takes place during days 1 to 5 of this phase.

Good time for sex? Yep. At the end of this phase, her endorphins peak, and increased estrogen gives her ample vaginal lubrication, says Laurel Stadtmauer, M.D., Ph.D., a reproductive endocrinologist in Cary, North Carolina. Opt for morning sex, as her endorphins are highest from 6:00 A.M. to 10:00 A.M.

● **Ovulatory phase**

When it occurs: Days 13 to 15

What's happening: She's in full baby-making mode. An egg moves into one of her fallopian tubes, and her cervical mucus thins, making it easier for sperm to reach the egg, says Valerie Montgomery Rice, M.D., a reproductive endocrinologist at the University of Kansas Medical Center in Kansas City. She may also produce more testosterone, which is nature's way of increasing her sex drive.

Good time for sex? The combination of estrogen, testosterone, and progesterone may make her euphoric and sexually aggressive. These 3 days could bring you the lustiest sex of the month.

● **Luteal phase**
When it occurs: Days 16 to 30

What's happening: She produces progesterone, a hormone that thickens the uterine lining and inhibits endorphins. This can make her irritable, Dr. Stadtmauer says. We trust that you're familiar with this stage.

Good time for sex? The perils of PMS aside, it could be. Some women—again, thanks to a kick of hormones—may feel sexually aggressive during the middle of the phase, says Dr. Stadtmauer.

DEAR DR. MANLY

Q: *I did everything right on our first few dates, so when we went back to her place last night, things got steamy during* Notting Hill. *But when she asked me to unhook her bra, things got complicated. I fumbled, fiddled, pulled, and pinched. Finally, she rolled her eyes and said, "Oh, for god's sake, let me do it." So tell me, how does one finesse 'de-bra-ing' a woman?*

—R. C., TRENTON, NEW JERSEY

A: If you're lucky, she's wearing a bra with a front clasp. That type comes off easily if you just slip one finger underneath and give a slight twist.

But if you're working blind on a back-clasp, may I suggest a brief moment of Zen-like contemplation. "Relax. Don't rush it, and don't get frustrated," says Cindy Cipriano, promotions director for Coquette Lingerie in Waterloo, Ontario. Easy for her to say.

A typical bra uses a hook-and-eye closure—and you need to envision how it works in order to unsnap it single-handedly, says Cipriano. Think of the bungee cord that you use to hold down the trunk of your car. It's elastic, it has a hook, and the rust hole that you wedge the hook into can be considered an eye. No matter how you tug, pull, or haul on it, it's going to stay put unless you back the hook out of the hole the same way it went in. The same is true of a bra.

Here's what you need to do.

1 If you're right-handed, nonchalantly let your right hand work its way around her to the clasp.

2 Feel for the bump where the hook and eye meet.

3 Place your thumb on one side of the bump, your forefinger and middle finger on the other.

4 Pressing against the strap, slide your thumb under your forefinger. It's kind of like snapping your fingers in slow motion.

5 The clasp should slide apart. Remember, the straps are elasticized and may fly outward with some speed. Keep your face, eyes, and small items of furniture a safe distance away.

Q: *I'm not (normally) a slob, but when I get nervous on a date, I usually end up dropping, knocking, spilling, or pouring something onto my shirt, coat, or pants. I can always get a laugh out of it (I play the bumbling-but-sincere type very well), but I end up wearing a highly visible reminder of my wine or marinara sauce for the rest of the evening. <u>What's the best way to destain while on location?</u>*

—A. G., New York City

A: Congratulations on finding a shtick that wows the babes, Columbo, and for realizing that though you may charm your date with the old meatball-on-the-tie trick, the rest of the world doesn't want to see the results. Before you attack that puddle of grease, it's important to understand the nine rules of stain warfare, to wit:

● Faster is better.
Remove a stain just after impact, before it has time to penetrate the fabric and set.

● Blot, don't scrub.
Scrubbing damages the fabric and drives the stain deeper.

● Use hot water on a grease stain.
Heat dissolves the grease. Cold just solidifies it.

● Use cold water on a wet stain.
That's any water-based spot, including wine or grape juice.

● Spit on your tie.
The enzymes in saliva help break down protein-based stains. Don't use soap and water on a silk tie. And don't spit while you're at the table—or when your mouth is full.

● Suck it up.
A liquid stain will spread, so put a napkin under the stained section to absorb the liquid before your shirt does.

● Go easy on the club soda.
Despite what you may have heard, club soda works no better than tap water.

● When all else fails, go to a pro.
If the stain is getting bigger or looks worse, stop—then take it to a cleaner as soon as possible.

● **Concede defeat in style.**

A number of companies make cotton shirts coated with Teflon to prevent oil- and water-based stains from penetrating. The shirts are supple, comfy, and fashionable—nothing at all like a frying pan.

Dr. Manly is a fictional character.
The actual advice was provided by a variety of
medical doctors and other qualified experts.

6

SEX
IN THE
PUBLIC EYE

 The year 2000 seemed tame compared to the White House shenanigans of 1999, which kept Bill Clinton and Monica Lewinsky in the news 24-7. Yes, millions watched what seemed to be a perfectly rational woman agree to marry a multimillionaire—and total stranger—on national television, but that just doesn't have the same voyeuristic value as a blue dress, a pizza, and a good cigar.

Perhaps that's all for the best.

Among other nuggets in this section, you'll read about a growing trend: More and more middle-aged men are forgoing their financial salad days to start a second family—with a younger woman. You'll also discover the names of the most important people to change the course of sex in the 20th century—a list, incidentally, that's a great conversation starter with younger women . . . in case you're thinking about starting a second family.

TOP TEN

Viagra Books

Step aside, Prozac—your thunder has been stolen by a little blue wonder diamond responsible for more new erections than Lego or Lincoln Logs put together. In 1998, there were fewer than 6 Viagra books listed with online bookseller Amazon.com. In 2000, more than 20. Here are 10 of the most popular.

1 *Viagra: A Guide to the Phenomenal Potency-Promoting Drug,* by Susan Vaughan, M.D.

2 *Beyond Viagra: Plain Talk about Treating Male and Female Sexual Dysfunction,* by Alfred J. Newman, M.D., Ph.D.

3 *Beyond Viagra: A Commonsense Guide to Building a Healthy Sexual Relationship for Both Men and Women,* by Gerald Melchiode, M.D., with Bill Sloan

4 *Viagra Nation: The Definitive Guide to Life in the New Sexual Utopia,* by Bruce McCall and Lee Eisenberg

5 *The Virility Solution: Everything You Need to Know about Viagra, the Potency Pill That Can Restore and Enhance Male Sexuality,* by Steven Lamm, M.D., and Gerald Couzens

6 *Viagra: The Wonder Drug for Peak Performance,* by E. Douglas Whitehead, M.D., and Terry Malloy

SEX IN THE PUBLIC EYE: **TOP TEN** 169

7 *Viagra and the Quest for Potency,* by Brian Drew

8 *Viagra: How the Miracle Drug Happened and What It Can Do for You,* by Jonathan Jarow, M.D.; Robert A. Kloner, M.D., Ph.D.; and Ann M. Holmes

9 *Viagra: The Potency Promise,* by Larry Katzenstein

10 *Viagra and You: New Treatments for Potency and Sexual Health,* by Mark Stolar, M.D.

MUST READS

A Century of Moving and Shaking

Who influenced your ideas of sex: the schoolgirl-recipient of your first kiss or the cousin who played "show-me-yours-and-I'll-show-you-mine"? The bombshell center-fold in the magazine you found in your dad's toolbox or the high school Spanish teacher with the largest breasts you'd ever seen with your own two eyes? No doubt all of the above. James R. Petersen, author of The Century of Sex: Playboy's History of the Sexual Revolution, *cast his gaze further afield. In this article from* Playboy *maga-zine, he ranks the men and women, heroes and villains, who changed the face of sex for each and every one of us during the past 100 years.*

● Thomas Edison
Electricity powered the amusement halls and introduced downtown Saturday night, giving men and women a destination for dates, and created, in effect, a single sexual culture. Moving pictures taught the nation about romance, how and when to kiss.

● Anthony Comstock
In 1873, Comstock persuaded Congress to beef up a law that prohibited mailing obscenity, which included information and items concerning contra-ceptives and "things intended for immoral use." As a special agent for the Post Office and secretary of the New York Society for the Suppression of Vice, he arrested those who sold "immoral" books, art, and photographs. He threw abortionists and advocates of birth control into jail. More than 80 years after his death in 1915, his influence is still felt. The Communications Decency Act of 1996, which would have crippled free expression online, merely added the word *computers* to the original Comstock Act.

● Havelock Ellis
At the turn of the century, the first modern sexologist enthusiastically attacked Victorian stereotypes—the ideas that modesty is a virtue, that women have no desire, that masturbation is a disease, and that the state has a right to intervene in the behavior of consenting adults. His style—collecting case histories and anecdotes from other cultures—expanded the universe, showing that sex was not only completely natural but also infinitely varied.

● **Henry Ford**

Who changed sex more: Sigmund Freud or Ford? Easily, it was Ford. Americans were doing backseats long before they took to talking about it on a psychoanalyst's couch. The automobile gave lovers mobility and privacy. Away from prying eyes, anything was possible.

● **Margaret Sanger**

She argued for "family limitation" in 1914 and had to flee the country. She opened the nation's first birth control clinic in 1916 and went to jail. She wrestled with doctors to make birth control a medical concern and lobbied Congress and the Post Office to dismantle the Comstock Act. During Prohibition, she smuggled diaphragms into the country among shipments of contraband Holland gin. She founded what would become Planned Parenthood. In 1950, Sanger persuaded benefactor Katharine McCormick to underwrite research for a form of birth control that would be as simple as taking aspirin. Within 10 years, gynecologist John Rock and endocrinologist Gregory Pincus had developed the Pill.

perfect figures

A British survey of 400 travelers found that women were 18 percent more likely than men to have unsafe sex while traveling abroad.

● **Sigmund Freud**

Hero or villain? The jury is still out. Freud visited the United States once, in 1909. His works were translated into English during the 1910s. By the 1920s, flappers and philosophers had grasped the essentials: Repression was bad, inhibitions were to be shed, and sex lay at the root of everything. Desire was a drive equal to thirst or hunger—nothing more, nothing less. Avoiding sex caused horrible neuroses. During the 1950s, Freud was resurrected by conservatives to herd women back into traditional sex roles. One team of Freudians claimed that for men sex was as easy as falling off a log, for women it was like being the log. In the 1960s, after Masters and Johnson rediscovered the clitoris, radical feminists such as Shere Hite and Anne Koedt labeled Freud the ultimate sexist oppressor. The good doctor had claimed that only vaginal orgasms (and not clitoral) were mature.

● **Alexander Graham Bell**

His 1876 invention was a coast-to-coast party line by 1915. Dial telephones (1919) and private lines added convenience and intimacy. The telephone put your lover's voice on the pillow next to your ear. If she wasn't there, you had a way to reach the other names in your black book. It moved commercial sex from the tawdry world of brothels and bars to the more sequestered world of call girls. In the 1980s, dial-a-porn reminded the nation of the erotic power of aural sex. By the 1990s, novels such as Nicholson Baker's *Vox* and government documents such as the Starr report were devoted to phone sex.

● Dr. Prince Morrow

In 1901, this controversial physician approached venereal disease as a medical problem, not a moral one. No longer would the wages of sin include death and disease. Dr. Morrow estimated that 75 out of every 100 men in New York City had been infected with gonorrhea, and between 5 and 18 percent with syphilis. To battle the scourge, he organized the American Society of Social and Moral Prophylaxis, which later became the American Social Hygiene Association.

● Dr. John Mahoney

In 1941, at the onset of World War II, Howard Florey, Ernst Chain, and Norman Heatley turned Alexander Fleming's penicillin into a viable drug, a miracle cure for infection. In 1943, Army physician Dr. Mahoney discovered that penicillin cures syphilis. Shortly after, Monroe Romansky and George Rittman found that penicillin also cures gonorrhea.

● James Mann

The United States has periodically been swept by moral panics. Mann exploited the first of the century, a rabid belief in the existence of a white slave trade ("60,000 daughters kidnapped into prostitution!"). In 1910, he pushed a bill through Congress that made it against the law to transport a woman across state lines for the "purpose of prostitution or debauchery or for any other immoral purpose." The Mann Act launched a national vice force, the Bureau of Investigation, later known as the FBI.

● J. Edgar Hoover

From 1924 to 1972, he was the nation's top sex cop. He raided brothels, locked up doctors who treated prostitutes, selectively enforced the Mann Act (from Charlie Chaplin to Chuck Berry), kept secret files on political enemies, and fanned the homosexual panic of the 1950s with a sexual witch-hunt of "deviants" in government. Hoover was a master of sexual politics (read: blackmail).

● Will Hays and Joe Breen

In 1922, former Postmaster General Hays left Washington to become the moral guardian of cinema. He created a list of do's and don'ts for directors, but it lacked teeth. In 1932, after the Legion of Decency threatened a boycott of Hollywood, Hays and Breen enforced the Motion Picture Production Code, which kept couples in separate beds, cut the length of a screen kiss from 4 seconds to 1.5 seconds, forbade nudity and any depiction of sexual pleasure, and censored any mention of abortion, breastfeeding, pregnancy, or childbirth. The code controlled Hollywood for more than three decades.

● Mae West

She went to jail for her words, serving 8 days for starring in a Broadway play called "Sex" in 1927. She challenged sexual stereotypes—what we now view as camp was revolutionary in its time. She played with the Hays office and was the nation's first shock jock—an appearance on Edgar Bergen's radio show led to a Federal Communications Commission investigation. West was subsequently banned by 130 stations.

● Morris Ernst

This lawyer for the fledgling American Civil Liberties Union believed that sexual expression was a civil liberty, an essential freedom. He defended Mary Ware Dennett's right to provide sex education to young people (1929), fought U.S. Customs to free literary lust (he championed James Joyce's *Ulysses* in 1933), and worked with Dr. Hannah Stone to allow the importation of birth control devices in 1933. Following the publication of the Kinsey report in 1948, Ernst advocated reform of repressive state sex laws.

● Margaret Mead

The anthropologist tested Freud's theories of repression and neurosis in the field. She depicted a sexual paradise, free of the restrictions of puritan culture, in *Coming of Age in Samoa,* published in 1928. Here was an educated, adventurous woman saying that "sex is a natural, pleasurable thing."

● Alfred Kinsey

His landmark surveys in 1948 and 1953 gave a statistical portrait of sex in America—the way it was, not the way it ought to be—and punctured centuries of hypocrisy.

● Hugh Hefner

In 1953, when other magazines were promoting family togetherness and the middle class was in flight to the suburbs, Hefner started a magazine for the urban male. He was the unabashed bachelor who believed that sex was good and that the unmarried had a right to a sex life.

⊙ William O. Douglas, Harry Blackmun, William Brennan, and Thurgood Marshall

The liberal heart of the Supreme Court worked the concept of privacy into the law of the land. First articulated by Justice Louis Brandeis in 1928, the "right to be let alone" grew to encompass the right to possess erotica, the right to obtain birth control, and the right to choose when and whether to bear children. While credit also goes to the individuals who launched test cases (lawyers such as Charles Rembar, who defended *Lady Chatterley's Lover* and *Fanny Hill,* and Sarah Weddington, who argued before the Court in *Roe v. Wade*), these men in black heard them out and agreed.

⊙ Alex Comfort

The direct heir of Havelock Ellis, this eccentric English writer served up a wonderful dish in his best-selling book *The Joy of Sex* in 1972. He introduced a culture locked in the missionary position to sexual exotica: bondage, sex in swings, "mouth music," grope suits, and techniques such as pompoir (milking the penis with vaginal contractions).

⊙ Betty Friedan

Her 1963 bestseller, *The Feminine Mystique,* exposed the trap of family togetherness, the plight of housewives living in suburbia. She founded the National Organization for Women, inspiring a second wave of feminism among women who were seeking fulfillment outside the home.

⊙ Masters and Johnson

In the 1960s, this couple provided a detailed description of the physiology of sex. They placed sex in the whole body, rediscovered the clitoris, and cataloged multiple orgasms in women. They devised cures for premature ejaculation and treated nonorgasmic women, and, in doing so, created the field of sex therapy.

⊙ "J"

The author of the 1969 classic *The Sensuous Woman* taught that oral sex was delicious. Some nine million women got the point. Her prosex female voice helped launch the second sexual revolution, paving the way for the likes of Germaine Greer, Nancy Friday, and Lonnie Barbach.

⊙ Linda Lovelace and Marilyn Chambers

In 1972, Gerard Damiano's *Deep Throat* and the Mitchell brothers' *Behind the Green Door* made porn chic, taking stag films from the all-male world of smokers and frat parties and transforming them into feature-length couples' fare. These movies depicted wholesome, prurient fun, everything from enthusiastic oral sex to shaving pubic hair. When Sony introduced the VCR in 1976, the visual revolution was complete.

Catharine MacKinnon
She pioneered the concept of sexual harassment, bringing law to bear on sex in the workplace. What the Mann Act was for the 20th century, sexual harassment law will be for the 21st century.

Newt Baker
The Secretary of War in 1917 ordered the closing of New Orleans' Storyville district and San Francisco's Barbary Coast as a prelude to World War I (unintentionally spreading jazz throughout the world). Red-light abatement laws coupled with "Keep fit to fight" patriotism drove commercial sex underground. Baker also launched the Commission on Training Camp Activities; the military's training pamphlets on venereal disease were the nation's first formal sex education.

W. E. Robie
During the 1920s, this doctor was a one-man sex industry, writing manuals such as *Rational Sex Ethics for Men in the Army and Navy* and *Sex Histories: Authentic Sex Experiences of Men and Women Showing How Fear and Ignorance of the Sex Life Lead to Individual Misery and Social Depravity*. Eventually, he summarized his knowledge in the less wieldy tome *The Art of Love*. The so-called doctor books were seduction manuals celebrated by everyone from Edmund Wilson to James Thurber and E. B. White.

Elvis Presley
Elvis was sex for sex's sake, an heir to Valentino, wearing out his pants from the inside, showing that men could move.

Anaïs Nin
Delta of Venus and *Little Birds*, short stories written for a connoisseur of erotica, along with Nin's intimate diaries, made sex an adventure in self-discovery for generations of women. For that

hot **TIP!**

If you have children and you or your wife work the graveyard shift, think seriously about switching to a day job. Among couples where Mom or Dad works midnight to 8:00 A.M., the divorce rate is six times higher than among couples where both hold day jobs. Factors at play include sleep deprivation, negative impact on the family's social life, and the lack of time alone as a couple. Child-free couples, on the other hand, were immune to the phenomenon, according to a 5-year study of nearly 7,000 married people.

reason, she was more important than her lover Henry Miller. She challenged women to take up pen and typewriter to record their fantasies.

● Helen Gurley Brown
The female Hefner, her *Sex and the Single Girl* (1962) gave young women permission to embark on sexual adventures.

● Ida Craddock
She wrote a series of advice manuals for newlyweds at the turn of the century, in which she recommended "an hour of tender, gentle, self-restrained coition." She described female orgasm and counseled that women take an active role in intercourse. Arrested in 1902 and convicted of violating the Comstock Act, she commited suicide rather than go to jail.

● D. H. Lawrence
In 1928, he published the first great dirty book, *Lady Chatterley's Lover,* immortalizing the notion that sex is natural. In 1959, when the courts ruled that *Lady Chatterley* was not obscene, literature was at last free.

● Hedy Lamarr
Her on-screen orgasm in the Czech film *Ecstasy* (released in 1932) flickered in more than 400 theaters over a 20-year span, a beautiful portrayal of a woman liberated by sex. It would take American filmmakers three decades to reach this level of expression.

● Jane Fonda
She and Brigitte Bardot toppled the 1950s bombshells, moving America's eyes from a breast fetish to total-body impishness. The successor to Hedy Lamarr, Fonda's on-screen orgasms ranged from camp (*Barbarella*) to political (*Coming Home*). Her exercise videos launched the fitness revolution.

● The American Law Institute
They were the unsung heroes of the sexual revolution. In 1960, this group of legal scholars drafted a model penal code that decriminalized sexual activity (from sodomy to fornication) between consenting adults.

● The Stonewall Rioters
In 1969, these patrons of a gay bar in New York resisted police and launched gay pride. In 1974, the American Psychiatric Association dropped its definition of homosexuality as a "sexual deviation."

● Mary Ware Dennett
She founded the Voluntary Parenthood League and petitioned Congress to dismantle the Comstock Act. In 1915, she wrote *The Sex Side of Life,* a primer on

the facts of life, for her sons. In 1929, the Post Office put Dennett on trial for sending the pamphlet through the mails. The court that reversed her conviction ruled that "an accurate exposition of the relevant facts of the sex side of life in decent language cannot ordinarily be regarded as obscene."

perfect figures

Percentage of Americans who will contract a sexually transmitted disease: 25

● Pope Pius XI

His *Casti Connubii* in 1930 tied sex to procreation. "Any use whatsoever of matrimony exercised in such a way that the [sex] act is deliberately frustrated in its natural power to generate life is an offense against the law of God and of nature, and those who indulge in such are branded with the guilt of a grave sin." He sentenced Catholics to Vatican roulette. In 1966, a papal commission voted 60 to 4 to change the church position and allow birth control. Pope Paul VI ignored their advice, and in *Humanae Vitae* banned the pill for Catholic women.

● Merrill Youngs

In the 1920s, this producer of condoms challenged the Comstock Act and won. Establishing rubbers as legitimate, he persuaded pharmacies to sell Trojans. Before that, condoms were sold primarily in gas stations, bars, and barbershops.

● Runners-Up

The inventors of the waterbed, the personal vibrator, Polaroid and video cameras, Viagra, cable TV, and the Internet. Thanks.

Good Old Dad—And Fresh Young Mom

If there's one thing that baby boomers will be remembered for, it's an unrelenting stamina and dogged pursuit of the pleasures of youth. For their fathers, the onslaught of middle age meant an empty nest, peaking career, new bass boat, a couple of weeks in France. But the sons of World War II have other ideas about living on the far side of 50, as Joanne Cleaver reveals in this article from American Demographics. *Today, many middle-aged men are returning to their oat-sowing days of young women, diapers, late-night feedings, and* Green Eggs and Ham.

Berkeley business school professor William Sonnenschein is living in a bit of a time warp. He's 50, and he has two adult children, ages 28 and 24, who are on their own. Finally, he's getting to travel. He's at the peak of his career. He no longer aspires to a bigger house and a fancier car. He's satisfied with the ones he has.

Two decades ago, Sonnenschein figured he'd be coasting toward retirement right about now. But just as the finish line came into view, it moved. In fact, Sonnenschein himself moved it when he and his second wife, Ericka Lutz, 38, decided to have a child. Now, instead of indulging himself with custom-made golf clubs and other accoutrements of middle age, Sonnenschein is helping 6-year-old Annie learn to ride her bike.

"If you'd asked me 20 years ago, I'd have told you that I wanted to retire at 50. But having another child, there's no doubt that I won't retire until she's through college," he says. "Finance is the key issue that determines whether you bring children into the world. I didn't really think about finances ahead of time, perhaps as much as I should have." He sighs. "I love teaching, and I have no desire to retire. On the other hand, sometimes I think, 'God, those hippie days were nice.'"

Parenting's a long haul for everyone, but some men have considerably lengthened their course. Men who raise one family, then remarry and go on to raise another with a new set of biological children, are starting over in more ways than one. They have to adjust to their new wife's expectations for how they'll share the parenting load. They have to explain to their older kids that they're not being abandoned, even if it looks as though that's precisely what's happening. And, as Sonnenschein knows all too well, they start coming to grips with the fact that they've just taken on a 21-year commitment that completely alters their future.

Hitting the Rewind Button

Celebrities like singer Julio Iglesias, 55, the father of three twentysomethings who has just welcomed his second child by current wife Miranda Rijnsburger, 33, can afford to have proof of their virility running around the living room in diapers. Reality is a little more sobering for most older second-time dads, say sociologists who have studied relationships among divorced fathers and their children. After all, they have not one, but two very diverse sets of children who have dramatically different financial and emotional needs. It's a touchy balancing act.

It's difficult to pin down exactly how many men are taking on this particular version of midlife crisis. For sure, the total pool of second-generation dads isn't all that big . . . yet. By definition, a man's second marriage that produces biological children must be to a woman of childbearing age. Excepting the occasional petri-dish mix of donated ovum and mechanically added sperm, that means those fertile second wives are most likely ages 25 to 44. According to the March 1998 Census Bureau tally of married couples, 25.6 percent of White men ages 45 to 59 are married to women ages 25 to 44; 33.2 percent of Black men are in the same situation, as are 31.7 percent of Hispanic men. But does this mean that there are a lot of old guys hooking up with the younger gals? Again, not yet. Only 1.8 percent of all men ages 45 to 59 are married to women between 25 and 34.

The Census Bureau, however, doesn't report on how many of those are second marriages and then how many children those married men have by their first and second wives. Ascertaining those numbers would mean surveying a population not only about their current family situations but also about preexisting biological children and prior wives.

There is evidence, however, based on other federal statistics, that the population of older, second-generation dads is growing. The percentage of marriages, for example, between never-married women and divorced men increased between 1970 and 1990, the latest data available from the National Center for Health Statistics, up from 6.9 percent to 10.9 percent. At the same time, the number of men remarrying in their forties and fifties also edged upward: In 1990, 10.5 percent of men ages 45 to 49 and 6.5 percent of men ages 50 to 54 had returned to the altar, up from 7.4 percent and 5.2 percent, respectively, in 1980. Not surprisingly, birth rates tracked by the age of the father indicate that the ranks of older dads doing diaper duty are also growing.

Whose Dad Are You, Anyway?

While numerous reports have examined the emotional complications of stepparenting, few researchers have zeroed in on the equally convoluted relationships between fathers and two separate biological families. One who has is Elizabeth Cooksey, associate professor of sociology at Ohio State University in Columbus, who has discovered some intriguing clues about who these dads are. In "Parenting

SEX TRENDS

TIME TO SCHEDULE THAT TRIP TO TOKYO

The birth control pill finally went on sale in Japan—four decades after it appeared in the West. Japan was the only major industrialized nation not to have approved the standard low-dose contraceptive form of the drug.

from a Distance: Effects of Paternal Characteristics on Contact Between Non-residential Fathers and Their Children," published in the May 1998 issue of *Demography,* Cooksey and her coauthor, Harvard researcher Patricia Craig, analyzed data gathered between 1992 and 1994 by the National Survey of Families and Households.

They report that of the 474 fathers who were no longer living with their children, 39.5 percent had more than a high school education, 41.9 percent completed high school, 34.5 percent were currently married, and 25.7 percent had a (new) biological child currently residing in the household. Cooksey and Craig also report that fathers who have one biological family (children between the ages of zero and 17), then remarry and have another set of kids, are actually far less likely to spend time with their first biological children.

The arrival of a new baby may signal the beginning of the cooling of the relationship with the dad's first set of kids, Cooksey says. In sociologist-speak, "The biological children they fathered at an earlier time tend to be displaced." Curiously, the presence of stepchildren doesn't seem to alter the picture much. When a man's new household includes only stepchildren, he is just as inclined to spend time with his own biological children as if there were no children present in his new marriage. And when both new biological and stepchildren are present in the new household, the father's commitment to maintaining a relationship with his first set of kids falls somewhere in between the two scenarios.

Enough about You—What about Me?

Other factors play into a dad's tendency to stay in close contact with his first-generation family. The closer the kids live to him, for example, the more likely they are to see him. And the higher the father's education level, the more likely he is to maintain close relationships with these children. (Cooksey didn't track the impact of court-mandated visitation arrangements, which obviously dictate terms of the relationship for many dads.)

So, when the first kids complain that they were shoved aside when Junior II arrived on the scene, well, they're probably right. "It's when [a father] settles down in the relationship and has new children with the new partner that the crowding out happens," says Cooksey. "We don't know why he's not seeing the first kids—we don't know how old the kids were when the relationship split or the nature of the relationship with the first partner."

Whew! It's hard enough sorting out the relationships on paper, never mind in real life. One thing's for sure: Dads with two biological families are stretched in two different directions.

Stanford University economics professor Martin Carnoy, who remarried when he was 52 and now has a 7-year-old daughter, was taken aback when his adult son, David, had decidedly mixed feelings about the arrival of his new sister. "It takes a lot of money to raise a kid, and he's generous with us, but it can evoke a lot of jealousy," says David, a 34-year-old editor for etown.com, a consumer electronics Web site. "Usually the older parents, when they were raising the first kids, were working hard, and now they have more money. She certainly has more stuffed animals than I ever had." (David Carnoy was 14 when his parents divorced and 22 when his father remarried.)

Once Again, With Feeling

The Carnoys know as much as anyone about the "refathers," as they call them, because they coauthored what may be the only book on the topic: *Fathers of a Certain Age.* "Most men do this because they love their wives," says Martin Carnoy, who interviewed 30 men who were at least 40 when they had biological children. "Most men aren't choosing to do this because they discovered late in life a need to father." Nevertheless, he adds, "most of them find this experience really great and have more time to spend with the kids than they had before. I just met a guy who's 67 and on his third marriage, and the father of a 4-month-old."

As well, the dads' younger wives usually have quite different expectations for their family life than did the first wives. For one thing, they are usually working mothers, sociologists say, and fully expect their husbands to share equally with childrearing tasks. In addition, these working moms have their own money to indulge their craving for cute baby clothes, European strollers, and educational toys.

So in a very real sense, these refathers are often learning how to parent all over again. North Carolina State University sociology professor Barbara J. Risman, who has researched the changing patterns in American families, speculates that there's a "generational difference between the husbands and wives. The husbands may have to learn the new way of raising children," she says.

"Second-time dads feel that they used to be part of the old male model— you work, you support, you're the disciplinarian," says Rachel Geller, chief strategic officer for the Geppetto Group, a New York City marketing firm that specializes in children and teens. "They bonded with their sons more than their daughters. Now, they're grateful that they have a second chance, and that's not the same as the first. They're really patterning themselves after current models of fatherhood."

Out with the Old, In with the New?

Meanwhile, the first brood observes this largesse with a jaundiced eye. "One major source of conflict with the older kids is that all of a sudden, they're having to share what they thought was theirs," says Martin Carnoy. "The older children were expecting to get this and that, and it's getting divided yet another way."

Therein lies the prime irony of the two-family dads: The unexpected blessing of the second family is inevitably accompanied by reduced expectations on the part of the first. Dad may have more money to spend because his career is in full bloom, but unless he has a lot of money to burn, the younger set gets first dibs. Older kids may have assumed that they'd get help with college or the down payment on a house, but now they learn that they're on their own. Talk about stretched resources.

Dad and his second wife are probably both working, so they're expecting to spend like a typical two-earner household: eating out more frequently, indulging in a few more personal luxuries, lining up a cleaning service. But what doesn't show up on most research radar screens is that the dad may well have significant financial obligations to his first children, points out Robert Klopfer, director of Stepping Stones Counseling Center, a Ridgewood, New Jersey–based therapy center for stepfamilies. Klopfer, a social worker, frequently sees second-time-around families that don't have nearly as much money as they should have because the father is paying child support for his other children, who are probably living with their biological mother.

Of course, the combination of a prime-of-life father with a younger, working mom does mean that the dad probably has more resources at his immediate disposal than he did when he started his first family, particularly if he was then in his twenties. But wait a minute, says Klopfer. Things aren't as rich as they seem. Not only is Dad paying child support for his older kids, but they may be moving into the most expensive years of their lives: college. And most states allow colleges to count the income of the biological parents and their mates (up to four wage earners) toward payment of tuition. (California has recently passed a law that allows stepmothers to exempt their income from the familial pool, for college tuition purposes, a campaign led by second wives' advocacy groups.)

What—Am I Made of Money?

Even in families with plenty of material resources and amicable relations among all the parents and stepparents, the first family can feel disenfranchised. New Jersey executive recruiter Richard Barkauskas first wed at age 21 and has two sons, ages 29 and 26, and a grandson from that marriage. He's also dad to a second family—a son, 16, and a daughter, 15. Though Barkauskas and his second wife have made their Vermont home constantly available to the two older children, invite them along on overseas vacations, and recently gave one a substantial sum toward a house down payment, the issue of Barkauskas' will is still a sore point. Currently, his affairs are arranged so that if he and his wife die, the two younger children will each get more than the two older ones, who also stand to inherit from their biological mother.

"As the [younger] kids move on toward grad school, then the plan changes. But right now, the younger ones are in a much more vulnerable position. The older boys aren't thrilled about it," admits Barkauskas, adding that he is sticking to what he believes is a fair division of assets.

Tensions erupt over how dads divide their time among the two families as well. "If the father is in his midforties or older, frequently he has made it already [careerwise]," observes Klopfer. "He has more time for all the kids, where he can go to the ball games or dance recitals . . . and the first-family kids can benefit from that, if they're local. If they're a long way off, there's frequently jealousy." The sentiment of the first children, he says, is, "He's giving a lot more to those kids than he gave to us."

With the paternal resources so picked over, what's left for marketers? Financial and estate planning and legal work are logical categories; given the knotty relationships they're locked into, it's hard to imagine how older second-time dads couldn't use some expert help in sorting out their wills and investments. Life insurance, too—lots and lots of life insurance.

It's a Thin Line between Young and Old

Because they straddle two life stages that are usually mutually exclusive—parenting young children and nearing retirement—these dads are likely to choose a bit from both. Berkeley professor Sonnenschein says he's not willing to give up his aspiration to travel frequently; he just brings his wife and young daughter along. Martin Carnoy is teaching his daughter how to ski, though he also notes that a common complaint among his circle of older dads is that they don't have many

SEX TRENDS

MARRIAGE, SCHMARRIAGE

Living together without the formality of getting hitched is now the norm in the United States, according to a University of Michigan study. Cohabitation increased from 10 percent of all households in 1965 to more than 50 percent in 1998, reported *USA Today.*

relatives up to the task of babysitting. "My adult kids? No way. They're into their own things," he says.

Fortunately, as the older kids mature, the big blended family does get a bit happier. After all, says David Carnoy, "It's hard not to like the kids. It's not their fault."

SEX WARS

"We've been married a long time in Hollywood years."

HELP ONLINE

WHO'S DOING WHO?

The latest, hottest gossip of the *National Enquirer* variety delivered free by, of course, the *National Enquirer.* Subscribe to the "Insider News" newsletter on the Enquirer Online site, and while there you can peruse top stories with headlines like "Madonna Didn't Shave Her Armpits" and "Willie Nelson's Wife Stole My Wife" and so on. You get the story but no juicy pictures. For that, you've gotta buy the rag.

www.nationalenquirer.com

UP WITH PEOPLE

The online version of *People* magazine offers daily reports and a 5-year archive of issues of the magazine—the stories, the pictures, plus online reader chat about stories, and even some video.

www.people.com

WEBCAM WORLD

Webcams are, of course, those little video eyes that people connect to their computers. Suddenly, the world can peek into their twisted lives and fascinations and whatever else they think is ready for prime time. Sign up for the Webcam World Web ring, and you can—*click, click*— jump all over the world, with video images (and sometimes sound) from great theater companies videocasting live to an updated snapshot every 30 minutes of a resplendent quetzal incubating and hatching an egg live high in a Costa Rican rain forest to—*click, click*—Cathouse Catcam, where you "watch cats sleeping live on camera" (sorry). It's a wild world out there, pal—no telling what you'll see next.

Http://webring.webcamworld.com/tryit.html

MAN'S GUIDE INTERVIEW

Must-Lust TV: The Bottom's Dropped

An Interview with *Chicago Tribune* TV Critic Steve Johnson

Now we've done it. Beauty pageants and dating shows individually weren't enough. We actually combined the two concepts, more or less, with Who Wants to Marry a Multimillionaire? *A bunch of woman competing on television over a moneyed guy they had never met.*

Certainly a low point in TV history. But wait, there's more . . .

Shows like The Dating Game *and* Love Connection *didn't go far enough, apparently, because now we have* Blind Date, *a show that televises actual dates—and makes snide comments about the participants.*

The talk shows weren't sufficient for our dysfunctional-relationship needs, so someone created Change of Heart, *which sends a man and a woman with relationship problems on separate dates. Then the dysfunctional couple, accompanied by the dates, comes to the show to talk about the experience, rag on each other, and decide on the air whether to continue the original relationship.*

And MTV, the channel that used to have music videos, offers us Loveline, *which attempts to handle sexual and interpersonal problems over the phone with a team that consists of a smart-aleck, a physician, a female sidekick, and guest stars from the worlds of television and music.*

And that's just the tip of the iceberg. Looking for insight, we turned to Chicago Tribune *TV critic Steve Johnson. We figured that working in the third-largest media market in the country gave him clout, while his midwestern roots might put him more in tune with the general population than critics influenced by constant exposure to Los Angeles or New York City.*

MAN'S GUIDE: First of all, because it was so high-profile and so controversial for a one-episode show, let's talk a little about *Who Wants to Marry a Multimillionaire?* Why was this concept so wildly popular to begin with?

JOHNSON: Essentially, it was train-wreck television. It was the kind of thing that many people came across as they were flipping through channels. And once you landed on that show, you'd just sort of sit there, open-mouthed and staring, saying to yourself, "I can't believe what I'm actually seeing here."

It was absolutely unbelievable to the viewers that people were going through with this process of competing for a husband on TV. So a lot of people stumbled across the show who weren't actually seeking it out. And the show continued to gain viewers in droves the longer it was on. It just kept sucking in people who were stunned by the spectacle of it all.

MAN'S GUIDE: Is this the *Jerry Springer* phenomenon? We watch the program because deep down we really want to, but then later we have to save face by reviling the show?

JOHNSON: I think there's a whole lot of that phenomenon going on. But I want to go on record as saying that I was appalled at the concept from the very start.

MAN'S GUIDE: We're with you there.

JOHNSON: Still, I did like the comment made by my colleague Barbara Broadman, who wrote a column about the program. As she put it, more or less, "If these people are willing to debase themselves for my entertainment, I'm willing to be entertained."

MAN'S GUIDE: Yeah, but it seemed kind of disgusting to parade a bunch of women out to fight over an unknown millionaire, the prize being what amounts to a shotgun wedding without having a bun in the oven.

JOHNSON: And without the angry father-in-law. But that pretty much hits the nail on the head.

MAN'S GUIDE: So are we just prudes, the two of us, being offended by this televised gold-digging—or bride-buying, depending on your perspective? Or should we just be disgusted with the stupidity and mediocrity that spawned the show to begin with?

JOHNSON: I think at heart, most people were offended at the whole concept. I think most people who watch *Springer,* for example, are watching in part because they're offended. Those shows always come down pretty firmly on the side of conventional morality. It's the two-timer whom the crowd boos. It's the person who behaves in a more virtuous manner who gets the support of the crowd.

So I think even if people enjoyed the marry-a-rich-guy show, they were not necessarily endorsing the concept. I guess the question is, where do we go from here? Will we end up with more of these kinds of things on the air?

MAN'S GUIDE: What's your prediction?

JOHNSON: Well, the show had 31 million viewers. So I think we'll see something very similar, very soon. FOX has sworn off the concept of *Who Wants to Marry a Multimillionaire?*—but I'll believe that when I don't see it.

But even if FOX doesn't return to this concept, there are enough television networks out there these days that someone else is going to pick up that rather tainted ball and run with it. I mean, you have dozens of cable channels out there, all of which would love nothing more than to cut through the clutter and get people like me writing about them. And one sure way to do that is to make a show called something like *Who* Else *Wants to Marry a Multimillionaire?*

MAN'S GUIDE: Let's take a little different tack here. What about something like *Change of Heart,* where a couple of folks agree to date outside their relationship with some cookie-cutter southern California types handpicked by the show's producers—and then they go on the air to talk trash about each other? Or what about any number of daytime talk shows, in which people publicly air the kind of dirty laundry most folks would hesitate to share with their closest friends?

JOHNSON: I think what those shows really tell us is that you don't need a lot of viewers to mount a viable program. There are a whole lot of channels out there. Besides, we are in a period where we are just declining, I think. I don't want to say declining morally because that seems too harsh. But our standards of what is acceptable have certainly been slipping several notches.

All the trends on TV point toward voyeurism and more voyeurism, so I suspect we'll only see more and more of these kinds of shows. *Who Wants to Marry a Multimillionaire?* will only be the tip of the iceberg. Five years from now, we may be looking back and saying, "Wow, wasn't that a sweet kind of show?"

MAN'S GUIDE: We've touched on marrying for money on TV. We've talked about game-show adultery with *Change of Heart*. We've talked about getting your 15 minutes of fame by embarrassing yourself and your family on any number of TV talk shows.

JOHNSON: What could possibly be left to talk about?

> " It took something like this to make the Miss America Pageant look good to me. "
>
> —Patricia Ireland, president of the National Organization for Women, referring to the would-be brides on parade during the FOX network special *Who Wants to Marry a Multimillionaire?*

MAN'S GUIDE: What is bringing on this recent spate of male-oriented programs like *The Man Show*?

JOHNSON: That's a good question. I think it's partly this notion of serving just a small chunk of the overall TV-viewing audience. It's also part of something in the air culturally right now. We're seeing the same kind of male-oriented material on the newsstands with a lot of the new men's magazines right now, like *Maxim* and *FHM* and all the other panting-but-not-quite-pornographic magazines. Obviously, there's some pent-up male thing happening here. You might even put the popularity of the WWF and the other wrestling shows into this same kind of realm. It's all a similar breed of numb, macho posturing.

MAN'S GUIDE: Is it a good thing that men have shows about beer, belching, bikini-clad women, and all those other guy things? After all, it seems like women have been bashing men at least as much, if not more so, in our more politically correct present than they ever have in the past.

JOHNSON: I suppose there's something to that—a televised outlet for your urges and a place to be a guy. It's a lot better to get it out

> **"** I don't like any female comedians. . . . A woman doing comedy doesn't offend me, but sets me back a bit. . . . I think of her as a producing machine that brings babies into the world. **"**
>
> —Comedian Jerry Lewis, quoted in *Newsweek*, from the U.S. Comedy Arts Festival in Aspen, Colorado, where he was the subject of a tribute that followed awards given to female comedians

while watching *The X Show* or *The Man Show* than to actually go out to a bar and act up. Which is something I suspect that 80 percent of the guys who watch those shows would never dare do in real life.

If most of them were confronted with scantily clad attractive women bouncing on trampolines, like you see in *The Man Show,* they would just be like little boys—they'd be puppies with their tails between their legs.

MAN'S GUIDE: My feeling, though, is that it goes beyond the theory of "I can watch TV and get the 'bar experience' without getting in trouble with my girl by going out to the bar." I think it's a little bit of a backlash.

In fact, I suspect that many of these male viewers are smarter than we give them credit for. Aren't they kind of having fun with their own stereotypes? I mean, if the women are going to dog us about them anyway, shouldn't we make light of our stereotypes and enjoy the situation as much as we can?

JOHNSON: In some ways, it's an extension of the stuff that comedians have been doing for decades, pointing out the differences between men and women. Except that instead of merely talking about the differences, as comedians do, you get the actual physical representation in the form of guzzling beer or showing big-breasted, bikini-clad women bouncing on trampolines.

It's totally gratuitous, but I have to admit that I actually don't hate that show. There is a level at which it really is smart. It not only pokes fun at guy things but also pokes fun at itself. It's winking at the whole concept even while it is reveling in it.

Some of the other shows, however, I cannot give that kind of credit. *The X Show* is an example of a show that isn't nearly as smart and is much more offensive.

MAN'S GUIDE: Still, it seems like there's an awful lot of crap out there. What does this decline in standards mean for us as a society? What does it say about our evolutionary direction?

> **JOHNSON:** Are you talking about the decline of the culture? Something like the collapse of the Roman Empire?

MAN'S GUIDE: Kind of. Are we giving media too much credit for undermining us?

> **JOHNSON:** Yeah, I think you might be. I think that when people decide, "Hey, I have to pull a hood over my head and run away"—I think that they end up giving television a little too much credit.
>
> There are so many other influences in our lives and in our kids' lives. And chief among those influences are parents and friends. So I don't think we can presume that just because there's a whole new kind of area of discussion on TV—however seedy it may be—that we're necessarily going to create a generation of morons.
>
> And the truth is that American TV is one of the last places that has held out against running a lot of the really obnoxious programming. Other countries are far more advanced than us at exploiting people. There is a desperate willingness among people to be on television and to do stupid and embarrassing things on TV.
>
> I think that as we get more cable channels and as we get more convergence between the Internet and television, there is just going to be more and more outrageous and tasteless programming. The fact is, with the increasing number of channel choices, you have to be that much more outrageous to grab an audience.
>
> Nowadays, you don't have to worry about achieving a general level of taste as you did in the 1960s and 1970s, when there were essentially three networks. Because now you're never going to get 30 percent of the audience on any given day. You only have to amuse 10 percent of the people on the networks now, and maybe 1 or 2 percent on most of the cable channels.

MAN'S GUIDE: Well, you review television for a living. Why don't you tell us what the best of the worst has been recently? What's the cream of the crap?

JOHNSON: Well, the FOX Network has been a horrible offender. But what's kind of funny is that FOX has a split personality. On the one hand, the network does *The Simpsons,* which is as smart as anything that's ever been on television. And FOX does *Ally McBeal,* which I think is a very smart show that takes a lot of chances in exploring the territory of modern sexual relationships.

On the other hand, FOX runs all of these gruesome reality specials, showing us animals attacking humans and things like that. And they give us *Who Wants to Marry a Multimillionaire?* They even showed Robbie Kneivel jumping from building to building while his wife and kids watched live—just so that we'd be able to see their horrified reactions if he crashed and died.

So I would have to rate FOX as the worst offender. But I also have to point out that NBC is pretty embarrassing in terms of its heavy reliance on sexual context. Too many of their shows are driven by pointless and heavy-handed sexual situations.

There is some good stuff. *Friends* is a very sexual show, but it's done cleverly. There is a huge gap between writing a sexual joke that has some flair, clever misdirection, and hints at sexual stuff, compared to one that tells the joke directly, bluntly, and blatantly—using shock value instead of cleverness or suggestion.

MAN'S GUIDE: Any signs of hope on the idiot box?

JOHNSON: The fact is, there is just a lot more TV now than ever before. So even if there is more of this outrageous, shocking material—and likely more to come—there is also more good television right now than there has ever been. Some people who study and review television have termed the current era as a kind of "second golden age" of television. And I tend to agree. With the proliferation of really smart shows out there, it's pretty hard to dismiss the whole medium.

And what is really encouraging is that if you look at the Top 20 in any given week, those shows tend to be the quality shows. The show *60 Minutes,* for one, basically has been a Top 10 show forever, and it's a terrific program. *ER* is a very well done, highly rated program. *Friends* and *Frasier* are popular, and they are excellent, smart, sharp comedies. *Law and Order* does well and is worth watching. And there are a lot of others, including *Ally McBeal* and *The Simpsons.*

If you are selective about what you watch, this is really a great time to be watching TV. There's more good, free entertainment out there than we've ever had before.

MAN'S GUIDE: As long as we're talking about the wide range of television offerings on broadcast and cable TV, what about gender niches? We've had Lifetime for a while now on cable, which targets a female audience, and now we have another woman-oriented channel on cable called Oxygen. How long before we get some male equivalent? Do you think that will ever happen— or do we already have that in channels like USA Network and FOX?

JOHNSON: Don't forget Spice and the other sex networks on cable.

MAN'S GUIDE: Yes, but those are pay-per-view—and they can get pretty expensive. I was thinking more along the lines of readily accessible stuff that comes to your television free—or at least comes with your basic cable subscription.

JOHNSON: That's true. Spice does cost extra. Well, ESPN is certainly a male-oriented channel.

MAN'S GUIDE: Well, I guess with men's fascination over sports, a case could be made that ESPN is our flagship men's channel . . .

JOHNSON: And then you have ESPN Classic and other sports networks. But I know what you're getting at—a general interest male channel. It probably won't happen.

For one thing, women are more clearly identifiable as a niche group to which you can market programming and products. They come across as a more cohesive group in terms of their interests and concerns compared to men. You'll probably never see a channel that is the flip side of Lifetime, something that blatantly advertises itself as "Television for Men."

QUICKIES

THE BEST, WORST, AND MOST DEEPLY DISTURBING

In what may be the best news we've heard all year, researchers report that women who have had breast implants tend to be more promiscuous and drink more alcohol. But in an investigative debacle of immense proportions, the scientists did not get their phone numbers. This steamy nugget of groundbreaking science is just one of many news stories that the *Man's Guide* staff has double-checked for reliability over the course of the year.

● Dutch gynecologists have found that women who frequently performed oral sex on their partners had about a 50 percent lower risk of developing preeclampsia, a potentially fatal disease. Researchers suggest that sperm may help build immunity to the condition.

● A recent finding from the eighth World Meeting on Impotence Research: "The woman who conveys an attitude of disgust and repugnance for the male genitals or for sex in general may dramatically affect her partner's sexual performance."

● A Florida man sued the stripper Tawny Peaks and the club at which she disrobed, seeking $15,000 for bodily injury after Tawny slammed her 69HH breasts into his head. The case was tossed after a court-appointed expert found her breasts too soft to cause injury.

● Members of the Australian women's national soccer team bared their "down-unders" for a year 2000 fully nude calendar. The team expects to net $1 million in royalties and double their yearly attendance at games. Warren Fisher, chief executive officer of the Australian Women's Soccer League, said that the team agreed to the calendar to "promote the image of the sport as being powerful yet graceful; modern yet timeless. In other words, feminine."

● In Pikeville, Kentucky, all hired escorts are now required to wear a sign that reads "escort." The sign must be visible at all times.

● Mary Frost, a 33-year-old Kansas City woman who stabbed 77-year-old Oscar Fingers to death with a kitchen knife, pleaded innocent by reason of Viagra. Seems that her "housemate," while in the throes of the erection-causing medication, asked her politely for sex, then begged her on his hands and knees. When that tactic failed, he got more "forceful." Frost testified that she first lobbed a ceramic rooster at him, then "stuck him" with a steak knife. The jury convicted her of third-degree murder.

● The Philadelphia Museum of Art featured 100 photographs of men's feet taken during orgasm.

● Alex Comfort, author of *The Joy of Sex* and the man who made it possible for millions of teenagers to get wildly horny by looking at line drawings of naked people, died at age 80. Comfort, who was also an anarchist, nuclear disarmament protester, and author of 50 books, once said, "Before my book [*The Joy of Sex*], any writing about sex gave the impression that it was written by nonplaying coaches."

● According to the USDA Livestock Behavior Research Unit at Purdue University in West Lafayette, Indiana, earlier castration reduces stress.

● In a study published in *Nature,* male faces with feminine features were found to be more attractive than more masculine mugs—by both sexes. Theoretically, the Leonardo DiCaprios of the world get more sex than rough-looking dudes like us.

● Add this job to the list of careers you only dreamed about in high school: Utah governor Michael Leavitt signed a law creating the position of "porn czar," whose responsibility it will be to restrict (or eliminate) the amount of naked flesh being seen by state residents, 70 percent of whom belong to the Mormon Church.

● Manatee County, Florida, made it illegal for women to expose 75 percent of their breasts or 66 percent of their butts in public. In an effort to shut down strip clubs, county officials have set the penalty for baring flesh at up to 60 days in jail. Dave Bristow, a spokesman for the Manatee County sheriff's department, admits that he doesn't yet know how the police will estimate exposure. We suggest a hands-on approach.

● A Georgia mother filed an obscenity complaint against Toys "R" Us. Seems the talking Austin Powers doll that her 11-year-old son was playing with had quite a mouth on him. In addition to "Would you fancy a shag?" the doll inquired, "Do I make you horny, baby? Do I?"

DEAR DR. MANLY

Q: *All I read about anymore is AIDS. <u>Are there any new sexually transmitted diseases I should be worrying about, too?</u>*
—T. M., Phoenix

A: New ones? The old ones are bad enough. Remember syphilis? It's an old friend that's taking its show on the road. Interstate 95, to be exact. Researchers at the University of North Carolina found that syphilis rates were almost double in counties that I-95 ran through, compared with non-I-95 counties. Lesson: Take the back roads.

Still, there is at least one new STD running about, and it can really bring you to your knees. According to *New Scientist* magazine, a disease called SARA (Sexually Acquired Reactive Arthritis), also known as Reiter's syndrome, has been targeting, among others, soccer players in England. SARA is most commonly seen in athletes and entertainers— meaning men who get laid a lot. (I've told the guys here at *Man's Guide* that they have nothing to worry about.) The disease often resembles a knee injury and can inflame the sacroiliac and the vertebrae in the spinal column, creating back pain. It can wreak havoc with the eyes, bring on prostatitis, and cause skin lesions and even serious heart problems, all of that triggered by the same sexually transmitted bacteria that cause nonspecific urethritis, an inflammation of the urethra. The most common bacteria responsible for Reiter's is *Chlamydia trachomatis,* and the Reiter's symptoms may appear within 3 weeks of a chlamydia infection. When chlamydia triggers the disease, prolonged antibiotic therapy is effective in lessening symptoms. Reiter's is difficult to diagnose because there is no specific test for it.

Treatment involves several medical specialties, including ophthalmology, urology, dermatology, and orthopedics. Most men who contact Reiter's recover from the initial flare-up of symptoms and can return to normal activities within 2 to 6 months. About 20 percent of people develop chronic arthritis, and up to 50 percent will experience recurring symptoms such as arthritis and back pain. In a small percentage, the disease is crippling.

Reiter's is not contagious, but the infective agents responsible for it (such as chlamydia) are, so you need to clear the original infection before engaging in unprotected sex with your partner.

Q: *My girlfriend is after me to share my sexual fantasies, but I'm nervous. Hers run more toward chaste "splendor in the grass" sort of images, while mine tend to feature handcuffs, matadors, police uniforms, and* Xena: Warrior Princess. *What's a naughty guy like me to tell such a nice girl like her?*

—L. L., RACINE, WISCONSIN

A: Your girlfriend may well be giving you a rated-PG version of her own wild desires. Most people's erotic reveries aren't always what Mom would refer to as appropriate, according to a study by Cheryl Renaud, Ph.D., a psychology professor at the University of New Brunswick in Canada. "We found that many men and women have had thoughts of doing things that, if they actually did them, would be illegal," she said.

Dr. Renaud gave students a hit list of nearly 60 different sexual actions—kissing an authority figure, spanking someone, making love somewhere besides the bedroom—and asked how many of the students had ever thought about each situation. "Everybody had positive sexual thoughts, and 97 percent admitted to negative sexual thoughts," said coauthor Sandra Byers, another psychologist at the University.

Most surprising finding: More than 45 percent of both sexes said that they had fantasies about either seducing an "innocent" or being seduced as an "innocent," the definition of which was left to respondents. Least surprising: Men were twice as likely as women to fantasize about partner swapping, spanking someone, or forcing another adult to engage in a sexual act.

The upshot? Confess your unique visions. Start out mild (with making love on the kitchen table or, depending upon what's "mild" in your world, *while* making love on the table) and work toward wild (making love on the kitchen table while wearing the coyote mask), judging her reactions along the way.

Dr. Manly is a fictional character.
The actual advice was provided by a variety of
medical doctors and other qualified experts.

7

SIDESTEP
THE SEX POLICE

 *If it has to do with sex, you can bet there's either a law or an organi-
zation dedicated to ending, altering, sanitizing, or regulating it. Take
Poland and Utah. Both places banned pornography in prisons last
year and are considering banning T&A altogether. And with the Olympics coming
to Salt Lake City in 2002, the Utah government has been cracking down on its
dwindling population of polygamists—men brave, stalwart, and crazy enough to
marry more than one woman.*

*From workplace dating to cheating spouses, from your secret crushes (and
what they mean) to the best advice for keeping five wives happy at once, if the sex
police are after it, you'll find it here.*

Husbands' Rights

The government fiercely protects the rights of owls, salmon, and stranded Cuban children, which is precisely why our man Brian Alexander believes that Uncle Sam should enact these 10 laws to protect the rights of husbands, a much larger voting bloc.

1. Any store selling women's clothing must provide a "husband chair," which shall be positioned within close range of the dressing rooms. This will enable Married Guys to sit down between outfit viewings, rather than having to lean on a rack of 34C smooth-cup underwires. Stores reporting more than $1 million profits must also include an end table and recent issues of *The Sporting News*.

2. The knee-length and ankle-length flannel nightgown shall be outlawed nationwide. Collection centers shall be established at all post offices and Clinique cosmetic counters, and wives shall be awarded "lingerie stamps" to subsidize any replacement garments purchased at Victoria's Secret.

3. Husbands shall receive two free sessions with a personal trainer each month to combat the public health menace known as PMGWG (Pernicious Married Guy Weight Gain). To encourage sports participation, Married Guys shall receive their choice of (a) a three-stroke bonus on every round of golf; (b) an extra "H" for every game of HORSE; or (c) four strikes and five balls for every game of softball.

4. A public education campaign shall instruct wives to say, "Honey, I think you'd be great at that!" when a husband argues—after a

frustrating workday or too much ESPN2—that he's been thinking of giving up the practice of law to pursue a career as a professional NASCAR driver, circus juggler, or rodeo clown. (Note: Because there is the proverbial snowball's chance in hell of such a career change actually occurring, women have little to fear. Such statements shall be construed merely as "venting.")

5 Hollywood shall assign a new movie rating—HWA (Husband Wariness Advised)—to any film labeled by critics as "the feel-good movie of the year" and to all movies starring Antonio Banderas, Julia Roberts, or Hugh Grant.

6 A not-guilty plea of self-defense shall automatically be accepted for any Married Guy who delivers a physical reprimand to that beer-swilling, back-slapping brother-in-law who, at the family get-together, shouts, "Hey, big guy! How they hangin'?"

7 Failure to kiss his wife for any period shorter than 24 hours shall not be interpreted as a slur on her attractiveness or a sign of impending divorce.

8 Any Single Guy driving a Porsche, Jaguar, BMW, or V-twin motorcycle who is seen sniggering at a Married Guy in a minivan shall have his license suspended immediately.

9 A friendly guy named Gus, Hank, or Jimbo shall be assigned to each newly Married Guy for a period of 6 months after the wedding date to patiently explain such intricacies as leaky-faucet repair, ceiling fan installation, gas grill assembly, and cockroach eradication.

10 Single women will be fined $50 if caught staring at our ring fingers and then smiling patronizingly, as if we were cute little old men in Miami Beach. The Ad Council shall broadcast public service announcements reminding single women that Single Guys are, by definition, emotionally stunted and unfulfilled, while Married Guys, though unavailable, are by definition more highly evolved and irrefutably sexy.

MUST READS

Keep Your Wives Happy

Think one woman is all you can handle? Try living with five, each of them half your age. Add 25 young children and just a pinch of money. Now put yourself in the middle of the desert, with no other men around for miles. Throw in the scorn of an entire religion and a state that's trying to drive you out before the Olympics come to town. Stir, bake, cool. When you're finished, you'll have a pretty good description of Tom Green's life, as author Tom Zoellner reveals.

Most of us have a hard time keeping one woman satisfied. So what does polygamist Tom Green know that we don't? He is a practicing polygamist, one of an estimated 30,000 in North America. Polygamists believe that a man's fidelity, affections, and seed are all too precious to be the exclusive property of one woman. The Green family lives out this doctrine in a cluster of house trailers on a ranch in the Utah desert, almost 60 miles from the nearest paved road.

It's not a life for the timid or the weak. In fact, do not try this at home. It can be a living domestic hell for everyone in the family portrait. Some folks think that modern polygamists are on the same plane as Charlie Manson, minus the murder and mayhem; but even on a less extreme level, it's just too complicated for most men. It's complicated in terms of morality, obviously, but it's also complicated in terms of logistics. You have the crowds, plus you have the jealousy. It's one thing to spend Saturday night playing poker over at your pal's apartment. But it's another to spend Saturday night having rowdy carnal relations with your wife's sister while your wife sits quietly next door tending your children. And to smile at both women over breakfast the next morning. No wonder Brigham Young, that diehard patrician with his intermountain empire and his 27 wives, said that polygamy could "send thousands to hell."

Green may not count himself as damned, but he's one tapped-out hombre. He has now spent more years married than he has spent breathing. He has been with Linda 12 years, LeeAnn 9, Hannah and Cari 7 each, and Shirley 13. Count 13 years of monogamy with his first wife (a traditional Mormon girl who divorced him when he "turned polyg") and 10 apiece with two plural wives who are no longer part of what Green calls his "management team," and you have a 50-year-old man united in matrimony for 81 years.

By the Numbers

Lots of men can't figure out a girlfriend, let alone a wife, let alone a pack of wives. Sitting there in an embarrassingly small living room with a bunch of good-looking young women and their husband, one might reasonably think that maybe this guy, no matter how anyone feels about his lifestyle, has learned a thing or two about a marriage or two. Here are the marital secrets of a polygamist.

● Don't mix them up.

Green loves each woman for different things. Shirley has an urbane wit, for instance. Hannah is demure and thoughtful. LeeAnn has beautiful hair. Add Green to any of these and you don't get Tom-plus-wife, you get a whole new couple. "I'm a different husband with each of them," he says. "Each one of them has different demands. I'm like oxygen, okay? I mean, for example, if Cari is hydrogen and we get together, then we become water."

● Make choosing easy.

Green never wakes up disoriented in an unfamiliar bedroom, wondering whose house he was in last night. Nor does he prowl the hallways playing eenie-meenie-mynie-moe when the lights go out. Sex scheduling is not his department. The women decide among themselves who will come to his bed on any particular night. It could be anybody.

"It's like, 'Well, *you* haven't been with him for a while,'" Linda explains. "'Why don't you take him tonight?'" The only disorientation comes when he slips his arm around somebody in the dark without knowing who it is. He thinks of it as his nightly surprise.

perfect figures

Percentage of currently married men who have had an extramarital affair: 4.8. (For women, it's 2.2.)

Percentage of now-divorced men who had an affair: 21.3. (For women, it's 12.5.)

● Make her do all the work.

Once a wife is chosen to spend the night with Green, the problems become more familiar: For example, who makes the first move? "I never initiate intimacies," he says. He quotes Genesis 3:16, in which God says to Eve, "Your desire shall be for your husband." He interprets that to mean that the man's role is not to chase but to be chased. "If a man pursues the woman, then she has all the power," he says. "If a monogamous man had the intestinal fortitude to wait for it, he'd have a much happier marriage." That's easy for Green to say, of course. He has to wait all of 24 hours before another wife shows up in his bed.

● Schedule your duties.

At age 50, Green can't quite keep up with his twentysomething wives, even when he works into the wee hours. So he often sets his alarm an hour early, to do in

perfect figures

Number of embryos created from in vitro fertilization that are currently in storage: 100,000

Number of frozen embryos awaiting resolution of disputes, usually the divorce of the parents: 20,000

• • • • • • • • •

the morning what he was too tired to do the night before. "Never in all my adolescent fantasies did I dream of this," he muses.

❍ Consult a higher authority.
Old-time Mormon theology holds that adding another wife to your family is a God-given right. The multiwived Mormon prophet Joseph Smith believed this so strongly that he approached one Mary Elizabeth Rollins in 1842 and told her he had received a divine command to marry her. In fact, he said, an angel had drawn a long sword and threatened to behead him if he didn't marry her.

These days, if you want to get exponentially hitched, you don't have to be touched by an angel. You just ask permission from a "living prophet" of one of Utah's secret polygamist churches, who will sign off only if he is sure that you're not having, as they say, "a revelation in the pants." If the official Church of Jesus Christ of Latter-Day Saints finds out that you're a mister with more than one missus, though, you're out of there.

❍ Make God your management consultant.
Green is not a practicing Mormon. He never consulted a "living prophet" either. Nonetheless, the Lord spoke to him one day and gave him the secret to a happy household—not in the language of *shalts* and *begats,* but in a catchy, alliterative formula that would look good on an overhead projector in a corporate boardroom. The secret is the four Cs: communication, coordination, cooperation, and compromise. This came to him as he argued with a wife long-distance from a telephone booth outside a bowling alley in Barstow, California.

"The words just came into my mind, just like with the Bee Gees when they compose their songs. They wake up with the tune in their minds." The four Cs are now posted on the kitchen cabinet.

❍ Bend the rules.
Green has an affection for divorcées. In fact, he circumvented the state's bigamy laws by legally marrying each woman and then divorcing her to marry the next. In Utah, the legal age for marriage is 14. "I wish I could have gotten married sooner," says LeeAnn, who is now 23. "At 13, I would have been ready."

○ Make them wait.

Green made Shirley, LeeAnn's sister, wait until she was 15 before he married her. Really.

○ Decide who's boss.

Somebody has to be in charge of the ranch. When Green is around, it's him. When he's out of town, his viceroy is Linda, the wife with seniority (following polygamist tradition). But Green uses the wives' collective wisdom to help guide his ark of a family. "I'd be foolish not to use them as a resource," he says. "They have brains, in addition to being babes."

○ Share the labor.

They're not only babes, they're telemarketers. Green used to take his wives from city to city to help sell magazine subscriptions over the phone. (They had especially good luck selling to military wives.) But the Green family has stopped the traveling life now that the phone company plans to run a line up to the ranch. As far as day-to-day duties go, his wives are happily employed, one way or another.

○ Keep the kids in line.

Everybody, Green included, minds the children. A standing rule states that any mother can discipline any other mother's child.

○ Put the family first.

Nobody understands this better than the wives. "In a monogamous relationship, if a woman wants something, she'll throw a fit and pout until he gives in," says Linda, 26. "But in plural marriage, if a woman does that, she'll find herself alone." Indeed, a depressed wife tends to be ostracized not just by the husband but by the other wives as well. "It's like driving down the road with a flat tire," says Hannah.

○ Don't be a pushover.

Green makes it a point to pursue a Pattonesque paternalism toward his wives: He doesn't explain much, and he rarely apologizes. It works. "If I didn't have Tom, I'd be married to some yesman," says LeeAnn. "I'd rather have a little of a real man than all of a jerk." Her sister agrees. "None of us would want a man who is P-W," Shirley says.

hot **TIP!**

Go with instinct, Dad. Fear of criticism from their wives has led many fathers to mistrust their own parental instincts. So they don't toss their children as high, laugh as loud, or tickle them as wildly. The result is that fathers often give up their natural exuberance and vitality.

"What's P-W?" we ask.

Shirley smiles demurely.

● Share the romance.

When Green is trying to woo a new woman into the family, he'll often bring his other wives along on dates. The wives spend more time with one another than they do with him, anyway. "It's a package deal," says Linda. "If she marries him, she marries all of us."

● Eliminate performance anxiety.

Green is more than the head of the household; he's the entertainer-in-chief. He once piled the whole brood into a pair of vans for a trip to Disneyland—a journey that was in itself like a collision of "It's a Small World" and "Mr. Toad's Wild Ride." When they finally made it off the dirt roads and onto the asphalt, Green got out of the driver's seat and danced a little jig in the road while his wives just shook their heads. Why? Because nothing brightens a routine existence like an occasional surprise. "You have to do something a little dumb every now and then to keep them guessing."

What Your Secret Crushes Mean

She passes you in the hall without even glancing your way, but you know every single freckle on the back of her right hand. That's because come Monday you'll connive yet again to sit across from her in the weekly meeting. She's partial to silk shirts and silver jewelry. She doodles, bites her nails, and sucks the end of her pen. And, oh, those ruby red lips. . . . She's in your head like a tinny Top 40 tune, but should she be in your bed, too? Colin McEnroe, who delved into the tawdry world of the secret crush, helps you figure out whether to go big or stay at home.

My doctor was, for years, a woman. Wait—she was *always* a woman, but she was my doctor for years. She was blonde, cute, younger than me, foreign accent, first name Ingrid.

She had all the makings of a good crush, except for the part where she would say, "This is going to feel a little cold" and then do something unpleasant.

A woman who is surprising, inventive, who slips past your usual defenses—

that woman can be a crush object, but the guy has to have some control over the relationship. With Ingrid, I had no control, except for tensing certain muscles, and that never worked for very long.

Control. That's the whole deal with a secret crush, right? You're thinking about her in a certain way, and she doesn't know it. (If, while this is happening, you're wearing a Napoleon hat and peering through her window at 11:23 P.M., the control thing has kind of spilled over the lip of the crush container.)

The Two Types of Crush-Bearing Men

● The attached guy (AG)

If you are married (or something) but are still having crushes, you may be using them as a multivitamin to make up for deficiencies in your primary relationship. This does not mean that your primary relationship is undernourished. You may just need a little bit more zinc or riboflavin. Or you may be genuinely on the make. Only you know the truth, and maybe even you don't.

● The unattached guy (UG)

If you're unattached, you are free to have crushes without guilt, but the downside is that people will assign more meaning to your crushes. The Unattached Guy is like JFK in the first months of his presidency, when his staff watched his every move and jumped to conclusions. ("He shifted in his chair! He wants to invade Cuba!") If the Unattached Guy's crush is picked up by the social radar, everybody will expect him to launch missiles, even if the crush is really kind of a vague, daydreamy one.

The Eight You're After

But enough about you. What about her? Who's out there to have crushes on? And what do your choices say about you? You may be drawn to certain occupations.

● Waitresses

Movie paradigm: Helen Hunt in *As Good as It Gets.*

You lunch there a lot, alone. You sit at the counter. She brings you your favorite soup before you even ask for it. She has athletic legs; she wears cute tops. She takes care of you. The good ones treat their regulars like dance partners, adjusting the amount of chitchat and hovering to fit the customer.

Subtext: If you're sitting and she's standing, where are your eyes? At breast level. This is not a lecherous observation. Waitress fixations are about nurturing, nursing, suckling. A guy may take Thai cooking courses and pick out his own Le Creuset cookware, but some less-evolved giblet inside him is always a little sad that women have stopped feeding him.

● **Librarians**

Movie paradigm: What I'm about to describe happens in about 40 percent of all movies, TV shows, and even commercials.

Most guys who use libraries start thinking about using a librarian. Why? Because of the whole fantasy motif of the librarian unpinning her hair, taking off her glasses, letting her tightly buttoned jacket slip off her shoulders and . . .

Going Public: Is It Time to Confess Your Crush?

My friend Shelley (recognized internationally as a woman) says that men should confess their crushes, and do it early.

"Depending on the man," she says, "it can actually be a delightful thing to find out. It can really, really be a turn-on." Well, what else are women going to say? If you lay it on the table, that's information. It's helpful to them.

But it may not be in your best interest, especially if she gets a restraining order. That's why I've developed a more subtle strategy. I call it "making a mist."

Let us imagine that you have a crush on Melissa.

You're not sure what it means or how important it is. You're not sure how Melissa feels.

So you make a mist around Melissa: of good intentions, support, comfort. If she has car problems, job problems, existential doubts, open-heart surgery, an

Interpol jacket, you're there for her. Even if she has romantic problems with some other guy, you're there for her.

And this is very important: You're there for her with a pure heart! You're not secretly sabotaging her other relationship. You're totally committed to her happiness.

This will make you feel very good. It will even make you a better person. And it will cause Melissa to see you as a lifeline. The less needy and wanting you are, the better this whole thing will work.

Two things can happen.

❶ Someday, Melissa will be coming out of another relationship (or a nunnery or a coma or something), and you will be in a certain place in your life, and the two of you will suddenly see, in a bolt of clarity,

Whoo! Why does this image contain such power? Because librarians become symbols of repression starting around third grade, from the first time one of them goes "Shhhh!" at us. This motif is so ingrained that a fake fashion version of it has evolved. Consider the Nelle character on *Ally McBeal*, who pins up her hair and wears ugly librarian glasses to provoke the librarian sexual-transformation fantasy. (Superman is sort of a male version of this.)

Subtext: Librarians suggest a scenario in which we overthrow order and substitute sexual chaos. They also imply that intellect (books) and sexuality (unpinned hair) could somehow intertwine. That would be gratifying. Hell, either one would be gratifying.

❍ Bank tellers

Movie paradigm: None that I'm aware of, but I have a project at FOX with Sandra Bullock written all over it.

The deal with bank tellers is that you get to look at them more than they get to look at you. She has to keep her eyes on what she's doing, so you can look at her—in a noncreepy way, we hope—without attracting too much notice from her or others around you. So bank tellers appeal to the mild voyeur in us.

Subtext: The fact that her nether regions are obscured is probably significant. Bank-teller crushes are kind of pregenital and therefore passive. A true Freudian would say that they're anal (the crushes) because money is a symbol for excrement. So the teller is symbolically inspecting and possibly emptying your diaper. Look how much you made! Look at your deposit!

This is very embarrassing, and now that I've really thought it through, I may start using ATMs.

that you are much, much more than supportive friends.

❷ Nothing of the sort will happen, in which case you will have a wonderful friendship for years, and how bad is that?

But, you ask, what if I am not capable of the selflessness implied by possibility number two? You don't have to be.

Because you are going to be making a mist around several other women at the same time. Perhaps even 8 or 10 women. Mist, mist, mist. This does not make you a Lothario, because what, after all, are we talking about? Being nice. With no particular expectations.

Making a mist, by the way, seems to work on all kinds of people. You can even try it on your wife.

That said, some crushes have less to do with an occupation and more to do with a general vibe.

● Miss Filthy Mouth

Movie paradigm: Bette Midler in almost any role.

A friend of mine has a crush on his hairdresser because she tells him filthy jokes and sticks her breasts in his face while she's lunging around to lop off his locks. (I used to have the same kind of relationship with Janet Reno, but that's a private thing.)

I've met that hairdresser. She's bawdy. She's not especially hot, nor is she on the make. She even has a picture of her two kids taped to the mirror. But I can see how you would look forward to seeing her if you needed to be reminded that sex is fun. My friend is, of all things, a sex therapist specializing in deviance. So his patients tend to be locked into unhappy, abusive relationships with their Cuisinarts. He might need a little reminding that sex can be a good giggle.

Subtext: If you're attracted to Miss Filthy Mouth—the woman with the dirty jokes and the lewd flirting—chances are that sex, in the main part of your life, has become burdened with baggage, complications, inhibitions, and disappointment, which pretty well describes all middle-aged married men, and almost everyone else to boot.

● The undervalued property

Movie paradigm: Jill Clayburgh in *Starting Over*.

You know Jill. She sits three cubicles down at work. She trains for marathons. Yesterday, you had some of her couscous, because last night's date wouldn't eat it, and she brought the Tupperware container in to share with the office staff. She's cute but not hot.

Actually, Jill doesn't date that often. She's so terrific, why can't she find a nice guy? She's funny, and she wears those cool outfits she gets for a steal on clearance. Boy, that was good couscous. Last week, she went to see *Life Is Beautiful* by herself. Can you beat that? I mean, she'd be so much fun to see a movie with, it's ridiculous she goes alone.

> **"** My fear [of Oprah] is not a personal fear; it's a fear for the nation. Oprah has a lot of power. If Oprah said, 'Ladies, enough is enough. It's time to start chopping off testicles,' I guarantee you'd be hearing them hit the floor like gumballs all over the country. **"**
> —Jimmy Kimmel, costar of *The Man Show* on Comedy Central

You go home and ask your wife or girlfriend, "Don't we know any guy who would be great for Jill?"

She may give you a wry smile and say, "Well, there's you."

Subtext: You have a crush on Jill.

There may be lots of reasons:

a. She really is a terrific kid.

b. She's exactly the sort of diamond in the rough you used to be so good at spotting, approaching, and dating. I mean, it's no great accomplishment to notice Cameron Diaz. But to notice, say, Renee Zellweger before *Jerry Maguire* is the equivalent of picking a stock just before it jumps from $5\frac{3}{4}$ to $27\frac{5}{8}$.

c. Jill reminds you of one of your favorite people: you. That is, you back when you were unattached and inventing your life on the fly and anything seemed possible. As opposed to now, when you're settled down and basically marking time until death.

d. Lacking a steady beau, Jill may be doing something your current partner is not doing: trimming her nose hair. No! I mean: making an effort. When you're looking for buyers, you tend to keep the house painted and clean.

● Miss Aerobics

Movie paradigm: Has there been an *SI* swimsuit-issue movie yet? We'll settle for Sarah Jessica Parker in *L.A. Story.*

Miss Aerobics is the Muse of Crunches, guiding you through the passage from bellies to Bally's. She spends 2 hours a day in the gym, working out in a Greco-Roman spandex thing in the pattern of the American flag. Her hair is bleached ash blonde, and she's at least 5 years younger than you. She could crush you like a walnut between those rock-hard thighs.

Why do you have a crush on her?

Gee, let me think.

Subtext: Maybe *subtext* is too subtle a word for this.

As you grow older, more accomplished, more confident, less vulnerable, you will attract women who

SEX TRENDS

PUTTING THE PERK BACK IN THE PYRAMIDS

Airport officials in Cairo recently arrested a man who was trying to smuggle Viagra from England into Egypt, where the drug is illegal. Officers found a bag filled with 15,000 Viagra pills, and another with 45,000 sedatives, no doubt intended as chasers. The total haul was worth about $290,000.

would have been beyond your reach in your younger days, when you were sort of trying too hard.

As these other things—your personality, charm, experience, polish, money, prestige—begin to attract women, you may drift out of touch with the one and only thing you used to (try to) use to attract women: your body. If Miss Aerobics seems to beckon to you, crooking her finger at the door of the health club, it is not only because her body is perfect but also because you're ready to rediscover yours.

● Zelda. As in Fitzgerald, not the video game

Movie paradigm: Courtney Love as Larry Flynt's wife, Althea. Or maybe Melanie Griffith in *Something Wild*.

Stationed way down at the other end of the hall from Miss Aerobics, Zelda smokes, drinks, does drugs, eats what she likes. She's tattooed and pierced in all the right places. She still looks pretty good, but she's on a spinning, dizzy trip to hell, laughing ruefully all the way. She's about as likely to climb on a Cybex machine as Jane Fonda is to marry Ted Turner. Wait. That happened, right?

Subtext: What did F. Scott say about our thinning briefcases of enthusiasm? Zelda gives you permission to break out of the quiet desperation of acceptable adult life and, instead, spend Saturday night watching her have her stomach pumped.

She gives you two kinds of permission, really. The first is to abandon all self-discipline and self-denial and plunge into Dionysian hedonism. (Note: If you're already there, proceed directly to Miss Aerobics or a librarian.)

The second is to see life as fundamentally tragic, instead of giving it the wan, nodding assent that is demanded of us every day. If you have a crush on Zelda, maybe you're kind of sick of pretending that life is beautiful when you suspect that, in the words of John Cusack, it's really all just sex and food hurtling toward a necropolis.

If you're planning to take your Zelda crush very far, I advise having what the United States lacked in Somalia: an exit strategy. Leave one of those "If I'm not heard from in 10 days" envelopes with a trustworthy friend.

SEX TRENDS

LORENA BOBBITT ORDERED ONE THE NEXT DAY

Canadian tourist Edward Skwarek, 37, sued a Manhattan Starbucks coffee shop for $1.5 million, claiming his penis was crushed by a "faulty toilet seat."

● Ingrid the doctor

It sounds kinky, but ask someone else about the details. I could never be comfortable with a person who might, at a given moment, find the missing keys to my old Toyota. Besides, I'm afraid she'd refer to making love as "copulation."

SEX WARS

"Please listen carefully to the available options."

HELP ONLINE

SEX ON THE JOB

This is sexual legal insurance, basically. Determine your rights
and boundaries and what constitutes sexual harassment or sexual
discrimination with this employment-law resource.
www.discriminationattorney.com

FUN, SURE, BUT IS IT LEGAL?

Stuff here on *any* legal issue? Findlaw features thousands of legal sites,
cases, codes, forms, law reviews, law schools, bar associations,
law firms, experts, courses, and more.
www.findlaw.com

PERVERT POINTER

Find your closest neighborhood sex offender by sleuthing the lists
at Stop Sex Offenders. This site offers links to sex offender registries;
college and neighborhood crime checks; safety tips for women, children,
and seniors; news; discussions; and more. Not our idea of a pleasant way
to spend the afternoon Web surfing, but it's there if you need it.
http://stopsexoffenders.com

Coloring outside the Lines

An Interview with *Multiracial Activist* editor and publisher James Landrith

Even a few decades after the Civil Rights era, almost nothing will attract more curious glances, even sometimes nasty ones, than two people of different races who are obviously in a relationship with each other.

And the starker the color contrast between their respective skins, the more frequent and longer the looks. And the more likely that those looks will drip venom.

It wasn't all that long ago that relations between Blacks and Whites were illegal. One of the most famous and groundbreaking cases was Loving v. Virginia. *In 1958, two residents of Virginia married in the District of Columbia, where interracial marriages were legal. Shortly thereafter, they returned to Virginia, where they were indicted for violating Virginia's ban on interracial marriages. In 1959, they were sentenced to a year in jail but suspended on the condition that they leave the state and not return together for 25 years.*

In March 1966, the Virginia Supreme Court of Appeals upheld the law. But in June 1967, the U.S. Supreme Court unanimously ruled the law unconstitutional, and the 16 states that still had what were called antimiscegenation laws on their books were forced to remove them.

But removing the laws did not remove persistent societal bias against mixed-race unions. Although U.S. Census data tells us that the number of interracial marriages more than tripled from 321,000 in 1970 to one million in 1980, that growth quickly leveled off. Between 1980 and 1990, the number of interracial marriages rose to only 1.1 million and still represented only 2 percent of marriages overall.

Nationwide, the bad attitudes toward interracial marriage have softened, but they haven't gone away, says multiracial advocate James Landrith, who is white.

Landrith is the editor and publisher of the Multiracial Activist, *an online publication located at www.multiracial.com. He also is the former Washington, D.C., director of Project RACE (Reclassify All Children Equally).*

Oh, and by the way, the woman who captured his heart is his African-American wife of 7 years, with whom he is raising two boys.

MAN'S GUIDE: It seems like the most highly charged and most potentially challenging interracial relationships are the Black-White ones. Is that a fair assumption?

LANDRITH: I'd say that's a pretty accurate assessment. Many types of interracial relationships draw attention and controversy, of course. But no interracial relationships have ever been as controversial as the Black-White relationship.

MAN'S GUIDE: Why is that?

LANDRITH: Well, for one thing, relationships between Blacks and Whites are complicated by about two centuries of slavery in this country. Blacks are the only racial group in this country to have had the dubious honor of being enslaved. That wound still cuts deep. And inequality continues to exist in terms of income and opportunities for Whites versus Blacks.

There are a fair number of people in the Black community who will say that you're a sellout if you're Black and dating a White person. There are a lot of people in the White community who will ask you, if you are White and dating someone Black, "Well, what about the children?"

You don't get many of those kinds of comments with the other types of interracial relationships. And I don't know exactly what it's going to take for us as a society to get past this.

> **"** If you're only going to have 10 rules, I don't know if adultery should be one of them. **"**
>
> —Media mogul Ted Turner, suggesting revisions to the 10 Commandments (he later apologized)

MAN'S GUIDE: Of the Black-White relationships, which tend to be the more potentially problematic: White man and Black woman, or Black man and White woman?

LANDRITH: Well, as far as backlash, it would be Black man, White woman.

MAN'S GUIDE: Is that because the Black women are lamenting the loss of another good Black man from the dating pool, while White men are looking at the Black man as if he has stolen one of their White women?

LANDRITH: Yeah, there is some of that, and then the underlying idea that the relationship is just some *Mandingo* love thing.

But what's interesting is that people aren't as willing to say that to a White man or even a Black woman—at least not directly. When I'm out with my wife, I can see the stares and the looks, and I can tell what they're thinking. But nobody comes right out with it.

Yet people don't seem to be as hesitant to go up to a Black male or a White female and say exactly what they feel about the pairing.

Also, from the Caucasian side, it's usually the White men who have the biggest problems with a Black man dating a White woman. Part of that is plain old jealousy. I think there's a bit of the "What's he got that I haven't got?" mentality going on.

MAN'S GUIDE: So one of the problems is the perception that it's all about exotic attraction and not about real love?

LANDRITH: That's definitely part of the problem, and that attitude can come from the White community and from the Black community.

MAN'S GUIDE: So, realizing that there is a lot of potential for misunderstanding and tension in an interracial relationship, what can a man do to help get the relationship started off on a good footing?

LANDRITH: First off, make sure that you don't date someone of another race just as a form of experimentation. This is not a lab project. Don't ever date outside your racial or ethnic group unless you specifically care about that person.

When a White man dates a Black woman, there is already an underlying thought among many people that he's "just visiting the ghetto for a little while." You don't want to perpetuate nasty ideas like that. You just make it harder for other people down the line who are in legitimate relationships.

Also, don't assume that your partner is going to hold political views that are stereotypically associated with her racial or ethnic group. Ignore the stereotypes and focus on the individual.

MAN'S GUIDE: For example, dating someone who is Black and assuming that she is a Democrat and a supporter of the Reverend Jesse Jackson.

LANDRITH: Exactly. There are also the religious issues to take into consideration. You need to be sensitive to those differences and be aware of them. If the woman you are with goes to church regularly, you should go to church with her—at least some of the time. And before you go, ask her if there is anything you should know regarding how you should dress, how you should behave, and so forth.

And when you get there, keep your mouth shut for a while and just pay attention to what's going on. Don't be critical of differences you might notice between a predominantly Black church and a predominantly White church, for example. Just go there and be open, and don't look for problems. You can worship with any color person in any kind of church.

MAN'S GUIDE: What are some of the biggest myths and misconceptions you should put out of your mind early on, especially as things start to become more intimate?

LANDRITH: Well, when you get involved physically, don't believe the sexual myths. For example, a White woman should not expect that all Black men are going be well-hung. And as far as Black men having more sexual prowess, that's not necessarily the case either.

MAN'S GUIDE: I suppose that Black men who date White women should be prepared for those assumptions, though. What about White men with Black women—or other minority women for that matter?

LANDRITH: The funny thing is, the stereotype is that Black women are freer and wilder in bed than White women. And that's a bunch of B.S. It all depends on the individual and her previous experiences.

MAN'S GUIDE: Some other minority women get the same rap. Interestingly, many minority women, such as Blacks and Hispanics, are less willing than White women to perform kinky sexual acts—or even milder acts like oral sex.

LANDRITH: Yeah, I agree with you on that point, and I've dated women of all colors.

To go into a relationship with someone of another race and be thinking, "Oh, this is going to be great; we're going to have kinky, wild sex; and it's going to be this great big, wonderful, liberating thing"—

that's just wrong. And if you build up the sexual stuff based on stereotypes, you're going to be disappointed eventually. You'll doom the relationship to failure.

MAN'S GUIDE: But not everything is stereotypes. Take hair, for example. You'll see Black women on TV shows or in movies freak out when it rains or when someone tries to splash them, because their hairdos will be destroyed. Black people's hair really is very different from White people's, and you want to be very careful before you mess with a Black woman's 'do.

LANDRITH: Oh, yeah. If it takes your Black partner 2 hours to get her hair ready in the morning or if she pays double or triple digits on its upkeep every week or so, then maybe you don't want to run your fingers through it.

MAN'S GUIDE: Are there any other legitimate physical differences that people should be aware of when it comes to women of other races?

LANDRITH: Hair is about the only significant one I can think of, really. I mean, women come in all body shapes, even though we have various ideas of what an Asian woman or a Hispanic woman or a Black woman generally looks like.

You can't buy into the stereotype, for example, that Black women are necessarily more curvy or more full-figured. That's something you get from watching too many videos and movies. And that's a pretty boneheaded way to base your expectations of what Black women are supposed to look like.

MAN'S GUIDE: What are the social differences? What can really kill a relationship or make it stronger?

LANDRITH: Awareness or lack thereof. Let's say that you have a girlfriend who's of a different race, and she complains about something that seems to her to be a racially motivated thing. Don't disregard that.

For example, maybe you got bad service at a restaurant, and she thinks it's because you're White and she's Black and the waiter had a problem with that. Pay attention to those perceptions. She's going to be a little more culturally attuned to that kind of thing than you are. She's going to see things that you aren't necessarily going to see.

MAN'S GUIDE: Do you think it just naturally happens that White men pick up on those subtle forms of racism as the relationship progresses? Or does a perpetual lack of sensitivity often kill interracial relationships?

LANDRITH: I wouldn't say often. But it can sometimes be an issue, particularly if you're not paying attention to what's going on.

But the man should take it upon himself, if the woman has a complaint, to believe her. Believe what she's saying when she suspects that a bad situation is racial in nature, and then find some way to rectify it. That might mean that you have to get up and complain to the manager. It might mean that you vote with your wallet and never give that place your business again.

Make sure that you don't allow mistreatment to continue by ignoring it, because ignoring it isn't going to make it go away. It's your responsibility to either do something about it or go somewhere else—or both.

The use of ethnic humor and things like that are in the same vein. Don't bring her around situations where that kind of thing is likely to occur. Never, never, *never* subject your date or your partner to anybody whom you think would not be respectful to her.

> **" Making love in cars has its own history and its dignity. Just think of drive-ins. "**
>
> —Riccardo Schicchi, manager of Italian porn star Cicciolina, on an Italian court ruling that makes having sex in a car an obscene act punishable by up to 3 years in jail

MAN'S GUIDE: Of course, racial jokes and mockery are bad, but what about picking up some of the linguistics and slang that might be more common to your girlfriend's racial group? Can that be a form of bonding, or is it more often divisive?

LANDRITH: That depends how you incorporate words and expressions and phrases that are associated with a specific racial group. You have to be careful. If you're doing it because it's coming naturally, that's one thing. But don't push it or make a special effort to speak in a stereotypically "racial" manner.

MAN'S GUIDE: Am I right in assuming that a White person using the *N*-word for any reason, no matter how closely aligned he or she is with the Black community and no matter whether they are using it themselves, as they do, is just asking for trouble?

> **LANDRITH:** Yes. And don't try to use the word and then cover your butt by couching it with, "Well, you know, I mean it the way you mean it."
>
> It's not going to mean the same thing to her when you say it as it does when she says it—ever. Don't do it.

MAN'S GUIDE: Don't misinterpret this next question, but "What about the children?" I don't mean that in the bigoted way you noted earlier. But if you and your partner are marriage-minded and you want to have kids, what are some of the things you should be aware of and should be doing to make things go as smoothly as possible?

> **LANDRITH:** Well, you want to be sure that you're going to be living in an environment that's safe for your kids. Not just literally in terms of physical safety—it should be a place where they feel comfortable and welcome and able to be themselves.
>
> Is the place you are going to live going to be a place that's conducive to your child's healthy upbringing? Is your child going to be deemed the "representative of the entire Black race" at every single discussion? Are your children likely to be ostracized by White kids and parents? You need to look into those things.
>
> You also need to talk to your spouse ahead of time about racial-identity issues. Are you going to raise your child to be both Black and White? Or are you going to raise your child to be one or the other? That's a big issue with a lot of couples.

MAN'S GUIDE: Sort of like a mixed-faith couple deciding whether to raise the child Christian or Jewish or neither.

> **LANDRITH:** Exactly.

MAN'S GUIDE: It seems like a tough issue, though, making concessions about where to live.

LANDRITH: It's a big country, and barring special economic or job-related situations you might have, there are plenty of places you can live. So unless you are out there trying to be the activist and change things—unless you *want* to be a blockbuster—don't put yourself out there so you can be abused.

Some people may consider that "selling out." They may accuse you of just giving up. But I can consider it being safe. Where you live is obviously a very personal decision, and you should make that with your spouse. But you have to keep in mind all those other issues. Is it physically safe to live there as an interracial couple or with mixed-raced kids? Is it going to be emotionally safe for your kids to be there?

Don't sit there and let somebody chastise you and tell you, "Well, they ran you out." You have to think of your family. And you know, you have only one life. Are you going to live it safely?

MAN'S GUIDE: What have we missed that we should talk about?

LANDRITH: One thing I always get asked—and it's almost always in a racial context—is "How did you meet your wife?"

Well, I said hello to her. It's not like I went to the White man/Black woman dating club.

And then people ask me, "Well, what would you say to a White woman instead?" And the answer is the same. I'd say hello or "Can I buy you a drink?"

I know people are often just curious when they ask me those things. They don't mean any harm, though it can get annoying at times. But it's really not that complicated. If you see a woman you are interested in, regardless of her race, talk to her. You don't need special pickup lines or anything like that.

QUICKIES

BAD MOON ON THE RISE

Lt. Patrick Callaghan, Ph.D., a career Navy officer, was given an official reprimand and a poor job evaluation by his superiors at the Naval Air Station in Pensacola, Florida, for mooning his buddy while jogging on the base. The 28-year-old was charged with indecent exposure and conduct unbecoming for an officer, and he was ordered to undergo psychological evaluations (which he passed). The Navy even considered booting Callaghan, who had a spotless 11-year record until the morning when he dropped his shorts in response to his friend's razzing.

Man's Guide concedes that mooning may not be the Navy's preferred form of salute, but what's the real problem here? Does the brass want to nip this mooning thing early, in case it turns into a fad, with fighter pilots flashing pressed hams at 40,000 feet? Or is it just another example of political correctness gone insane? The thing that really starches our shorts is that another Navy officer, Lt. Frederica Spilman, posed nude in *Playboy* the year before—and the Navy merely sent her a letter saying that it didn't approve of her actions. Sure, she looks good wearing nothing but camouflage panties, but is exposure "indecent" only if it's a man's?

THE HIDDEN HAZARDS OF PHONE SEX

If you've been scheming to get a few days off from work, here's a tactic that's better than spilling coffee in your lap. A Florida phone-sex operator won a controversial workers' compensation settlement after claiming she was injured by regular work-related masturbation.

Seems the 40-year-old talk-dirty professional developed carpal tunnel syndrome (also known, appropriately enough, as repetitive motion injury) in both hands after being required to diddle up to seven times a day while speaking with gentlemen callers. Reportedly, the woman used one hand to answer the phone and the other to perform such routine office tasks as recording customers' names, logging their fetishes, and, well, putting dew on the lily. Most "conversations" lasted 15 minutes, but regulars who asked for the woman by name got 15 minutes of bonus time. Whatever happened to faking it?

WHOSE SPERM IS IT, ANYWAY?

You can kiss your little swimmers goodbye once they leave the premises. New Mexico man Peter Wallis sued his former girlfriend for breach of contract and theft, saying she lied about being on birth control, then "stole" his sperm and became pregnant against his wishes after they'd had consensual sex. The court dismissed the case—and so did the readers of *New Woman* magazine. A poll of their readers found that 78 percent believed that sperm becomes the woman's property after it's ejaculated into her body.

"What does he intend to do with it? Reuse it? I think not," wrote one would-be owner. "If he was so concerned about his sperm, he had two options: Keep it in his own body or put it into a specially made little bag. It's called a condom." The other 22 percent agreed with the woman who wrote, "I think a woman 'owns' her eggs, so that means a man must 'own' his sperm, too." No word on who has rights to the little fellas left behind in the wet spot.

> " They are just a bunch of frustrated women who want to be men. "
>
> —Boxer and convicted rapist Mike Tyson, referring to the British women's groups who protested his presence in London before one of his fights

A TOOL OF THE REBELLION

Consider it just another way of saying, "I got your tyranny *right here!*" For several decades, fully clothed Indonesian administrators from the nation's capital, Jakarta, have tried to stop the Stone Age–style natives of the Irian Jaya province of western Papua New Guinea from wearing what the feds see as primitive, backward clothing. The bone of contention? Skimpy "penis gourds" that are proudly exhibited by Dani tribesmen as their sole item of apparel. Traditional Dani men form penis sheaths out of long, hollowed-out gourds, which are then kept in the upright and locked position by strings around the waist. Fashionable gourds are decorated with fur, feathers, shells and embroidery; some styles also double as pouches, holding cash and tobacco.

Thousands of Irian Jayan locals have already been massacred by the Indonesian Army as it exploits the region's rich mineral and forest resources. So far, Jakarta's efforts to eradicate the gourd-garb have failed, although the law does ban their bobbing display inside government offices. Today, the penis gourd is seen as an act of defiance against the Jakarta government. Recently an elder, Sopaluma Elosak, clutched his erect gourd and cried, "Freedom to Papua!" when a reporter asked him how he felt about Indonesia.

DEAR DR. MANLY

Q: *I just started dating a woman I work with. Do I have to tell my boss?*
—G. D., Santa Cruz, California

A: If she's your boss's wife, keep quiet until after the performance review. Otherwise, your decision to break the don't-ask-don't-tell rule depends on your work relationship with the woman. If she's a subordinate or a client, it's career-smart to mention it to your boss, regardless of where the relationship is headed. Better that you tell him you're dating the secretary than tell Ralph in accounting, who may editorialize on the situation.

When you do talk to your boss, don't make a big deal about it. Just say, "Look, I wanted to give you a heads-up on this in case it makes you uncomfortable." No apologies, no stammering. And whatever you do, try not to make an appointment to discuss it—a brief stop-by is the way to go.

Q: *Is there any way to tell if my wife is cheating on me?* **I have no hard evidence, just this feeling in the pit of my gut. Something's not right.**
—S. W., Oswego, New York

A: Don't ignore those gut feelings. Cheating spouses throw off more signals than a paranoid third-base coach, but they may be so subtle that all you get is an uneasy feeling. Have you been getting hang-up phone calls in the evening? Is she showering more than usual? Is she suddenly more critical of your behavior? Other signs to watch for: Changes in makeup or clothing tastes. Talking about some guy at work whom she's never mentioned before—or *not* talking about someone whom she used to talk about often. And if she's recently decided to take an adult education class twice a week at the local community college . . . well, you can imagine what kind of education she might be getting.

Also, if she's accusing you of cheating, she may have realized the value of a good offense. "It's like some lawyers," says my buddy Joe

Alercia, who works with the American Detective Agency. "Crooked lawyers are used to ripping people off, but they make the people who bill *them* account for every penny." That's because a cheater is naturally paranoid about everyone else being a cheater, too.

Here's one trick that psychics use to find out if they're hitting a nerve: Put her in a squeaky chair for your next conversation. She may not be saying anything out loud, but the squeaks will speak volumes. Why? Liars tend to fidget. The more squeaks, the more uncomfortable she is with the questions you're asking. So try a few innocent queries first, just to establish a squeak baseline.

Technology alert: Don't assume the worst just because the phone goes dead a few times when you pick it up. Everybody with a phone gets hang-up calls nowadays. That's because telephone solicitors use computerized dialers that call up to four phone numbers at once and then hang up on all but the one that answers first.

Q: *I have this thing for collecting a pair of panties from every woman I date. I'm not sneaking into houses in the middle of the night or anything, just retaining a pair that happens to get "kicked" under the bed. Well, last week my current girlfriend uncovered my stash. She was livid. She kept asking, "Why?" Nothing I said satisfied her, so she dumped me. Now I'm wondering: Why do men have fetishes in the first place?*
—W. C., WASHINGTON, D.C.

A: A nurse friend of mine told me about this guy who came to the emergency room complaining about decreased sexual desire. Seems this gent liked to masturbate on his TV. Literally. He'd actually bang his penis against the side of the set. The reason he visited the hospital was not to be cured of this behavior, however; he'd bought a new set, see, and well, *it just wasn't the same.* True story.

"Fetishism is the concentration on a sharply focused object instead of the real thing," says David Reuben, M.D. "A man obsessed with lace panties, for example, is really substituting the underwear for the woman's sex organs." (Yeah, but what about a TV set?) Seems that because men are highly visual thinkers when it comes to sex, it's easier for us to let fantasy take over and use objects as surrogate sexual partners.

For many men, these fetishes are mild. A quick poll around the office revealed a fitness buff who gets off on women who smoke cigars and an amateur chef who has a thing for aprons. As long as these fetishes don't put the kibosh on your real-life sex life, there's no need to worry. But if the women you meet are dumping you because of it, well, it's time to find a good sex therapist and get to the root of the matter.

Dr. Manly is a fictional character.
The actual advice was provided by a variety of
medical doctors and other qualified experts.

SPOT-CHECK
CYBERSEX

The dizzying evolution of the Internet will keep you spinning, and sex is right there at the forefront, hard-driving the momentum. Two decades ago, using snail-like 1200 baud modems, many of the Internet-savvy Boy Wonders leading the interactive tech boom were distributing compressed image files of naked women through members-only electronic bulletin boards known as BBSs.

Today, Internet-savvy porn dogs have gone broadband on cable and T3 with World Wide Web live sex shows, voyeur Web cams hidden inside showers and sorority houses, and more X-rated videos and pictures than you can shake a credit card at. Chat rooms, online singles classifieds with pictures, and e-mail have made it easier to get dates with flesh-and-blood women, too. Some of them are men pretending to be women, but, hey, it's an interactive world out there, so you'd expect some strange strangers to be interacting out fantasies, now wouldn't you?

TOP TEN

Cyberwooing Tips

Back in the olden days, an LDR (long-distance relationship) guaranteed guys one of two things: hand cramps from writing letters or outrageous telephone bills. Fortunately, millennial technology makes daily contact a no-brainer, leaving you to concentrate on becoming her latter-day Don Juan. Here's how to guarantee a flush in her cheeks and a flutter in her heart whenever she hears, "You've got mail!"

① She's a real person, so remember that. Take the extra effort to speak in whole words, not acronyms, initials, and sideways facial expressions (emoticons). She gets enough LOL, IMHO, and TTFN from her friends. You should be giving her polished prose, not codes and cyberdribble. (In case you're wondering, these stand for Laughing Out Loud, In My Humble Opinion, and Ta-Ta For Now.)

② Let her know what the message is about. Type something new in the subject line every time you send her e-mail, whether or not you're replying to her message. Never a woman roamed the Earth who was swept away by the romance of *Re: Re: Fw: [Fw: (Re: About last night . . .)]*. Which leads to point number three . . .

③ Always reply to her messages. Always, always, always. E-mail means never having to say, "Huh? I'm sorry, were you talking to me?" All you have to do is go back and reread the message. If she takes the time to write to you, then take the time to tell her the message was received and read—even if you have to put off a full reply till later. "I have a meeting in 10 minutes, but I wanted to let you know I got your note. I'll follow up tonight."

④ Feelings . . . nothing more than feelings . . . E-mail lacks important emotional indicators that we tend to take for granted in face-to-face conversation. She can't hear your sighs of enchantment or see your nods of agreement, so it's up to you to create that context by painting pictures with words. (In the old days, this was called poetry.) Check the difference between, "I thought about you today," and "I'm listening to your favorite Yanni CD as I write this. Can you smell the coffee, too? I just made a pot of that Amaretto Vanilla Almond French Roast you suggested . . ."

⑤ Follow with the change-up. A stirring, heartfelt epic can really set her soul to singing—unless it arrives back-to-back with five stirring, heartfelt epics in 5 days. Follow up the Romeo stuff with short, punchy, sparkling messages that reveal your witty, lighthearted nature—apropos jokes, top 10 lists, Web site links, and e-postcards. Which leads us to the next tip . . .

⑥ Don't serve spam, serve caviar. There's no shame in forwarding e-mails to your e-beloved, but they shouldn't look like forwards. Do some cleanup first. Copy the message into a word processor and make it look nice and purty: Spell-check it. Delete odd line breaks, unnecessary headers, and irritating coding. Leave nothing but the golden nuggets and a few thoughtful words of introduction.

⑦ Think of it as a conversation. E-mail is not the medium for monologues. Write with the purpose of eliciting a response. Ask insightful questions, but not too many at a time. Above all, answer all her questions, even if briefly—or you may give the impression that you're avoiding the subject. If you can't reply immediately, excerpt parts of her original e-mail into your own to refresh her memory.

⑧ Set up secret love accounts. Use a free browser-based e-mail service to create unique addresses. Rather than write to you at j_blow1303@some.bigcorp.com, she can send missives to joe_adores_jane@passion.com. (Best not to use your work e-mail anyway. Big Brother is not only watching your messages, he's saving them for later.) Create an e-mail account for her, too, using the same service. Then tell her how to change the password so she can keep it private if she so desires. And this leads to tip number nine . . .

⑨ Create a private Web retreat. Take advantage of free browser-based personal Web-site services to build a home page just for the two of you. Password-protect the site and give the URL to no one but her. Post all those (nonincriminating) photos you took at the beach last time you saw each other. Buy her a digital camera (you can find them online for less than the price of a nice dinner and cab fare) and teach her how to upload her own photos. Update the site as often as you can. '

⑩ Change media once in a while. Love cannot survive on pixels alone. No amount of digital lovey-dovey will ever replace a well-timed handwritten letter, a dozen long-stemmed roses, a box of Godiva chocolates, a custom CD of blues love songs, or a videotape of you performing Riverdance just for her.

MUST READS

Stripped and Whipped on the Wild, Wild Web

Sex online is the biggest thing since . . . well, sex. Of course, it's not real sex, but in some ways it's much better. And we'll never get rid of it. Internet sex is out of the box. You can't ban it. You can't bury it. You can't send it off to boarding school and hope it will return with manners. It's here to stay because it gives men exactly what they want: sex without commitment, emotional cost, or any real procurement effort. Web pornography has turned computers into sex objects. And men, by the millions, are hooking up. Should you? Writer Greg Gutfeld answers that question.

Walter bought a PC for his home office. Like any normal guy, when he found out that there were naked ladies in the box, he took a peek. Then he took another. And another. Then he fell into the 'net's deep end, first with Internet Relay Chat (IRC)—thousands of chat rooms filled to the brim with dirty talk. He traded pictures. Lots of pictures. Then he moved to NetMeeting, with its real-time, moving-picture sex. Finally, when his fast Internet connection had taken him miles and years away from his home, his job, and his marriage, his daughter caught him. Screwed for real. That's when he wrote to me.

Walter's first few downloads led to an infinite procession of wide-open women in entry-level positions. "The first month, I'd sneak a peek like any normal guy," says Walter, not his real name. "But it's endless." He started checking his favorite sites constantly, afraid something might happen without him. And the more he checked, the more focused his desires became. He started masturbating nonstop. And he wanted more. "At first, I was happy with Web sites, but then came the chat rooms, where I'd have computer sex with all sorts of women. Then I found this place—there is no other place like this on the Web."

It was IRC, a universe of text-only "rooms" filled to the last byte with naughty nurses, sexy schoolgirls, lesbian couples, and willing bi females. There's one room simply described as "a single hot lonely girl." Naturally, it's packed with men. It's more figment than fact, but Walter's there. "You can send pictures back and forth," he said. Suddenly, the fantasy has a pretty face.

Walter was careful. "A lot of guys pretend to be women so they can get pictures of men." He asked women to send pictures, with their clothes on and off. "If they can't send one with clothes, then it's a guy who has downloaded pictures of naked girls. He'd never have clothed shots."

Kicking It Up a Notch

But eventually, Walter grew bored with that, too. So NetMeeting came next, where you can look at sex partners in real time (if they have cameras). Walter had a camera. A really good camera. To Walter, this was like a great date that ends in great sex. "Videoconferencing is gas on the fire!" he blurts, before reconsidering. "If I don't do something, I will ruin my life and my marriage, and sink my business. I have two daughters. They deserve a better dad."

He's telling me this even after one of his daughters caught him "looking at something I shouldn't have been looking at." She told her mother. He confessed.

"This is a lot bigger problem than you think," he told his wife. "I'm spending hours a day sometimes—6 to 8, actually—when I should be doing the work that puts the roof over our heads and food in our mouths. I'm having problems."

And his wife? It broke her heart, he says, voice cracking. "We'll probably survive this, as long as I stay away from it." By the time I reached him, it had been only a few days. "I went back once for 30 seconds, got disgusted with myself, and shut it off." So he trashed his videoconference programming and dumped all the other stuff. He tells me that he's entering counseling. "I work at home. My kids are in school. My wife works. I'm here all by myself. I'm not a horn dog who hangs out at a strip club. This thing just grabbed me and sucked me in hard."

Walter's no weirdo. He's never bought porn before. Doesn't subscribe to the Playboy Channel. I doubt he even owns a raincoat. But now he can't look at a bland, beige computer without feeling a sexual charge. It starts in his groin and flows up his spine until his brain is dizzy with expectation. The computer may be off—no matter, it's classical conditioning, like Pavlov's dogs. He sits down, and the promise of gratification tingles through his nervous system. It's the chemistry of a sure thing. And for Walter it's replacing the real thing.

SEX TRENDS

COMPUTER VIRUS

Health officials in San Francisco tracked an outbreak of syphilis to an America Online chat room—the first time a disease has been traced to cyberspace. Six gay men were infected with the venereal disease through sexual encounters with partners they met online.

"The Internet chat room is becoming an important sexual network and one that poses particular challenges for us," says Dr. Jeffrey Klausner, director of the STD unit at the San Francisco public health department.

The Pros and Cons of Easy Access

Sex is the number one destination on the Internet. During a single month recently, 15 percent of the 57 million Americans using the World Wide Web accessed the 10 most popular adult Web sites. Porn is the Internet's first cash cow, all those tits doing for the Web what X-rated videos did for the VCR, turning the unknown into the undeniable.

To be sure, many surfers who frequent these sites are lonely losers, unwashed introverts, and skanked-out pervs, downloading the only sex they'll ever have. But a surprising number of normal guys—married, professional men, men whose taste for pornography has always stopped at the Victoria's Secret catalog—have plugged into this exotic new world of porn-on-demand and made it theirs.

Most of them have never had a problem with porn before. They certainly never felt like prisoners of a sexual compulsion. Until now. For some, curiosity has progressed to obsession. They don't mean to like electronic sex so much, but they do. And the need grows. They require more and more to keep from getting bored.

Sex on the Internet is hypnotic and timeless. At least TV has markers, like commercials and credits. Viewing the never-ending stream of nudity and sex on the 'net, you quickly lose track of time. It's like sitting in a windowless room with an unlimited supply of a powerful drug. Distinctions between day and night become irrelevant.

I could show you. We could go to clublove.com and check out hundreds of beautiful women—all young, all willing. Take your pick: "Free exclusive porn stars, full-length XXX movies, a 30,000-image archive" from the "smuttiest, wettest, nastiest, hottest, hardest sex site on the planet." The word "free" is all over the place, but the moment you click on an image ("free live sex show," the voyeuristic bathroom "pee cam") a credit card form pops up. I went to "Watch this babe masturbate!" only to discover that it would cost $24.95 a month for the luxury.

These women are not ugly ducklings (unless, of course, you're looking for ugly ducklings; you'll find them, too) but surgically enhanced, fully loaded sex machines. Here, "streaming" videos take on literal meaning. It's better than anything you can find on late-night cable porn, and less risky than driving to the Playtime Adult Boutique out by the underpass.

Here you can plug into these women figuratively. Get in, get off, and get out. And 10 minutes later, you can do it again, with a different woman. From Peru.

Stimulation versus Overstimulation

That's what makes sex online far more compelling than any shrink-wrapped smut. It's instant gratification in endless variety—you never get to the end of the

(*continued on page 238*)

Eyer Beware

When considering pay-to-play Web sites, keep one hand on your libido and the other on your wallet. It's hard to make sound financial decisions when all you want to do is look at dirty pictures. Sex-Web-site owners know this, and they play dirty when it comes to billing you for their services. Greg Gutfeld points out the perils of the porn.

● Adult Web sites overload you with small type.
The terms of a site's "free membership" are longer than a New York City lease. And you'll go blind trying to read them, which is why you won't. If you do, you might discover that "Free trials will renew automatically to a 1-month membership."

"The Web sites know you're too impatient to read the fine print because you want the naked pictures," says Gina Smith, an ABC News correspondent who reports on Web porn.

● They offer free memberships that aren't free.
The sites I surfed offer free memberships, then charge you if you don't call to cancel. One $45 charge, from peep.com, came only days after I signed up for a free 2-day trial. They credited my account after I complained.

This has happened to a number of men I spoke with. "I had a $19.95 charge for 3 months that I wasn't aware of," says Tom. The site said, in fine print, that it was free for a few days. But after that

they billed you unless you called and canceled on a special telephone number. "I never noticed it." He called to complain, so they offered him an additional month free instead of his money back.

His coworker really got nailed. "He visited a site where you can ask a girl to do anything on live video, and she complies. It was supposed to be free, but he received a telephone bill for $638. The fine print stated that a $3.99-per-minute charge would appear on your phone bill, for your convenience."

● They make it hard to cancel.
If you think it's difficult to cancel America Online, trying getting rid of a porn site. "You have to e-mail a certain address, but your messages are rejected or just ignored," says one man. "You continue to receive a monthly charge on your credit card. What saved me was that I kept all the e-mails that I sent and received. I supplied copies to my bank, and they voided all the charges."

● They know most people will be too embarrassed to fight back.

One man told me he'd signed up for a 1-week free preview, supplying his credit card number. "They sent me an access code for the site. But the code was seven numbers; they gave me five. I e-mailed my cancellation request numerous times, but they didn't respond. They charged me for membership 3 months in a row. It's going to be embarrassing to call my credit card company, but I've got to do it." Many victims of these scams simply pay up rather than fess up. It's like getting mugged by a prostitute you hired (not that I would know).

● **They blame you when they get caught.**
I signed up for Club Love's free 1-week membership, then canceled before the week ended. When I called to cancel, though, the smart-ass operator told me I had actually not clicked on the 1-week membership but rather the 1-month membership. I hadn't, and I wouldn't back down, so they canceled the $24.95 charge.

● **They reject your credit card, then they run up charges on it anyway.**

When I applied for a free membership at one porn site, they rejected my credit application. When I received my American Express bill, it included a $24.95 charge from a mysterious business called "DMR," located somewhere in North Dakota. I called and talked to an operator whose job, it seems, is to do nothing but embarrass perverts like me.

When I asked him what the charge was for, he relished saying, "Your membership to euroteensluts.com." He thought exposing my kinks would cause me to slink off. Think again!

"Oh yes!" I said. "Euroteensluts.com! I tried to join, but my card was rejected!" He transferred me to a nice woman, who explained that I would be charged for another month as well. "They just renew it every month." When I said that I would not pay and that, by the way, this was going to make a neat story in a magazine, she acknowledged that "sometimes there are glitches in the system." She agreed to credit me for the charges. To this day, I do not know what a euroteenslut is. And that's probably all for the best.

magazine and have to start looking at the same pictures again. With old porn, once you view it, you've consumed it. You've chewed the flavor out of the gum. This can't be done on the Internet. The gum never runs out of flavor. A new piece of flesh waits behind every old one, and expectation bids you to go further. Much further. Because as long as there's more to come, you'll keep coming.

This is all so new. No stimulus like this ever existed before. Evolution designed our bodies to deal with real people, not replicas. But now we have tricked the beast, and the beast doesn't seem to mind.

The point is that you can't look casually at porno. There's nothing casual about a pile of naked women on your desk. You can't just stand up and walk away. Instead, you get carried away. I've seen it. And I've talked to dozens of men who describe similar experiences, worried about the place their obsession has led them.

Before I go further, however, I should say that not every guy looks at a dirty picture on the Internet and gets hooked. One man said that 'net porn substituted nicely while his wife was pregnant. "My wife was so drained from the baby that she, by her own admission, left me to fend for myself," he says. Another guy used the Internet like a vitamin; a daily dose supplementing a dry spell. "I stopped when I found a girlfriend," he says. And then there are guys who hop on the 'net, hunt for stuff, and share with their wives. "I'm not comfortable soliciting sex information from friends, so the Internet is my only resource," says one man. "The information gathering has led my wife and me to experiment—sometimes right in front of the monitor." He suggests using a trackball.

perfect figures

A survey of female romance-book devotees found that just 3 percent have actually dated a guy they met online, while 83 percent say they would never even consider dating an Internet acquaintance.

• • • • • • • •

Still, the fact is, a lot of guys who become involved with online sex get in deep. If it were just the typical guy, looking on the 'net for one naked photo to satisfy himself, it would be no big deal. But it's never one photo. Nearly all of the men I talked with found they couldn't satisfy themselves with a quick look. "It's the intrigue that the next site might have something really exciting," says Carl, an oceanographer in his forties. "It usually isn't the case, but you never know."

What Carl is describing—the hope that there will be a sexier woman, a more bizarre position—is at the heart of this phenomenon, and it's what drives men to the 'net. It's what drives men, period.

Just ask Calvin Coolidge.

Presidential Pardon

It's an old story: The 30th president and his wife were visiting a government farm. When the missus saw a rooster mating, she asked the attending farmer how often the rooster copulated. Over a dozen times a day, he said. "Please tell that to the president," she said. When the president saw the same rooster and was told about the frequency, he asked, "Same hen every time?" Nope. Different sex partner each time. The president nodded. "Tell that to Mrs. Coolidge."

And so the Coolidge effect was born—a phrase scientists use to describe a phenomenon called male re-arousal. It's like this: Once a male mammal has sex with a female, his desire fades. He still wants to have sex, but not with her. Even if the female is disguised with perfume and a mask, the male knows—and remains unimpressed. But replace the old female with a new one, and the male perks up. And ruts again.

Continue this replacement, and the male will continue to rut—up to dozens of times.

This is the Coolidge effect. "The next female is equivalent to the first. He can do it again and again," says Donald Symons, Ph.D., professor of anthropology and author of *The Evolution of Human Sexuality.* "The effect is so strong that sexual limits of some animals haven't been found." No one has studied this effect in humans. "You couldn't get it by a human-subjects committee," says Dr. Symons, "although a lot of men would volunteer."

Technically, a lot already have—not in labs but in dens, offices, and work spaces all over the country. The Internet has tapped into the Coolidge effect in men everywhere, tickling the primal epicenter of male sexual response. And the men who respond soon find themselves cut off from everything else.

"I almost never talk to women, even if they are obviously attracted to me," says Neal, an accountant. "This habit has caused me feelings of alienation and isolation. I've wasted all my days and nights on this."

You sink deeper into this limitless supply, this vast library of opportunities, and soon your only sexual outlet is an electrical one. "I have become increasingly more dependent on an impersonal machine for my sexual release," says Dan, a college student, echoing many other men I interviewed.

"Every week, I try to stop, but it never works," says Mark, a 20-year-old student who masturbates daily to sex sites. "I feel guilty that I'm relying on this so much, and it affects my sex life."

"Every time she leaves the house, I'm logging on to porno Web sites," says Larry, a 23-year-old student. When he does have sex with his wife, "I just want to get off and be done with it."

When Alvin Cooper, Ph.D., a sex researcher, analyzed a group of more than

RTFM, Baby, RTFM

You know what it means when she licks her lips and flutters her eyelids—either she's hot for you or she's about to throw up. But what if you can't see her? How do you know what she's thinking? Because chat rooms lack the emotional signifiers we take for granted in a face-to-face encounter, chatters use a system of abbreviations and symbols to indicate actions or feelings. Consider how the statement "good job" changes meaning depending on which sideways facial expression, or "emoticon," you use. (Hint: Turn your head sideways to see the "face.")

Good job :^)	With "smile" implies congratulations	BTW	By the way
		BTDT	Been there, done that
Good job :^(	With "frown" implies satire	BRB	Be right back
		GGP	Gotta go pee (as in GGP/BRB)
Good job :^P	With "tongue sticking out" implies jealousy	IMHO	In my humble opinion
Good job 8°	With "eyes and mouth wide open" implies shock or surprise	NP	No problem
		CYA	See you later
		TTFN	Ta-ta for now

And because chatters are by nature lazy typists, they've developed common abbreviations for words and sayings. For example, words that sound like letters (why, you, be, see, are) are never written out—they're typed Y, U, B, C, and R. Other abbreviations:

		K	OK
		^5	High-five
		!	No kidding! Wow!
		?	Well? Explain yourself
,g.	Grin	RTFM	Read the freaking manual (usually said in reply to obvious questions)
LOL	(So funny I'm) laughing out loud		
ROFL	(Even funnier—I'm) rolling on the floor laughing	A/S or A/S/L	Request for your age/sex or age/sex/location; asked mostly by teens and preteens

9,000 people who frequented adult Web sites, he found that about half the group, which was 85 percent male, spent less than an hour a week online for sexual activities. These guys are fine, Dr. Cooper says. "To them it's like *Baywatch.*" But nearly 9 percent spent from 11 to 80 hours a week searching for online sex, and admitted it was causing serious trouble for them. "I have seen men who are online 4 to 6 hours a day just looking at sexual stuff and masturbating," says Dr. Cooper. "They choose to go there instead of to their wives."

The Big Letdown

Can you blame them? Consider the Internet's appeal: accessibility, anonymity, affordability. "There are no real-world obstacles," says John Suler, Ph.D., professor of psychology at Rider University in Lawrenceville, New Jersey. "You don't have to drive to a video store or bookstore, nor do you have to deal with people." And you don't have to buy dinner to persuade the blonde at peep.com to peel off her thong.

You can't touch her, of course, but you don't need to. The fantasy is intense enough once the barriers to gratification are gone. Where once there was effort, now there is ease. Internet porn is old porn sucked through a crack pipe.

When a man, after weeks of this, actually sleeps with his wife, he's in for a disappointment. "The Internet has set unrealistic expectations," says Terry, an executive. "I now believe that my girlfriend is not as adventurous as I'd like. She's now very boring." He didn't feel that way before. "I worry that cybersex may have skewed my reality of just how many people are running around having group sex." In the Internet sex world, we're all wallflowers at the dance.

What's left is pure self-gratification. "The more you have sex with yourself, the more the experience becomes centered around your penis and nowhere else," says Neal. "I actually get a little annoyed if my partner tries to stimulate other parts of my body." Soon, the only sex you're good at is the kind you have with the machine. "The longer I do this, the worse I'm getting at real sex," says Terry. "The drive just isn't there."

You can't hurt your laptop's feelings, but real relationships inevitably suffer. "I started telling my girlfriend not to come over," says Paul, a staff assistant. "There's no intimacy anymore," says Ben, a 27-year-old who works with computers. "I expect she would feel I am cheating."

From a purely physical perspective, he is. "It doesn't matter whether you're having sex with a real woman or with an endless stream of online pictures—it's going to be hard to maintain a relationship with your wife," says Dudley Seth Danoff, M.D., a urologic surgeon at Cedars-Sinai Medical Center in Los Angeles. Whether the sexual energy is drained by a nubile neighbor or a high-speed T3 line, your body doesn't know.

So it's no surprise that "roughly 65 percent of the people who visit the Center for Online Addiction do so because of marital problems created by cyberpornography," says Kimberly Young, founder of the center. "When a woman finds out that her husband has a double life, she's hurt. 'Why would he look at all that rather than sleep with me?' The man can't answer. He is ashamed." Should he be?

Out with the Old, In with the New

Is it a man's fault if he chooses easy gratification over what is hard to procure? Maybe he's doing what all men were designed to do, searching for sexual opportunity. This vast pornucopia has latched on to the sexual engine that drives our species: the insatiable desire for fresh features. From there, online sex can inflame desire at the very same time it gratifies it. You barely have time to go limp, as the endless expression of novelty supplies you with another fresh body. "And the women don't ask for the Neiman Marcus card afterward," says Dr. Danoff. "It's every man's dream!"

Male desire can be described simply: New women are hot, and they are hot because they are new. "But a woman who is attractive primarily because she is new loses everything once she is no longer new," says Dr. Symons. Which explains why, as Aaron, another sex surfer, says, "I spend a lot of time online looking for something that I know I will never get." Once the novelty wears off, all that remains is the need for more novelty.

Sexual novelty is powerful. Lack of it can cause impotence. A doctor may prescribe Viagra (sildenafil), say, to men who have trouble keeping it up for their wives but not for their mistresses. That's situational impotence, occurring only when novelty is missing. You don't need Viagra on the Internet.

Inevitably, this unending search for new sex "ups the ante," says Dr. Danoff. "It takes more to get you going." As Neal says, "Some of the things I've found, I'd never have even thought that anyone would enjoy, good and bad." First it's a girl, then two girls and a guy. Then two girls, a guy, and a speculum.

Is it an addiction to want sex all the time? Maybe. Maybe not. But clearly Walter's problem goes beyond a natural appetite that cannot be satisfied. Maybe it's because we're animals who spend our lives tracking, stalking, and bagging women. Now a man can spend hours enjoying the meal without going hunting. We've subverted the urge to compete and survive.

And so the Internet turns evolution on its head. According to the laws of reproductive competition, the man who seeks new partners will outpopulate the man with weaker desires. But now men with strong desires for sexual novelty can choose the Web over their wives. They'll end up reproducing pictures of nude starlets instead of producing kids. And disappear, genetically speaking, without a trace.

Maybe that's a good thing. Thin the herd. But if it's not, how do you stop?

Getting Out from Under

Perhaps the best way is to bring the mistress out in the open. Move the computer to the family room. Buy a laptop and work in public places. By limiting your privacy, you may not act on the urge, says Dana Putnam, Ph.D., a psychologist who counsels cybersex addicts at www.onlinesexaddict.com.

If that doesn't work, many people turn to software programs or Internet services that prevent access to smut in the first place. Paul tried one, after months of locking himself in a room and masturbating compulsively to porn sites. "After a few weeks, life got back to normal," he says. "My sex life with my girlfriend took a new and exciting turn, although some positions are not as easy or as comfortable as they look."

For most men hooked on cyberporn, it's a tough fight. "Every day is a struggle to keep this from becoming my primary sexual outlet," says Carl. "It is a constant battle to remind myself, when arousal material is so easily accessed, that to attain a higher level of real sexual fulfillment takes intimacy."

That's why we marry instead of meander. Marriage couples our sexual urges with the weight of responsibility. Without it, life would be a serial of senseless sex, interrupted by trips to the clinic. "The best advantage I have in overcoming this is an understanding wife," says Walter. "I told her what was going on, and she was hurt. But she agreed to help me get over it."

Walter hasn't been perfect. "I've spent 4 to 5 hours on the Internet in the past 2 weeks." But that's down from his 30-hour-a-week compulsion. Still, he told me that he'd seek counseling, and so far he has not. "I've tried to immerse myself in work. I think I'll be all right. I just have to keep my ass away from this PC all the time."

That sounds like a good idea, Walter. Now turn that thing off, go upstairs, and make love to your wife.

A Very Bad Way to Buy Viagra

Just about every newspaper in America carries ads offering Viagra (sildenafil) prescriptions by mail. But is it safe? Here's what's troubling: You can actually order the stuff without a physical checkup. That's hard to believe, since mixing Viagra with common nitrate heart medications can be deadly. Men's Health *magazine decided to investigate mail-order prescriptions sold through 800 numbers and Web sites and get to the root of the matter.*

It works like this: You send an e-mail or give some faceless voice your medical information and sign, or click on, a waiver of liability. The company then supposedly forwards your info to a doctor. The investigating editor for *Men's Health* magazine told each company that he has heart disease and takes isosorbide dinitrate, a cardiac drug that can cause a dangerous drop in blood pressure if mixed with Viagra. Based on that information, any doctor should have refused to give him a prescription.

Both of the 800 numbers and two of the three Web sites quickly denied his order. But the third Web site, run by Viapro, Inc., in Arizona, shipped his $185 order right away. When the package arrived, our editor called the site's customer service number to ask if they were sure that mixing Viagra with his heart drug wasn't dangerous. An operator said she thought it was safe, but she offered to check with the site's doctor.

Two days later, a Viapro representative, Bill Reeves, called and told our editor not to take Viagra. When we asked for a refund, Reeves agreed. "Your order was approved due to a computer glitch," said Reeves, reminding our editor that warnings about drug interactions are posted clearly on the Web site.

We contacted the Food and Drug Administration to see who's regulating these sites and the 800 numbers. The short answer: nobody. "The FDA is primarily responsible only for the labeling and marketing of drugs, not for how they're dispensed," says FDA spokesman Randy Wykoff, M.D. Prescribing and dispensing are regulated by state laws, but not all states specify whether doctors can prescribe drugs to people in other states without an actual visit, says Susan Winckler of the American Pharmaceutical Association. (Arizona is one state that doesn't specify.)

"Ordering prescription drugs without a face-to-face consultation or an established doctor-patient relationship is just plain dumb," says William H. Mahood, M.D., of the American Medical Association. It greatly increases the chances of fatal drug interactions, and it almost guarantees that a percentage of users will be taking prescription drugs that are unnecessary or dangerous. And since erection problems can be a sign of diabetes or heart disease, men may overlook real trouble if they consult their browsers instead of their doctors.

Furthermore, these mail-order companies are no bargain. They charge about the same as what you'd pay for the drug at a pharmacy—$10 each for ten

100-milligram pills—but you'll also pay a "consultation fee" of about $65 and roughly $20 for shipping. And your sexual problems may not be kept confidential. If you can't even be certain that a doctor will look at your medical history, how can you be sure that the site will keep your information private?

We're not the only ones worried about drugs being shipped to men who haven't seen a doctor. Congress began investigating these mail-order pharmacies last year, and the FDA is in the process of developing verification standards, so the laws regarding them may become much tighter.

The verdict: If you want to take advantage of this wonder drug, see your doctor. There's no shame in it. You have nothing to gain and everything to lose—your privacy, your money, your health, your life—by trying to sneak in the back door.

SEX WARS

"In your computer files you refer to me as a snoop."

HELP ONLINE

ART APPRECIATION 101

Feast your eyes on the world's greatest erotic and sensual art treasures
at this erotic bookstore and cybergallery. Glimpse exhibits
from great museums in Europe, the Far East, and the United States;
browse the bookstore; or send an erotic art postcard.
www.erotictraveler.com

REV YOUR ENGINES

LadyBiker.com. Need we say more? This is a grassroots site
(not a porn site) where women post pictures of themselves with their bikes.
Purely amateur photography. Odd mixture of leather, lace, chains,
sultry looks, and some we-wish-we-hadn't looked.
www.ladybiker.com

MAN'S GUIDE INTERVIEW

Smile: You're on Candidcam

An Interview with Cybervoyeur Seth Warshavsky

If that woman you left the bar with is stripping your clothes off in full view of her computer-mounted digital camera, make sure that the computer is turned off. Otherwise, you may have just become the feature attraction on the Web at "Rachel's Apartment: Live and Uncut."

If you are locking lips with a fine young thang on Bourbon Street, watch out. You might return home to find that your significant other was tuning in to a live Webcam to check out the nightlife in New Orleans . . . and she caught you doing your "client meeting."

And even if you don't end up live on camera, you never know if, or when, images of you might rear their ugly little heads. After all, naked pics have come back to haunt Vanessa Williams, Dr. Laura Schlessinger, and other high-profile folks.

To get a sense of the future of privacy, or lack thereof, in our media-hungry, Internet-speed society, we consulted with Seth Warshavsky, the chief executive officer of the Seattle-based Internet Entertainment Group. IEG has full ownership of more than 100 Internet porn sites (including its flagship site at www.clublove.com) and has its fingers in more than a thousand other online ventures—almost all sex-oriented.

If you're wondering why Warshavsky is a good commentator on the current state of privacy, bear in mind that he was first to break the honeymoon sex video of Tommy Lee and Pamela Anderson Lee, and he was the guy who posted the nudes of Dr. Laura. And he successfully defended those actions in court as well as winning many other high-profile privacy battles.

MAN'S GUIDE: Although I want to talk about privacy issues in the Internet Age in a general sense, I think I need to get a benchmark from you first.

You are famous—or perhaps infamous—for things like the Pamela and Tommy Lee video, the pictures of Dr. Laura when she was in her twenties, and reenactments of purported sexual encounters people have had with celebrities. Is everyone fair game, or is there still a line that can be drawn?

WARSHAVSKY: No, I do not believe that everybody is fair game.

MAN'S GUIDE: Then where do you draw the line?

> **WARSHAVSKY:** Most of the deals that we've done, the Dr. Laura
> photos being a good example, are deals in which the people who were
> recorded or photographed had signed away the intellectual property
> rights.
>
> If we don't have some way of obtaining the intellectual property
> rights to something or getting the people involved to forgo their right
> to privacy, we cannot display it. And we won't. So it's clearly not a sit-
> uation in which everyone is fair game.
>
> We are very selective about what we will take. We have standards. I
> don't think they are really any different from journalistic ethics and
> standards used by a *Time* magazine or *Newsweek* or *Hard Copy* or CNN.

MAN'S GUIDE: Admittedly, you have higher standards than a lot of
people in the sex business. I was impressed, for example, that you had testified before Congress on the need to establish a ".adult" extension for Internet
sites in order to better control kids' access to online porn.

> **WARSHAVSKY:** Yeah, yeah. That's very important to me, and to
> the company. But my point is that if *Hard Copy* or CNN could have
> shown Pam and Tommy Lee naked on the air, they would have done
> so. But these are easily accessible television programs. That kind of
> programming is not allowed by the Federal Communications Com-
> mission.
>
> However, later on they did show parts of the video on TV—they
> just blocked out the genitals. So when people say that I or the people
> at my company have no morals and have no ethics, that's completely
> untrue. In fact, we've turned down some stuff. We turned down the
> videotape of Dr. Jack Kevorkian performing an assisted suicide, which
> was later aired by *60 Minutes*.
>
> We were one of the first organizations that Dr. Kevorkian's people
> approached with the tape, and we turned them down. We really are
> very selective about what we will present to our audience. We look at
> every aspect, especially legal aspects, and we examine how we person-
> ally feel about the concept before we decide to run with it.

MAN'S GUIDE: I guess the reason I ask if the line is getting fuzzier is not
because of any legalistic stuff but because, well, consider the Dr. Laura pic-

tures versus the Pam and Tommy videotape. Tommy has promoted T&A in music videos, and Pamela Anderson Lee made a career on her boobs and other enhancements.

But Dr. Laura's career is not based on physical exposure. Why was she fair game? Because it seems that if a radio talk-show host is fair game for nudie pics, we're inching closer to making private folks fair game.

WARSHAVSKY: I think the Dr. Laura photos were something that people needed to see. Dr. Laura is such a hypocritical person. She judges people and makes statements about their beliefs and acts. So I think it's important for her audience to see how she's handled her own life. These photos were taken by a boyfriend while she was still married to another man.

And when we did present her with the pictures, she denied that it was her in the photos. It wasn't until we got into court that she said it was her. Then she said she owned the copyright. And then we presented the contract showing that we owned the copyright. She handled the situation very poorly. And I think that her audience really had the right to see how she handled sexuality in her own life, since that's what she preaches about.

> **" When you spend your time on the Internet, you don't hear a human voice, and you never get a hug. "**
>
> —Norman Nie, a political scientist at Stanford University and principal investigator for a study on the negative social consequences of America's increasing online activity, waxing nostalgic for the old days

MAN'S GUIDE: Well, here's the issue I primarily want to address: What about the proliferation of Webcams and the effect that's going to have on our privacy? More and more live cameras are being pointed at public places and those images are being beamed to Web sites.

WARSHAVSKY: The test as to whether material is considered private and whether you have a right to privacy is whether or not you're in public light. Were you in the public eye when you were acting out or doing whatever else you were doing?

If somebody chose to put a camera out his window and pointed it at the corner of First and Battery in Seattle, he'd have a right to do that.

And if the camera catches you, you wouldn't really have any rights to privacy because you're out in public. Everybody can see you anyway.

MAN'S GUIDE: Ah, but there's the crux of the problem. If you're in public, you may expect to be seen by people on the street. But you don't expect to be seen by dozens or hundreds or thousands of people on the Internet or on TV or wherever.

WARSHAVSKY: The laws dictate what constitutes a private place versus a public place. Personally, I really think that if people are out in public, you should be able to film them. I don't see anything wrong with that.

There are definitely going to be a lot more live cams out there in the coming years. And I think people are definitely going to want to tune in. People are voyeurs, by and large. People like to see what other people are doing. People are curious. And I think that as long as there's a demand for these live feeds, people are going to be providing live cameras and putting the images on the Web or on other media.

MAN'S GUIDE: Should we be concerned that we're increasingly under the scrutiny of cameras wherever we go? Why should we have to be on our 100 percent best behavior from the moment we step outside of our front doors until the moment we get back inside our homes?

WARSHAVSKY: If you don't want people to see what you're doing, you should do it in private. If you don't want something like sex between you and your wife to be shown on the Web or on TV, and if you don't want it sold as a videotape, then you shouldn't film the activity to begin with. Or if you do, you film only one copy, and you keep it somewhere safe and never let anyone else get their hands on it.

Because even though my company, IEG, won't show a video unless we have property rights to it . . .

MAN'S GUIDE: . . . someone else will?

WARSHAVSKY: That's right. Someone else will be willing to show it, even if they don't have the rights to it. You just have to be careful. As technology evolves, as anything evolves, situations change. The Internet has created a huge arena. It's an incredible resource for people. The Internet has made it so much easier to do a lot of things quickly that a few years ago would have taken three, four, five times more effort to do.

MAN'S GUIDE: So like it or not, we have to accept the good with the bad, and watch our backs?

> **WARSHAVSKY:** There are going to be negatives. There are going to be cons. But I think the advantages of the Internet far outweigh any of the problems that it causes.

MAN'S GUIDE: Dr. Laura may have signed away rights to her nude photos years ago, but if someone catches me on a live camera, I didn't sign anything at all. If I cannot stop a person from recording me, shouldn't I at least have a right to be paid if that person uses my image?

> **WARSHAVSKY:** Personally, I think it depends on the use of the material. I mean, legally, I don't think people are entitled to any such compensation. Now, on the personal side, I think that depending on how the material is used, maybe the person who was recorded should be entitled to compensation.

MAN'S GUIDE: So you don't see it as an obligation but more as a matter of politeness. If you want your company to be viewed in a positive light and you want to play fair, you might kick something back to the person. But you don't think there's a basis for legal entitlements.

> **WARSHAVSKY:** Exactly.

MAN'S GUIDE: I'm kind of interested in the relationship between the camera and your employees, especially the women doing the live nudity and sex shows for your sites. I understand you have a "Pee Cam." Now, I like to think of the bathroom as my one last refuge from work. When you've already got cameras everywhere else, why do you need to have one where the women take their bathroom breaks?

> **WARSHAVSKY:** That's just a stage. The women who work for us pose and perform sexual acts on a stage in front of a camera. The bath-

room and the toilet are just different stages for the performances. The woman is in front of the camera in one spot most of the day doing her thing, and then she goes to a new venue where people may also want to see her.

But I mean, if one of the performers is really embarrassed about people watching her take a pee, a regular bathroom is available for her to use without a camera. We're not taking advantage of anyone. The women who work for us are performers. This is the work that they have chosen to pursue.

We aren't tuning in to reality. We do fantasy. We don't put cameras in people's homes, or in places where people don't know the camera is there. Everything's very aboveboard. Everywhere that there is a camera, the people who work for us know about it. They know if there's a camera in the room.

MAN'S GUIDE: You've touched on the voyeuristic streak in humanity already, but what is the appeal? I myself am a little old-fashioned, I guess. I still prefer videotapes for my porn.

WARSHAVSKY: The Internet is an incredible medium for the distribution of adult material. And there are a couple of reasons for that. The first thing is . . . well, you said you liked the videos. The thing about the Internet is that with superfast connections and high-speed Internet access becoming available everywhere, you can see any video you want online.

You can see a video that is in the adult rental store down the street on your computer, in full-screen mode, with CD-quality audio—all without leaving your home.

The Internet is becoming a powerful vehicle for advertisers and for companies to project messages to consumers. So I think that various people and organizations are going to subsidize the implementation of high-speed networks that run into everyone's homes. I think if you at least have a television, you're going to have high-speed Internet access in the next 3 to 5 years, no problem.

MAN'S GUIDE: Leaving aside the sex cams, does online porn have a bright future?

WARSHAVSKY: Sure. It's the perfect medium. You don't have to go into the video store. You don't have to be embarrassed. It's totally instant gratification that is totally anonymous.

The Internet is also a great medium for this material because it combines all of the former media into one place. You can have the editorial content of a *Hustler* or *Playboy* or *Penthouse* magazine. You can have the videos online. You can have live scenarios like online strip clubs. And you also have the interactivity that you get with phone sex.

The Web wrapped all of these media into one, and it became a totally anonymous environment where people could get what they want right away.

QUICKIES

WIRED AMERICA

Which state has the highest number of homes with connections to the Internet? Forget California with its computer-rich Silicon Valley or the state that's home to the "information capital of the world," New York City. Instead, think of states where there's evidently not much else to do on a Saturday night. Following are the top 13 states, and their percentage of households with net access.

❶	Alaska	44.1
❷	New Hampshire	37.1
❸	Washington	36.6
❹	Utah	35.8
❺	Colorado	34.5
❻	Oregon	32.7
❼	Connecticut	31.8
❽	Vermont	31.8
❾	New Jersey	31.3
❿	Maryland	31.0
⓫	California	30.7
⓬	New York	23.7
⓭	Mississippi	13.6

TALK ABOUT MISTAKEN IDENTITY

Fortunately, Trevor Tasker, a lonely bloke living in England, fell madly in love with thirtysomething Wynema Faye Shumate over the Internet. Unfortunately, she lived inconveniently far away in Charleston, South Carolina. Fortunately, she agreed to marry him if he'd fly across the Atlantic to meet her. Unfortunately, Tasker discovered upon arrival that not only was dear Wynema actually 65 years old, she was also in prison on charges of "desecration of human remains." Seems police discovered the body of James O'Neil, 70, in her freezer, where he'd rested in peace for more than a year. Fortunately, an autopsy showed no foul play in O'Neil's death. Unfortunately, Shumate, who "helped take care of" the wheelchair-bound O'Neil before his demise, was also charged with stealing $4,200 from his bank accounts after he died.

BAD NEWS
FOR THE FLESH AND BLOOD

At this rate, the Internet may well become the solution for overpopulation. For years, it's been possible, using nothing but a credit card and Web browser, to see, hear, and even choreograph the X-rated antics of live, uninhibited women the world over without the inconvenience of being anywhere near them.

What's worse (or better, depending on your socialization skills), you can now pleasure a woman, in a remote-controlled sort of way, without actually touching her. "Cyberdildonics" (www.safesexplus.com) is a software package and $25 adapter that allows you to control a partner's sex toy—vibrator, dildo, plug, suction pump, you name it—via the Internet. Buy a setup for yourself, add voice chat and video, and you'll never have to risk procreation (or human contact, for that matter) again.

WORSE NEWS
FOR THE FLESH AND BLOOD

Elite, the company that launched the modeling careers of supervixens Cindy Crawford, Linda Evangelista, and Naomi Campbell has created the first "virtual fashion model," Webbie Tookay. Webbie, who along with Engelbert Humperdinck is burdened with the most ridiculous name in the history of spoken language, is a computer-generated animated mannequin, a politically correct amalgamation of a voluptuous blonde European, a Latina, and an Asian. Her handlers say that she's ready to participate in virtual fashion shows, fashion magazines, TV programs, feature films, electronic games, Internet projects, and bar mitzvahs—all without risk of weight gain, anorexia, jet lag, or a fiendish coke habit.

"We are very proud of her personality," said Luciana Abreu, a partner in Illusion 2K, the digital production company partnering with Elite. "She would never wear fur. She has environmental concerns, she is for birth control. And besides, she looks very pretty. She has well-defined breasts and hips."

While Webbie may indeed be the first virtual fashion model, she's hardly the first non-real-media personality (even if you don't count Dan Rather). Back in 1984, digital newsman M-M-M-Max Headroom made his TV debut. More recently, Lara Croft, the bodaciously buxom artificial star of the "Tomb Raider" video games, supplanted real-life vixens in many young men's nocturnal fancies. And one need look no further than *Star Wars: The Phantom Menace* to see that it's already possible to create an entire cast of fake actors, including most of the "real" ones. Check out Webbie's assets at www. illusion2k.com.

DEAR DR. MANLY

Q: *A guy I work with says that <u>the only thing making any money on</u> <u>the Web is pornography. Is he right?</u>*
—S. G., Niles, Illinois

A: Porn isn't the only thing making money, but it's still making an impressive haul. According to Forrester Research, so-called adult Web sites were a $1 billion industry in 1998. What's even more surprising is not the bucks involved but the fact that the Web has shifted the balance of power from the producer to the performer. As stripper-turned-porn-mogul Danni Ashe told *Newsweek*, "Virtually every woman in the business now has her own Web site."

Ashe took her own talents to the Web after getting arrested in a strip club back in 1995. Eager to get out of the hands-on side of the business, she bought a book on HTML coding and soon launched Danni's Hard Drive, which now has 25,000 members who each pay $20 a month for the privilege of virtually interacting with Danni and friends in X-rated photos, racy chat, and live video feeds. That's just a drop in the hanky, though, of the worldwide audience for online sex. More than half the requests on search engines are adult-oriented, according to the trade group United Adult Sites.

Still, the glut of smut seems to be leveling off. The number of new porn sites has doubled every year since 1994, with several hundred thousand sites now hawking sex with everything from humans to animals. But last year, the growth was just 40 percent, and signs indicate that it's falling fast.

"Putting up a new porn site is like opening up a coffee shop in the financial district between two Starbucks," said Caity McPherson of Bay Area Adult Web sites, a nonprofit association of sex-trepreneurs, in an interview with *Wired* online. Don't expect to see a concurrent decline in consumer demand, however. The ease and anonymity of to-your-monitor porn service isn't likely to wear off soon, when the alternative is parking your car in front of some joint called "The Peek-A-Boo-Tique," buying a *Hustler* from the 17-year-old kid at the quick-mart, or dropping $50 in ones at a topless bar.

Q: *My wife has always been a computer nut, but lately she stays up late 4 or 5 nights a week, "just surfing around" as she calls it. Last night, I found transcripts of explicit sex chats she'd had with someone named "Luv-Daddee." I call it an affair, even if she hasn't physically met the guy. What do you think?*
—B. B., PITTSBURGH

A: As much as guys get the rap for being sex hounds, it turns out that women are actually more likely to become compulsive about so-called cyberaffairs than heterosexual males, according to Dr. Al Cooper of the Marital and Sexuality Center in San Jose, California. Dr. Cooper did an online survey that suggested 200,000 people are addicted to online pornography or sexually explicit chat—many of them women, gay men, and other "sexually disenfranchised" groups. (Oddly enough, married men aren't considered "sexually disenfranchised." Shows how much he knows.) College students, who typically have ample free time, raging hormones, and fast Internet connections, are also at risk.

These groups "may not have the same skills built up that heterosexual men have to deal with sexual temptation and pornography," Dr. Cooper said. "It's like unleashing them in a candy store." He defined a cybersex compulsive as someone who spends more than 11 hours a week on the computer pursuing sexually oriented activities.

Cybersex compulsion is driven by the anonymity, convenience, and escape afforded by the Internet. There's a reason she's turning to the Web—and not to you—for titillation; keep that in mind before confronting your wife. To learn more about the problem, order the booklet "Infidelity Online: An Effective Guide for Dealing with Your Relationship after a Cyberaffair" from the Center for Online Addiction at www.netaddiction.com.

Dr. Manly is a fictional character.
The actual advice was provided by a variety of
medical doctors and other qualified experts.

credits

index

●D

R

Raincoats, 38
Rational Sex Ethics for Men in the Army and Navy, 175
Reiter's syndrome, 196
Relationships. *See also* Dating; Marriage
  e-mail, 230–32
  long-distance, 230–32
  past, reigniting, 14–15
  Web site on, 16
Rembar, Charles, 174
Replens, condoms and, <u>9</u>
Respect, conflict and, 3
Responsibility
  independence and, 13–14
  intimacy and, 14
  sex and, in marriage, 243
Riboflavin, for sex drive, 102
Robie, W. E., 175
Romance, 84–91
  cyberwooing and, 231–32
  generic vs. creative, 87
  obligatory vs. optional, 86–87
  passion and, 91, 155–56
  places to avoid, 159
  practical expressions of, 88–89
  sex and, 67, 90–91
  Web site on, 152
Romance novels, <u>24</u>
Romantic Mischief, 84
Rose petals on bed, 160

S

Salaries, by gender, <u>10</u>
Sanger, Margaret, 171
SARA, 196
Scents, as aphrodisiacs, 104
Seasons, sperm count and, 115
Sensitivity in men
  as quality women want, 9–10
  sex appeal and, 42–43
Sensuous Woman, The, 174
Serotonin, as aphrodisiac, 104–5
Sex. *See also* Intercourse; Orgasms
  aphrodisiacs and, 103–5
  for conception, 116–17
  cyberpornography and, 241–43

emotional bonding and, 69
on first dates, 139
flagging interest in, 66–69
food and, 102–6
frequency of, <u>112</u>
throughout house, 92–93
hypnosis and, 122–26
invention of phone and, 171–72
male desire for novelty in, 242
marriage and, 70–76
men's activities after, <u>105</u>, <u>106</u>
mortality rate and, 101
motherhood and, 67–68
penis size and, 95
public figures and, 167, 170–77
quiz about, <u>105</u>, <u>106</u>
romance and, 67, 90–91
seduction tricks and, 64–65
sharing fantasies about, 197
statistics about, <u>71</u>, <u>112</u>
surprise in, 79
talking about, 66–67
testicle size and, 127–28
touch and, 77–78
weather and, 94
Web site on, 152, 153
with wives vs. girlfriends, 73
women's monthly cycle and, 162–63
Sex and the Single Girl, 176
Sex appeal, 39–42
  acting your age and, 45
  attractiveness and, 39–40, 55–56
  body language and, 44–45
  bragging and, 42
  caring for children and, 43–44
  charisma and, 41, 54
  cultivating, 31–61
  elegance and grace as, 46–48
  fashion and style as, 32–38
  flirting and, 45
  grooming and, 50
  hormones and, 41
  humor and, 42
  psychological factors in, 41
  sensitivity and, 42–43
  Web site on, 49
Sex drive. *See* Libido
Sex education, first, 175
Sex Histories, 175